Seasons of Change

Seasons of Change

LABOR, TREATY RIGHTS, AND

OJIBWE NATIONHOOD

Chantal Norrgard

The University of North Carolina Press / Chapel Hill

First Peoples
New Directions in Indigenous Studies

Publication of this book was made possible, in part, by a grant from the Andrew W. Mellon Foundation.

Manufactured in the United States of America
Set in Utopia by codeMantra
The paper in this book meets the guidelines for permanence and durability
of the Committee on Production Guidelines for Book Longevity of the Council on
Library Resources. The University of North Carolina Press has been a member
of the Green Press Initiative since 2003.

Library of Congress Cataloging-in-Publication Data
Norrgard, Chantal.
Seasons of change : labor, treaty rights, and Ojibwe nationhood / Chantal Norrgard.
pages cm. — (First peoples: New directions in indigenous studies)
Includes bibliographical references and index.
ISBN 978-1-4696-1729-9 (pbk : alk. paper) — ISBN 978-1-4696-1730-5 (ebook)
1. Ojibwa Indians—History. 2. Ojibwa Indians—Employment. 3. Ojibwa Indians—
Government relations. I. Title.
E99.C6N64 2014
977.004'97333—dc23
2013047868

18 17 16 15 14   5 4 3 2 1

THIS BOOK WAS DIGITALLY PRINTED.

For Lorraine and Phillip Norrgard

Contents

A section of illustrations begins on page 83

A map of reservations and towns in the Lake Superior region
appears on page 18

Acknowledgments

This book is the culmination of a long journey that would not have been possible without the support of many people to whom I am incredibly indebted and appreciative. First and foremost, I must thank the Ojibwe people of the Grand Portage, Fond du Lac, Red Cliff, and Bad River communities whose stories inspired me to write this book—chi miigwetch.

The framework of this project began to take shape while I was a graduate student at the University of Minnesota. I was fortunate to work with Jean O'Brien, a dedicated adviser whose positive guidance has lead me to become the scholar and professional I am today. I thank her for her advice, time, and care, all of which have played a vital role in shaping this book. It was through an appointment as a research assistant under David Chang that I first learned about the craft of researching, writing, and revising a manuscript. I am grateful for his willingness to read multiple drafts and his insightful feedback on my work throughout all stages of this project. Brenda Child imparted her extensive knowledge of Ojibwe history, and her encouragement led me to consider the importance of the everyday experiences of the people I was writing about and why this history continues to matter to Ojibwe communities. Several other faculty members at the University of Minnesota had a hand in shaping the ideas that comprise this book and read chapters. Patricia Albers encouraged me to think further about the specific dynamics that led Native people to seek work in the American labor market and the consequences of how they have been perceived as workers; John Nichol's inspired me to explore the multifaceted definitions of labor in Ojibwe communities; Barbara Welke encouraged me to speak to American Labor history more broadly; and David Wilkins reminded me of the important role the struggle for sovereignty played in shaping American Indian economic actions. At Minnesota, I was also fortunate to be a part of a talented cohort of graduate students in the history department and American Indian workshop. I would especially like to thank Sarah Crabtree, Jill Doerfler, Heidi Kiiwetinepinesiik Stark, Jenny Tone Pah Hote, and Keith Richotte for the rich intellectual exchanges we shared as peers, as well as their humor and their friendship.

Internships at the Madeline Island Museum and the Great Lakes Indian Fish and Wildlife Commission (GLIFWC) provided me with essential insight into the history of the Lake Superior region and importance of treaty rights in Ojibwe communities. Steve Cotherman shared a great of information about the local history of the area and has continued to express enthusiasm for my work and my general progress. The staff at GLIFWC shared their invaluable knowledge, and Sue Erickson assigned me terrific projects that enabled me to engage further with Ojibwe history and culture and to learn more about the surrounding communities. Thomas Vennum Jr. also took the time to discuss his insights and experiences while I was working at the museum.

A predoctoral fellowship in American Indian Studies at Michigan State University allowed me to complete a draft of the manuscript. Susan Krouse, the director of American Indian Studies and her husband, Ned Krouse, provided endless support and a home away from home while I was living in East Lansing. Sadly, Susan passed away before the completion of this book. I will always be grateful for her kindness and guidance. I was welcomed by many other faculty members at MSU who were generous with their time and knowledge. They include Nancy DeJoy, Heather Howard, Kimberli Lee, William Lovis, Dylan Miner, Mindy Morgan, John Norder, and Susan Sleeper Smith.

A postdoctoral teaching fellowship at Lawrence University also enabled to me to complete my book proposal and to begin revising my manuscript. I would like to thank Peter Blitstein, Dominica Chang, Paul Cohen, Carla Daughtry, Jake Frederick, Karen Hoffman, Brigetta Miller, Jerald Podair, Stewart Purkey, Monica Rico, Asha Srinivasan, and Lifongo Vetinde for welcoming me into the Lawrence community and for their encouragement. Through the Fellows Program I also had the opportunity to develop wonderful friendships with Siobhan Brooks, Sonja Downing, Alison Guenther Pal, Nathan Hanna, and John Mayrose.

As a visiting assistant professor at Mount Holyoke College, I was fortunate to get to know a number of gifted scholars. Faculty in the history department offered support and advice that was indispensable in the process of making revisions to the manuscript. Fellow members of the Crossroads in the Studies of the Americas Colloquia engaged in rich intellectual discussions about comparative aspects of indigenous history and provided helpful feedback on Chapter 1. I am also grateful to have been invited to the meetings of the Five College Native American Studies Program. I would like to thank Kathleen Brown-Perez, Laura Furlan, Neal Salisbury, and Lauret Savoy in particular for welcoming me. It would have taken me much longer to finish revisions to the manuscript if I had not had the members of my writing group at the Five Colleges to cheerfully and persistently push me along. For this, I thank Jennifer Fronc, Andrea King, Barbara Krauthamer, and Edward Melillo, Dawn Peterson, and Elizabeth Stordeur Pryor.

At Northland College, Kelly La Venture and Clayton Russell offered vital support and encouragement during the final stages of revising the manuscript. Erica Hannickel also provided extremely helpful feedback on the introduction, and I thank her for the engaging discussions about American history, teaching, and the process of writing a book.

I have benefited greatly from being a part of the vibrant community of scholars in the field of Native American and Indigenous Studies. As a graduate student, I had the privilege of working with an array of leading scholars through the Committee on Institutional Cooperation–American Indian Consortium (CIC-AIS). Thank you to Philip Deloria, Gregory Dowd, Raymond Fogelson, Brian Hosmer, Larry Nesper, and Jacki Rand for listening to my presentations and commenting on parts of my chapters in their very early stages at the consortium meetings. I also developed wonderful friendships through the CIC-AIS with Qwo-Li Driskill, Angela Haas, John Low, Melissa Rinehart, Joseph Genetin-Pilawa, and Cristina Stanciu. I am fortunate to know such talented young scholars.

Along the way, many other scholars have read my work, commented on conference presentations, or shared their input and advice. Thank you to David Edmunds, Sasha Harmon, Martha Knack, Rebecca Kugel, Cary Miller, Colleen O'Neill, Jeffrey Ostler, David Rich Lewis, Alyssa Mt. Pleasant, Coll Thrush, and Bruce White. I am especially grateful to Jessica Cattelino for reading the manuscript and for her astute comments that helped me to transform it into a book. I would also like to thank the anonymous reader for the University of North Carolina Press, whose perceptive critiques and suggestions were of great assistance in finishing this project.

It would not have been possible to write this book without the assistance of the librarians, archivists, and staff at the Bayfield Heritage Association, the Grand Portage National Monument, Lawrence University, the Minnesota Historical Society, Mount Holyoke College, the Wisconsin Historical Society, the National Archives, the Newberry Library, the Northeastern Minnesota Historical Society, the Northern Great Lakes Visitor Center, the National Park Service, the Superior Public Library, and the University of Minnesota.

For their generous support in terms of time and funding I thank the Five Colleges Crossroads in the Study of Americas (CISA), Lawrence University, Michigan State University, Northland College, the University of Massachusetts, the University of Minnesota, the CIC-AIS/Newberry Library, and the First Peoples: New Directions in Indigenous Studies Initiative.

I am indebted to Mark Simpson-Vos at the University of North Carolina Press, who has been an outstanding editor, mentor, and supporter of this project from the beginning. I would also like to thank Tema Larter, Zachary Read, and Caitlin Bell-Butterfield for helping to usher my manuscript through the publication process and Mary Caviness for her adept copyediting, which has improved the clarity, prose, and style of this book.

Words cannot truly do justice to how grateful I am to my family for their love and support. My parents, Lorraine and Phillip Norrgard, have had a profound influence on my work as a scholar. Their commitment to social justice and their dedication to working with indigenous communities was instilled in me at an early age, and they motivated me to become the person I am today. My grandmothers, Martha Norrgard and Harriet Rueter, are an inspiration, and I thank them for cheering me on at every level of my education. I also cherish the memory of my loving grandfather Edward Rueter, whose hard work in part made it possible for me to go college. I credit my siblings, Ariane, Burgess, and Sören, with helping me to think critically and independently about the world around me, and I continually marvel at their creativity, steadfastness, and grace. Finally, I want to thank my partner, Aaron Windel, who has been a tremendous source of love and support. His calm presence, gentle humor, and sharp intellect enrich each day and mean more to me than I can express.

Seasons of Change

Introduction

In 1959, the Bad River Tribal Council issued a declaration of war against the Wisconsin Department of Conservation to protest state officials' arrest of Ojibwe hunters and fishers for exercising their treaty rights. The declaration was in part a response to the termination policy; the aims of federal policy-makers shifted from allowing Ojibwe self-determination to a renewed focus on detribalization and the dismissal of tribal sovereignty. As part of this policy, the federal government transferred its jurisdiction over tribes to states. State violation of treaty rights, however, was not new to Ojibwes.[1] Since the turn of the century, the governments of Minnesota and Wisconsin had seized control over Ojibwe lands and resources, while the federal government looked on. Using contemporary rhetoric from the Cold War to underscore its position, the council proclaimed:

> When in the course of human events, it becomes necessary to protect the rights and the liberties of certain peoples of this great nation from encroachment by other peoples, it is the duty of the Tribal Council, the governing body of the Bad River Band of Lake Superior Tribe of Chippewa Indians of Wisconsin, to take measures that will protect the members of said Band from unjust arrest by State Conservation officials.
>
> IT IS HEREBY DECLARED, that a state of cold war exists between the Bad River Band of Chippewa Indians and the officials of the Wisconsin Department of Conservation, and that such state will exist until such time as the State of Wisconsin shall recognize Federal treaties and statutes affording immunity to the members of this Band from State control over hunting and fishing within the boundaries of this reservation.
>
> During this period, state conservation officials shall be denied access to all tribal and restricted lands within the boundaries of this reservation.[2]

The council delivered the imperative message that hunting and fishing were critical economic rights that defined their sovereignty. These were rights designated by exclusive treaties between Ojibwes and the federal government. Therefore, state conservation officials had no historical precedent to arrest Ojibwe hunters and fishers for exercising them. Bad River's willingness to go so far as to declare war against the state of Wisconsin for violating their rights to hunt and fish illustrates the vital connection between Ojibwe livelihoods and their political autonomy. It raises questions about the economic and political history that lies behind this declaration. Namely, how did Ojibwe livelihoods become sites of political conflict and tension?

This book explores two key dimensions of Ojibwe history: labor and tribal sovereignty. Beginning with the negotiation of treaties in the mid-nineteenth century and ending with Ojibwe life during the Great Depression, it traces the role that labor played as a historically shifting dynamic shaped by Ojibwe struggles with colonialism. It charts Ojibwe efforts to retain their autonomy under the increasingly difficult conditions presented by containment on reservations, the dispossession of their lands, federal Indian policy focused on eliminating their traditional ways of life, and state encroachment on their treaty rights. It examines how Ojibwes enacted their sovereignty around the axis of labor. The connections between treaty rights and Ojibwe economic actions raise a critical yet largely unexplored question: How does our understanding of American labor history change when we recognize tribes' unique position as indigenous nations who were incorporated into the boundaries of the United States?

Scholarship on indigenous labor during this period remains underrepresented in American labor history. However, a number of works on American Indian labor history have put the building blocks in place for exploring this question. In their watershed collection on Native Americans and wage labor, Alice Littlefield and Martha Knack brought attention to the importance of Native American wage labor in American society as well as its significance in defining social relations between Indians and non-Indians.[3] More recently, a handful of scholars, including Colleen O'Neill, Brian Hosmer, Paige Raibmon, and William Bauer, have explored the role that labor has played in American Indian adaptability and perseverance.[4] These scholars have demonstrated that wage labor facilitated cultural production and community among Native peoples rather than a loss of identity. Rather than discarding their traditions, American Indians integrated new forms of labor into the social, political, and economic structures in place in their communities in ways that enabled their survival.

My book compliments this scholarship; I explore many examples of Ojibwe agency to illustrate how Ojibwes found meaning, sustained traditions, and built community through their work. But I also move in a new direction by examining the political dynamics that make American Indian labor history unique. Since the emergence of the "new labor history" in the 1960s, numerous studies have explored how workers of different races, ethnicities, classes, and genders have built community, sustained culture, and expressed identity through their labor.[5] While this approach to labor history has allowed us to think in valuable ways about how Native peoples sustained aspects of indigenous life oriented around culture and identity, it does not always provide an explanation for how their experiences were different from other workers based on their unique political relationship to the United States. As Alexandra Harmon, Colleen O'Neill, and Paul Rosier argue in their article on American Indians and economic development, "Making sense of Indians' economic circumstances and decisions frequently requires making sense of their unique and shifting status under the laws of colonial regimes.... Indians' expectation of sovereignty—an attribute of indigenous societies enshrined in U.S. law—differentiates Indian and non-Indian labor history."[6]

This is not a simple task. The unique political position of tribal nations has led many labor historians unfamiliar with American Indian history to exclude Native peoples from their work based on the difficulty of accounting for tribal sovereignty.[7] Inspired by the work of British historian E. P. Thompson in the 1960s, American labor historians focused on Euro-American workers' experiences in the industrial workforce and their transition from farmers to factory workers.[8] While labor history has expanded to account for the diverse experiences and backgrounds of workers, historians still largely examine labor through the frameworks of unions, class, economic citizenship, and the industrial workplace—areas in which Native peoples have either been invisible or marginalized.[9] Even when Native people could be found in these contexts, the assumption that workers desired equality or integration into the United States contrasts sharply with the premise of tribal sovereignty, the goal of which is cultural, social, and political autonomy.

Seasons of Change explores American Indian labor through a wider lens and uncovers the roles that tribal sovereignty and American colonialism play in shaping Ojibwe labor history. This history presents a rich picture of the diverse economic actions of indigenous people that do not necessarily fit into common categories used to analyze labor. Ojibwe labor consisted of a range of economic actions that changed over time as Ojibwes lived under and resisted the conditions of late-nineteenth- and early-twentieth-century U.S. colonialism.[10] It constituted a complex web of social, political, and ceremonial relations that governed their interactions with the natural world, with one another, and with other peoples. Ojibwe work was shaped by their culture and identity, but their work was also intertwined with their sovereignty and self-determination. Ojibwe struggles to exercise their treaty rights in the early twentieth century added yet another layer of complexity to this picture; it was through the process of economic transformation as well as political struggle that labor became intertwined with Ojibwe nationhood.[11]

OJIBWE LABOR IN TRANSFORMATION

Thinking about Ojibwe labor as part of a dynamic, shifting history enables us to consider how labor was defined by a variety of economic activities and how it became intertwined with American Indian assertions of sovereignty over time.[12] In Ojibwe communities, traditional forms of labor were structured by the concept *bimaadiziwin* or the "good life." Ojibwe scholar Lawrence Gross defines *bimaadiziwin* as a unifying concept that can be described as a "long and healthy life" that was "the life goal of the old Anishinaabe."[13] This life entailed a variety of subsistence activities governed by the shift in seasons and movement to locations where resources were available, also known as the seasonal round.

The seasonal round was heavily influenced by the climate and geography of the Lake Superior basin, which consists of the lake itself and the thousands of waterways and wetlands that flow into it. Because of its vast size, Lake Superior has its own localized maritime climate. The lake moderates the temperatures in the surrounding area and leads to significantly more precipitation, contributing to wet summers, heavy snow in the winters, and strong northeasters in the fall. Winters are long and cold and summers are warm; temperatures range from below zero Fahrenheit in the winter to 80 degrees Fahrenheit.[14] Prior to logging in the nineteenth century, most of the land surrounding Lake Superior was heavily forested and was part of an extensive boreal ecozone that stretched from the northeastern seaboard to the northern Rockies. The soil of the region contains a mixture of clay, sand, silt, gravel, and rock and is embedded with deposits of minerals, such as copper, iron, and silver.[15] The quality of the soil and the short growing season made it difficult for Ojibwes to rely on agriculture for their livelihood. However, the landscape harbored a seasonal abundance of plant and animal life on which the indigenous people of the region depended.

Ojibwes tailored their traditional livelihoods to these conditions. In the spring, they moved their family to sugaring camps to tap maple trees and boil the sap, and they speared and netted fish in rivers and lakes. Spearing took place in the evening by torchlight; the light from the torches illuminated the eyes of walleye pike that the spearers sought. In the warmer summer months, Ojibwe families moved to larger villages near waterways, where they netted and trapped fish, harvested a plethora of wild plants, including a variety of berries, and cut birch bark to be used for canoes, baskets, and wigwams. Summer was a time of social gathering, diplomacy, and warfare since the heavily forested territory in which they lived could be more easily traversed via open waterways. Then, as summer turned to fall, families once again moved to smaller camps on lakes, where they harvested wild rice and turned it into food through an intricate process of drying, parching, winnowing, and treading. In the winter, when temperatures dropped to below zero, families kept warm in well-crafted wigwams, and they relied on their stores of wild rice, maple sugar, and berries, as well as game and fish, to survive. Ojibwes were skilled at tracking and hunting or trapping a variety of animals, including beaver, otter, mink, marten, deer, elk, and moose, and they also went ice fishing to obtain food. During the winter, Ojibwe families constructed essential items, such as moccasins, clothing, rabbit-skin blankets, and snowshoes, and told stories to pass the long winter months.

The concept of a good life centered on an intricate system of social and ceremonial beliefs based on reciprocal relations between the animal, plant, and human worlds. Ojibwes established and sustained these relations through gift-giving. An individual or group gave thanks and offerings of tobacco or other gifts for taking resources from nature, such as picking berries or cutting birch bark. This belief in reciprocal relationships was also important to hunting and fishing. Tobacco was placed in the water prior to fishing. A proper funeral was conducted for an animal that had been killed, and gifts were offered to the animal for sustaining the hunters and their families. Similarly, people shared or gifted the products of their labor to cement political and social relationships. These actions were part of the view that humans and their environment were interrelated and that through gift-giving, individuals and communities established proper relations and balance in the world in which they lived.

These livelihoods underwent significant change during the fur trade. In the eighteenth century, Ojibwes became a central force in the extensive trade in beaver furs that gripped the western Great Lakes. While Ojibwes continued to rely on the seasonal round of subsistence activities, hunting, trapping, and processing hides grew in importance because of the fur trade. In addition, Ojibwes engaged in new economic strategies. Because fur traders were dependent on Indians' labor for furs and other commodities, they had to accommodate the custom of gift-giving in order to maintain beneficial trading alliances and intermarriage with Native people. Ojibwes continued to see this reciprocity in social and ceremonial terms, but they also used it as a means to obtain political leverage among competing traders and against other tribes. It was through the fur trade that Ojibwes became involved in early capitalist ventures. In the early decades of the nineteenth century, fur traders attempted to diversify their economic activities to incorporate the industrial market. Ojibwe headmen negotiated leases with traders who were interested in harvesting their timber, and they worked as commercial fishers for the American Fur Company. Several men of Ojibwe and European ancestry transformed trade into entrepreneurship, establishing businesses in the emerging settlements around Lake Superior.

In 1837 and 1842, the United States negotiated two major treaties with Ojibwes living in Minnesota, Wisconsin, and Michigan in order to further national economic interests and to fortify its political power in the western Great Lakes. In 1837, U.S. officials negotiated the Pine Tree treaty at St. Peters, Minnesota territory, to gain control of the pine timber in the Chippewa River valley via land cessions. U.S. officials negotiated another treaty in 1842 at La Pointe, known as the Copper treaty, to obtain additional land cessions and a hold over the valuable mineral resources located along the southern shores of Lake Superior. In turn, Ojibwe headmen reserved the right to continue their livelihoods in territory ceded to the United States. In Article 5 of the treaty of 1837, Ojibwe headmen reserved "the privilege of hunting, fishing, and gathering wild rice, upon the lands, the rivers and lakes included in the territory ceded."[16] In Article 2 of the treaty of 1842, Ojibwe headmen made a similar stipulation "for the right of hunting in ceded territory, with the other usual privileges of occupancy."[17] The treaties represented not only Ojibwe efforts to practice their livelihoods but also their exclusive nation-to-nation relationship with the United States.

Though the articles of the treaties were succinct, they set in motion the dramatic economic, environmental, and political changes that would take place in Ojibwe communities and the region as a whole. They became a tool for the federal government to extend settler sovereignty over the region while eliminating the political barriers that Ojibwe presence in the region presented. In 1850, President Zachary Taylor issued a removal order that called for Ojibwes living in northern Wisconsin and Michigan to move to Minnesota territory based on an article in the treaty of 1842 that stipulated the possibility of their relocation. Four hundred Ojibwe people perished of starvation, disease, and exposure in what is known as the Sandy Lake tragedy. The tragedy was the result of a scheme that local officials devised to trap Ojibwes in Minnesota over the winter by moving their annuity payments from La Pointe to Sandy Lake. Ojibwe headmen and a number of local citizens protested the removal order. Their efforts resulted in the treaty of 1854, which enabled Ojibwes to remain in their homelands by setting aside reservations and confirming their treaty rights. However, it also led to the cession of the remainder of Ojibwe lands along the north shore of Lake Superior, and it provisioned for the allotment of reservation lands.[18]

The treaties initiated the growth of industries that were to dominate the economy of the western Great Lakes, generated national economic growth, and defined the labor traditions of the region in the nineteenth century. Lumber companies moved in to harvest the vast stands of pine timber that made up the region's forests. Mining companies established an immense copper industry on the southern shore of Lake Superior to extract the mineral for a range of industrial and household uses. Commercial fishers took advantage of Lake Superior's rich fisheries to supply fish to urban centers to the south and east. The shipping and railroad industries capitalized on demands for infrastructure generated by the growth of Euro-American settlements, building extensive networks of transportation to connect the midwestern hinterland with the rest of the United States. All of this expansion was made possible by the treaties. The United States depended on the treaties to fuel the economic development of the Great Lakes and to establish its political power over a region that would become a center of national industrial development in the late nineteenth and early twentieth centuries.

In the midst of these transitions, treaty rights became critical to Ojibwe economies. They enabled Ojibwes to retain access to the lands and resources they depended onto survive even though they faced relocation to reservations that were miniscule in proportion to their original homelands. Ojibwes relied on treaty rights as means to navigate the changes that were taking place around them. Substantial numbers of Ojibwes began to make a living in the capitalist market through commercial fishing, hunting, and trapping, as well as by selling wild commodities, such as wild rice, maple sugar, and berries, to local settlers.

Ojibwes also took on wage labor that would allow them to continue exercise these rights and to mitigate the effects of federal Indian policy. Ojibwe men worked off-reservation in the lumber industry because they had been dispossessed of their own lands and timber through the process of allotment. Although they worked in some of the most dangerous jobs, many of them found that this work afforded them a measure of separation from Indian agents, valuable skills, and even a degree of prestige. Ojibwe men also worked on ships, on trains, and even for the postal service. Many Ojibwes used new forms of transportation, such as trains and ships, to access resources, begin new economic ventures, invigorate their connections to territory ceded in the treaties, and sustain relationships with one another outside of reservation boundaries.

Circumstances changed once again in the early twentieth century as the region's economy shifted from one centered on industrial capitalism to one dominated by tourism. This transition was largely due to the lack of resources left to extract; most of the region's lumber had been cut, its minerals had been mined, and its fisheries had been emptied, and there was little to transport other than the tourists who came to escape the congestion of urban life or rural people who were fleeing the area to find jobs in cities. In the interest of promoting tourism, state governments focused on restoring the environment and implementing conservation laws that favored recreation and discouraged commercial or subsistence land use. Ojibwes found work in the tourist industry, performing in dances and pageants, selling commodities, and working as domestic servants or as hunting and fishing guides. The tourist industry, however, ultimately contributed to the restriction of the Ojibwes' treaty rights.[19] State governments extended their jurisdiction over all resources and impeded the economic activities of Indians by restricting treaty rights. Against this backdrop, Ojibwe economic actions took on new meaning: they not only were a way of making a living; they also served as a form of resistance and a way to assert sovereignty against state encroachment. Ojibwes continued to hunt and fish despite arrests, fines, and the confiscation of equipment, and they challenged these arrests in the state and federal courts.[20]

RETHINKING THE PARAMETERS OF
LABOR AND THE NATION

Ojibwe economic actions included subsistence, trade, wage labor, and commerce to which Ojibwes ascribed unique meanings. Their actions were defined by their sense of place, culture, identity, kinship and community, survival, resistance, and sovereignty. These are factors that are not easily accounted for using traditional Western concepts of labor, which have contributed to the absence of American Indians in labor studies. As Thomas Berger explained in his report for the Alaska Native Review Commission, the social, cultural, ceremonial, and environmental relationships that indigenous subsistence practices alone entail are so extensive that "no one word can encompass all these related concepts."[21] But there are also clear political motivations behind the ways in which Americans have defined labor. Indeed, narrow definitions of labor have been deployed to categorize American Indians' economic actions as something other than work. Since early contact with American Indians, Euro-Americans deliberately undermined indigenous economic opportunities, choices, and rights by arguing that their economic actions did not constitute legitimate or authentic forms of labor.[22] This assertion has ultimately served colonial efforts to obtain indigenous lands and resources and to assert power over indigenous communities.

With these complexities in mind, I use the terms "livelihood," "labor," and "work" to describe a range of economic activities in which Ojibwes engaged. However, I recognize that there are differences between them. I define "livelihood" as comprising a set of economic actions as well as the social, cultural, material, and political resources on which individuals, families, and larger social groups draw to make a living.[23] Livelihood entails the social dynamics and values that shape people's economic choices and actions, and it allows us to account for indigenous labor *and* its connections to the broader social and cultural values of indigenous societies.

I use the terms "work" and "labor" interchangeably to describe the strategies Native peoples have developed to make a living. Building on Daniel Usner's scholarship, I understand these terms as capturing "various activities pursued by American Indians for subsistence, commerce, and income."[24] My intent is not to undermine the political gains or goals of workers who were in labor unions or the importance of scholarship on the American labor movement by defining labor and work in broader terms. However, I do use these terms to bring attention to the exclusion of American Indians from American labor history. I apply both terms to American Indian economic actions as way of asserting an indigenous presence in American labor history and dismantling Euro-American definitions of labor and work that have been deliberately deployed to restrict and undercut Native people's economic agency and to further the initiatives of settler colonialism and federal Indian policy.[25] In doing so, I hope to move in the new direction of indigenizing American labor history.

This book shows how the different forms of labor in which Ojibwes engaged became sites for the construction, expression, and practice of indigenous nationhood, that is, how Ojibwes asserted their political distinctiveness and identity through labor.[26] A number of Ojibwe economic actions exemplify what Audra Simpson terms "everyday nationalism," or the ways in which nationhood is understood, practiced, and narrated by indigenous peoples based on their day-to-day, lived experiences.[27] In Ojibwe communities, these lived experiences frequently centered on labor, whether it entailed hunting, fishing, and gathering as part of the seasonal round, cutting timber in a lumber camp, carrying mail to local towns, or guiding eager sportsmen to the best fishing spots in the region. My intent here is not to generalize about the meaning behind Ojibwe labor; certainly not all of the economic actions of Ojibwes were directly focused on nation-building or sovereignty. Rather, I approach this concept as a way of understanding how some forms of labor became politicized and central to Ojibwe identity over time. Moreover, I show that even where work was not politicized, Ojibwes still performed and attached meaning to labor in ways that were intertwined with their indigeneity and the conditions of colonialism that they lived under.

Examining how Ojibwes enacted their nationhood through their labor allows us to understand how American Indians found meaning and political power in their work in ways that were different from those of non-Indians. This approach should not be taken to mean, however, that American Indian history should be studied in isolation from U.S. history. On the contrary, recognizing the historical relationships between American Indian labor, indigenous nationhood, and U.S. colonialism opens new avenues of exploration in American labor history. It allows us to understand how American economic and political life developed around the process of delineating political sovereignty in relation to indigenous people and to recognize the role that treaties played in shaping both indigenous and non-indigenous economies.

There is a significant body of literature on the role that labor and policy have played in the construction of the boundaries of the American nation-state and the ways in which diverse populations within the United States have contested and reshaped these boundaries through their work. Historians such as Mae Ngai, Evelyn Nakano Glenn, Sarah Duetsch, and Leon Fink have emphasized the national, transnational, and colonial dynamics that shape the conditions under which immigrant and migrant laborers worked, as well as the ways in which their experiences were shaped by race, gender, class, community, and citizenship.[28] Similarly, Alice Kessler-Harris and Jacqueline Jones have illustrated the ways in which U.S. ideologies about race and gender have shaped and restricted the boundaries of what Kessler-Harris has termed "economic citizenship" in the United States.[29] This literature has opened new categories of analysis, but it fails to account for workers who did not seek incorporation in the nation-state or to have their rights validated in settler society.

This book intersects with this literature by examining the ways that settler sovereignty, which targeted indigenous resources and indigenous sovereignty, shaped economic citizenship for Americans during the nineteenth and twentieth centuries. It also reveals the ways that the United States structured its own economic and political systems in relation to indigenous nations. Historians recognize that immigration policy, as well as race- and gender-based policy, has shaped the boundaries of economic citizenship, but few have considered the political dynamics of settler colonialism that made economic citizenship possible in the first place. Patrick Wolfe has defined settler colonialism as a process in which the aim of European powers is to replace Natives on their own land based on the logic of elimination.[30] This logic of elimination was fundamental to colonial structures with which Europeans incorporated American Indians and other indigenous people into the nation; incorporation became the tool for elimination.[31]

In the United States, the federal government focused on eradicating American Indians through outright violence as well as federal Indian policy. Assimilation policy focused on the erasure of indigenous people's way of life in favor of absorbing them into American society and preparing them for citizenship. Allotment policy sought to eradicate tribal identity and American Indian assimilation by dividing tribal lands held in common into individual holdings and selling surplus lands to settlers. The United States determined that Native people were "competent" enough to sell their individual landholdings and, by granting them citizenship as part of the process, made them subject to the jurisdiction of the federal and state governments. American economic citizenship not only depended on the dispossession of indigenous lands and resources; it also became a tool through which the United States attempted to eradicate the identity and distinct political rights of indigenous people. Recognizing this history allows us to explore the political contexts surrounding economic citizenship more fully and to understand its limitations.

This context also presents new opportunities to rethink the political, geographic, and economic boundaries of the nation in American labor history. Labor historians have begun to explore labor through a transnational framework with the intent of interrogating the "origins and authority of the nation-state."[32] This development offers fruitful possibilities for greater inclusion of American Indian labor in this picture as well as new opportunities to reconsider how indigenous nationhood reconfigures the history of the nation-state. There has already been some interest in how this framework might apply to indigenous communities: Andrew Parnaby, for example, has written an insightful article that compares the work of the Mi'kmaq of Cape Breton and the Squamish of British Columbia, demonstrating how their histories of interaction with colonial powers determined their differing positions in the economies of the East Coast and West Coast, cutting across the political borders of the Canadian nation-state.[33] More broadly, scholars in American Indian studies have started to draw connections between the experiences of indigenous nations within nation-states. Jace Weaver recognized in his assessment of American Indian studies that one of the most important trends in the field is a "borderless discourse" that links indigenous peoples through their struggles with colonialism.[34]

Nevertheless, transnational history largely focuses on Western understandings of the nation. In the process of clarifying how transnational history is salient to U.S. labor history, Julie Greene writes that "transnational history looks at the processes and actors that move across the territorial boundaries of the nation-state. These processes are themselves extremely diverse: They may include economies, demographic movements, capital flows, ideas, cultures, and commodities."[35] Transnational history offers numerous possibilities to examine the history of the United States in a broader context and to explore categories that transcend national boundaries or challenge national mythologies about the formation of the American nation-state.[36] The presence of American Indian workers in U.S. history raises an important but unexamined question: How do we account for the diverse political and economic histories of more than five hundred indigenous nations located *within* the boundaries of United States? Sven Beckert has suggested that more work could be done on the transnational dimensions of American Indian history.[37] I suspect that some historians might be hesitant to include American Indians in this picture because they view American Indian labor is *subnational* since tribal nations are encompassed by the United States; they might categorize indigenous peoples as subjects of the nation-state. However, this assumption is largely based on colonial definitions of American Indian nationhood.

An important step toward placing American Indian history in a transnational perspective is recognizing the differences between nation-states and indigenous nations. Scholars in American Indian Studies have made distinctions between indigenous nations and the nation-state. David Wilkins distinguishes between Western concepts of sovereignty exercised by nation-states versus tribal sovereignty exercised by American Indian nations. He writes that sovereignty is a "Western concept, both complex and contested" and that "sovereignty in modern times more accurately connotes legal competence: the power of a culturally and territorially distinct group of people to develop institution arrangements that both protect and limit personal freedoms by social control."[38] But he explains that tribal sovereignty is "the spiritual, moral, and dynamic cultural force within a given tribal community empowering the group toward political, economic, and most important, cultural integrity, and toward maturity in the group's relationships with its own members, with other peoples and their governments, and with the environment."[39]

Self-determination is a key component of tribal sovereignty. Following David Kamper, I understand self-determination as a process, as means to describe the historically specific ways that American Indian individuals and communities have enacted their sovereignty and their "collective rights" as nations.[40] Some tribal nations exercised a great deal of power and in some cases, adopted some of the practices of western governments. However, they were different from western nation-states.[41]

As indigenous people, Ojibwes constituted themselves as nations based on their own political structures. They were also recognized as nations by other indigenous peoples as well as nation-states.[42] At the time of sustained contact with Europeans in the early seventeenth century, Ojibwes exercised a great deal of political power in the expansive territory of the Great Lakes, or what Michael Witgen calls "Anishinaabeaki," a term that means both a place and a social formation.[43] While Europeans emphasized that they had conquered Native peoples within this territory, in reality, they were highly dependent on their partnerships with them.[44] From the seventeenth century to the nineteenth century, Ojibwes exercised political power through a variety of fluid social structures at local and regional levels that enabled them to attain advantages in a world of shifting empires and alliances in ways that cofounded European assertions of hegemony over them.[45]

In the early nineteenth century, the United States negotiated treaties with Ojibwes based on the recognition of their nationhood and their political autonomy. However, treaties also were tools of empire, marking U.S. efforts to assert power over tribes to undermine their sovereignty, and to obtain their lands and resources. Treaties essentially made the formation of the nation-state possible. While Ojibwe leaders interpreted treaties as agreements in which they granted U.S. citizens permission to utilize resources on their lands, American officials interpreted treaties as permanent cessions of land and power. The United States asserted its own settler sovereignty based on what the federal government deemed as the cession of indigenous title and jurisdiction. It is this history that differentiates indigenous nations from nation-states yet also links their histories. Audra

Simpson argues: "The nation hood of indigenous people is made from the bare parts of consciousness and history. However, unlike the nationhood of western states, the nationhood of indigenous peoples has been bifurcated and dissembled with global processes of colonisation."[46] A critical component of American Indian history is how even under these conditions Native people persisted and became distinct and vibrant communities. I demonstrate how in the midst of these processes of colonization, Ojibwes found new ways to constitute and articulate their position as an indigenous nation while challenging the initiatives of the U.S. federal and state governments through their labor.

I structure this book around forms of labor that were prominent in the daily life of Ojibwes during the nineteenth and early twentieth centuries. These were periods of American history distinguished by unprecedented economic growth, imperial expansion, and the extension of the nation-state authority over most aspects of American life. I demonstrate how the negotiation of treaties in the mid-nineteenth century fundamentally influenced the larger contexts of U.S. economic and political expansion during this period, as well as the labor Ojibwes performed. I focus on five prominent livelihoods that were codified in or made possible by treaties: hunting, fishing, and gathering and wage labor in the lumber and tourist industries. Though Ojibwes found work in many additional occupations, I focus on these livelihoods because they most clearly illuminate how Ojibwe work came to exemplify aspects of their self-determination and nationhood via the treaties and show how they were different from those of Euro-American workers based on their distinct political struggles.

The book is divided into two sections. The first section examines livelihoods reserved under treaty rights and how they became politicized as a result of treaty rights struggles. It explores how Ojibwes transformed the subsistence activities of hunting, fishing, and gathering into commercial activities and continued to exercise their sovereignty in the midst of federal and state colonialism. Chapter 1, examines the social and cultural significance of berrying as a form of gathering that Ojibwes adapted to mechanized agriculture and the capitalist market. Chapter 2 shows how hunting and trapping grew in importance as commercial activities following the fur trade and became a site of political resistance as states focused on restricting treaty rights. In particular, it demonstrates how debates over American Indian economic citizenship and the validity of hunting as labor were intertwined with Ojibwe struggles to exercise their rights. Chapter 3 examines Ojibwes work in the Lake Superior commercial fishing industry and the challenges that the growth of fishing monopolies presented to Ojibwe autonomy over their labor.

The second section explores wage labor that Ojibwes took up and incorporated into the seasonal round as a means of navigating the changes caused by the dispossession of their lands and resources following the treaties. Chapter 4 investigates what it meant for Ojibwes to become laborers on lands that were once their own and workers in an industry that depended on cessions of their land and timber for its success. Chapter 5 examines the politics of Ojibwe work in the tourist industry as the regional economy shifted from industrial capitalism to tourism in the early twentieth century. Because tourists associated the presence of Indians with an authentic wilderness experience, many Ojibwes found opportunities to work in the industry. However, tourist expectations also influenced the increasing privatization of local lands and the restriction of treaty rights that made it difficult for Ojibwes to make a living.[47] I examine how the opportunities and conflicts presented by the growth of the tourism shaped the experiences of Ojibwe workers and in the industry. I conclude *Seasons of Change* by looking at the connections between Ojibwe assertions of sovereignty through their labor and the activism of later generations of Ojibwes as part of the treaty rights movement that began in the 1970s and continues today.

LAKE SUPERIOR OJIBWES: PEOPLE AND PLACES

The terms "Anishinaabe" (plural, "Anishinaabeg"), "Ojibwe," and "Chippewa" have all been used at different times to describe the same people. I use "Ojibwe" because it is the most specific term to describe the people residing in the area this book focuses on. As Larry Nesper and other scholars point out, there are a number of explanations for the origin of the name Ojibwe. The renowned mixed-blood Ojibwe historian and interpreter William Warren explained in his nineteenth-century account of Ojibwe life that the term referred to the kind of moccasin they wore, which puckered at the toes, or to the practice of roasting captives "till puckered up."[48] More recently, Harold Hickerson and Theresa Schenck have suggested that this term comes from the Crane clan and suggests the sound of the crane's voice.[49] Many Ojibwes to refer to themselves as Anishinaabe. However, Anishinaabeg also refers to the Ottawas and Potawatomis who speak similar dialects and were the political allies of Ojibwe people.[50] The term "Chippewa" is an American corruption of the word Ojibwe. It was used in treaty negotiations, in federal documents, and in dialogue between Ojibwes and state and federal officials. Though the term has fallen out of use in Ojibwe communities in contemporary times, Ojibwes living in the nineteenth and the early twentieth century used the terms "Chippewa" or "Indian" in public documents and correspondence with non-Indians. Therefore, it appears in many of the quotations included in this book.

I focus primarily (though not exclusively) on the histories of Ojibwe people from the Bad River and Red Cliff reservations in Wisconsin and the Fond du Lac and Grand Portage reservations in Minnesota. I utilize a range of sources that provide insight into everyday life in these communities, including Works Progress Administration collections, published oral histories, autobiographies, local histories, and the reports of Indian agents and inspectors for the Office of Indian Affairs. I've chosen to focus on these communities because they share similar (but not identical) histories due to their close proximity to Lake Superior and their interactions with the once bustling towns that border them. These "border towns" include Grand Marais, Cloquet, and Duluth in Minnesota and Superior, Bayfield, and Ashland in Wisconsin. I look at multiple communities to provide a bigger picture of the ways in which the dramatic changes of the nineteenth and twentieth centuries affected Ojibwes in the region. Despite the imposition of reservation and state boundaries in the nineteenth century, as I demonstrate in this book, these communities were never isolated from one another.

Prior to the mid-nineteenth century, Ojibwes were part of bands whose organization was based on the use of a particular territory by cooperating families.[51] The configuration of these bands was flexible. Ojibwe people depended on interband alliances as a defense against enemies. These alliances were cemented by intermarriage between people from different bands. Though the bands were distinct, they were linked by a common culture, language, and system of beliefs.[52] As early as the eighteenth century, the bands began to form regional identities: the bands living near the north shore of Lake Superior were known as the Sugwaundugahwininewug, or Men of the Thick Fir Woods, and the bands residing on the lake's south shore were called the Kechegumwininewag, or Men of Great Water.[53]

The United States imposed the larger sociopolitical designation of "tribe" on Ojibwes as part of its extension of power in the region. As was common practice, U.S. officials mapped out tribal territories in the Great Lakes as a means of establishing hegemony and to negotiate treaties efficiently. The federal government found it advantageous to treat with tribes rather than to negotiate the shifting political dynamics of bands and to interact with a handful men they deemed the leaders of tribes, despite the fact that Ojibwes designated many different leaders for different purposes. The treaty of 1837 referred to the Ojibwes who were present at the negotiations as the "Chippewa nation of Indians."[54] In the treaties of 1842 and 1854, the United States divided Ojibwe bands into the "Chippewa Indians of Mississippi and Lake Superior" as a way of designating two main territories in which they lived and negotiating for cessions of land.[55] In the treaty of 1854, the United States set aside reservations for bands of Ojibwes living in the Lake Superior region.[56] From this point on, the term "band" has referred to Ojibwes located on specific reservations, and the terms "tribe" and "band" have been used interchangeably. "Tribe" has also been used to refer to Ojibwe bands collectively.

The landscapes of the reservations vary based on their locations. The Grand Portage reservation is located on the north shore of Lake Superior in Minnesota, about six miles from the Canadian border. It is situated on extremely rocky, forested land. The Fond du Lac reservation is located twenty miles west of Lake Superior near the mouth of the St. Louis River in St. Louis County, Minnesota. It is comprised of a mixture of forest, marshland, rivers, and lakes. The Red Cliff reservation is located on forested land on the northern tip of Bayfield County, running along the southern shore of Lake Superior and, as the name suggests, is known for its red sandstone cliffs. The Bad River reservation is located southeast of Red Cliff in Ashland County along the southern shore of Lake Superior. Bad River reservation includes five townships of dense forestland drained by the Bad, Marengo, Potato, and White Rivers, as well as two hundred acres of land on Madeline Island near Amnicon Point, which is a valuable fishing ground.[57] Local people know Bad River for its sloughs, which yield significant wild rice harvests and cranberry crops, and the old Ojibwe village of Odanah.

The size and location of the reservations influenced the external pressures faced by these communities and the ways in which they engaged with economic change. In comparison to the size of the territory that Ojibwes held prior to the treaties, the land set aside for reservations was miniscule. Charles Cleland estimates that in 1854 approximately 4,000 Ojibwes were living in the region. The treaties of 1842 and 1854 ceded roughly 22,167,000 acres of their land. The reservations set aside in the 1854 treaty equaled a combined area of 287,520 acres, meaning that the land available to Ojibwes was reduced by 98.7 percent. Allotment in the 1870s and 1880s decreased the size of these reservations even further.[58] This meant that Ojibwes frequently traveled off-reservation to make a living because they could not support themselves on the reservation land base alone. Moreover, living on or near the lake and developing towns and cities encouraged this mobility and led many families and individuals to engage in new economic activities.

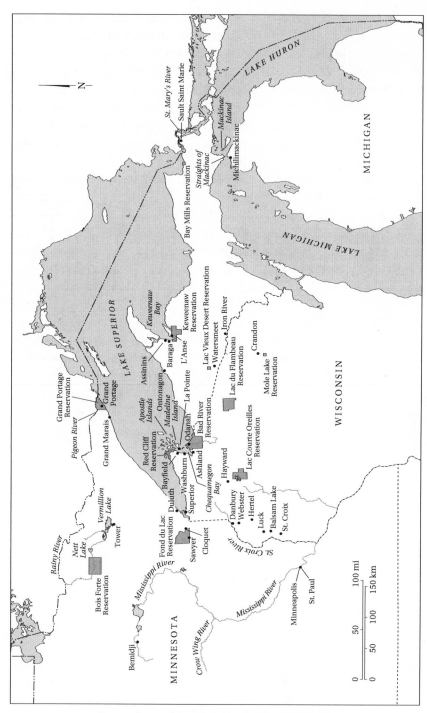

Reservations and Towns in the Lake Superior Region

The Grand Portage, Fond du Lac, Red Cliff, and Bad River Ojibwe bands also maintained kinship ties with one another as indicated by the similarity of family names in these communities, contributing to inter-reservation mobility.[59] These bands were located under Bayfield and later the La Pointe Indian agency. In the 1870s and 1880s, external interest in reservation timber, coupled with allotment policy, led to a dramatic re-duction in reservation lands and checkerboarding of Indian and non-Indian landownership within reservation boundaries. Even with federal and tribal efforts since the 1930s to restore the land base of reservations, such as Red Cliff, tribal lands are still smaller than their original size. Yet all four reservations remain vibrant communities in which band members have sustained their cultural traditions and exercise their treaty rights in contemporary contexts.

What follows is the story of how Ojibwes from these communities en-dured and engaged with the dramatic changes of the nineteenth and twen-tieth centuries, a history that is still significant as Ojibwes exercise their treaty rights today. Tracing this history, *Seasons of Change* reshapes the boundaries of labor history to consider the relationship between eco-nomic transformation and Ojibwe sovereignty. It explores this history from a new angle. Looking at historical transition through the lens sovereignty it illuminates how Ojibwes exercised political agency through the labor they performed. Most importantly, it shows how labor was central to Ojibwes' resistance to American colonialism and their continuing presence as an indigenous nation.

CHAPTER ONE

From Berries to Orchards

The Transformation of Gathering

During the Great Depression, Ojibwe families journeyed to the berry patches of northern Minnesota and Wisconsin to make a much needed income from the fruit they harvested. They picked berries for days and even weeks, occasionally pausing to enjoy the summer weather or to socialize in berry camps that consisted of makeshift shelters and tents. In 1938, Florina Denomie of Bad River described the economic importance of berry picking, or berrying. "One of the leading industries of the Chippewas of Lake Superior is blueberry picking," she wrote.[1] Indeed it became an important source of seasonal income. "This, of course, like other occupations which are the endowments of nature, is seasonal, and outside of the more substantial industries, such as farming and lumbering; blueberry picking ranks first in the point of dollars and cents," wrote Denomie.[2] Denomie's statement speaks to the importance of berrying as both a form of subsistence and a substantial commercial industry that emerged in late nineteenth century and continued through the 1930s.

The history of berrying illustrates how Ojibwes transformed traditional forms of subsistence into commercial activities as they experienced the pressures and constraints imparted by federal Indian policy and settler colonialism. Berrying was one of many forms of labor that constituted "gathering."[3] Ojibwe headmen reserved the rights to gather in the treaties of 1837 and 1842, recognizing the importance of these activities to the economies of their communities.

During treaty negotiations, Ojibwe headmen emphasized the importance of these plant resources. In 1837, Flat Mouth, an important headman from Leech Lake, spoke for all the Ojibwe leaders present when he said: "My Father. Your children are willing to let you have their lands, but they wish to reserve the privilege of making sugar from the trees and getting their living from the Lakes and Rivers, as they have done heretofore, and of remaining in this Country. It is hard to give up the lands. They will remain, and cannot be destroyed—but you may cut down the Trees, and others will grow up. You know we cannot live, deprived Lakes and Rivers; there is some game on the lands yet; & for that reason also, we wish to remain upon them, to get a living. Sometimes we scrape the trees and eat of the bark. The Great Spirit above, made the Earth, and causes it to produce, which enables us to live."[4] By reserving the rights to continue to practice seasonal subsistence activities and granting the United States access to certain resources on their lands, such as pine timber, Ojibwe headmen believed that they had assured their people's ability to continue to pursue their customary lifeways in their homelands. The right to gather was a crucial part of Ojibwe survival. Flat Mouth made specific reference to the harvest of maple sugar, and by employing the phrase "getting a living from the lakes and rivers," he was quite likely referring to the harvest of wild rice and fishing.

Ojibwe headmen also emphasized the importance of gathering rights alongside hunting and fishing rights in the negotiations leading up to the treaty of 1842. When Marten, the head leader of the La Court Oreilles Band of Ojibwe, signed the treaty, he did so under the condition that "we should remain on the land, as long as we are peaceable."[5] Elaborating on this point, he explained, "We have no objections to the white man's working the mines, and the timber and making farms, but we reserve the birch bark and cedar for canoes, the rice and sugar tree and the privilege of hunting without being disturbed by the whites."[6] Just as Ojibwe leaders had done in 1837, Marten outlined the importance of having access to birch bark, cedar, maple trees, and wild rice. He made it clear that gathering was a key part of their survival, and by reserving it in the treaty, he designated it as a right to a specific form of livelihood.

The emergence of a berry industry in Ojibwe communities began with their relocation to reservations in the 1870s and ended during World War II, when the market for berries changed drastically as the result of the expansion of mechanized agriculture on the West Coast and in some areas of the South. While northern Wisconsin and Minnesota never became agricultural centers due to the short growing season and soil quality, the opening of Indian lands to logging and, subsequently, the availability of cutover acreage generated a regional interest in farming in the early twentieth century. Many local Euro-Americans tried their hands at growing a range of crops as well as dairy farming.

In the process, Ojibwe berrying practices underwent dramatic changes. The federal government capitalized on the agricultural movement to farm the cutover to transform Ojibwe livelihoods. Federal officials observed that Ojibwe subsistence practices encouraged a sense of tribalism that interfered with assimilation. They tried to instill a sense of individualism and economic competition among Ojibwe people. They encouraged Ojibwes to make a living in the capitalist market and to farm in hopes that these economic activities would replace traditional livelihoods and undermine the extensive web of social connections that held Ojibwe communities together. Some Ojibwes adapted berrying to mechanized agriculture, growing and selling berries in response to the pressures by the Indian Service to turn to farming. Large numbers of Ojibwe men and women also traveled to berry fields to pick berries for a wage or to sell them to commercial buyers.

What Indian agents failed to recognize were the ways in which traditional livelihoods could be transformed instead of being erased. It might have appeared that Ojibwes who planted rows of berry plants in plowed fields or cultivated orchards or picked berries and sold them in local cities and towns were no different from Euro-Americans who engaged in the same economic activities. Yet, the larger purposes that these activities served for Ojibwe people distinguished them from Euro-Americans. Despite Indian agent efforts to contain Ojibwes on reservations and to undermine community networks, Ojibwe people continued to exercise their treaty rights, traveling to familiar places off-reservation to pick and sell berries and to socialize in berry camps. Instead of subscribing to the ideas of individualism and economic production embedded in the agricultural activities the federal government promoted, some Ojibwes utilized fruit farming as means to retain connections to their lands and to share resources with others.

As a form of gathering, berrying was central to the traditional economies of Ojibwe people. However, it took on new importance under the conditions of colonialism that Ojibwes faced following the treaties. By transforming berrying into a number of different livelihoods, Ojibwes withstood Indian agents' pressure to farm and navigated the capitalist market in ways that served their own interests. In the process, this labor became a vehicle through which Ojibwes sustained and built community and articulated their sense of identity.

GATHERING

Historically, gathering was a critical component of Ojibwe subsistence. Ojibwe women oversaw and took part in a majority of the labor that fell under the category of gathering, as well as the activities that took place in sugaring, ricing, and berrying camps. Women allocated the stands of maple trees used for sugaring to specific families, and they tended to the process of boiling the sap and turning the sap into sugar.[7] They designated rice beds, harvested rice, and oversaw the drying process, which involved parching it, jigging on it to loosen the husks, and winnowing it to get rid of the chaff.[8] Women and children picked berries and dried them for later consumption. Ojibwe women essentially held authority over the labor that gathering encompassed and the distribution of food.[9]

Gathering took place from early spring until late fall. In early autumn, Ojibwe women navigated the shallows of rivers and lakes to harvest wild rice. With two people in the canoe, one person stood in the back of canoe, poling and navigating the craft, while the other folded the rice plants over the edge of the canoe and gently tapped the hulls of the rice into the canoe using knocking sticks. Once they filled the canoes, they hauled the rice ashore to begin a complex process of drying, parching, dancing on, and winnowing it so that the wind would blow the husks away. When they completed the process, they stored extra rice underground in containers made of birch bark, woven cedar, or animal skins. As a staple food, wild rice was a critical resource year-round. In 1852, William Warren made note of the "large quantities [of wild rice] of which the Indian women gather sufficient for the winter consumption of their families."[10]

In early spring, Ojibwe families moved to sugar camps where the women tapped maple trees to collect the sweet, nutritious sap. The extent to which the sap flowed depended on a precise combination of freezing nights and warm days that usually occurred between February and March. Through a process that was as complex as harvesting and preserving wild rice, Ojibwe women tapped the maple trees, collected the sap in birch-bark baskets, and boiled it until it became a fine, condensed sugar. Prior to contact with Europeans, the sugar was boiled in birch-bark baskets filled with hot rocks. Following contact, Ojibwe women used large cast-iron kettles to boil the sap. Like wild rice, maple sugar was stored and consumed throughout the year.

From the late spring until the early fall, Ojibwe women harvested a plethora of wild plants that they used for foods and medicines or dried and stored for future use. Among these plants were a wide range of berries that grew in abundance in the forests and marshes of the western Great Lakes. The kinds of berries that Ojibwes harvested depended on their geographical location and the time of year during which particular berries were ripe. Blueberries, raspberries, blackberries, and strawberries were available in the summer months and grew abundantly in the clay and sandy soils of the region. High-bush and low-bush cranberries grew in the wetlands and ripened in the summer and early fall. These berries were a key source of food, but Ojibwe women also harvested many other species of berries, such as bane, bear, bunch, June, snow, and thimble berries, for medicine.[11]

Traditionally, when Ojibwe women harvested blueberries, raspberries, blackberries, or strawberries they dropped them into a small birch-bark basket, or "mak-kak," which could be carried or hung on a sash around their waist. They would then empty the smaller basket into a larger basket shared by the group.[12] Berries could then be eaten immediately or dried and stored for winter use.[13] Later, as Ojibwes began to harvest berries on a larger scale for cash, individuals used ten-quart buckets that they would empty into a thirty- to forty-quart box.[14] Ojibwes picked low-bush cranberries by hand as well. Later, as the berry industry grew, some pickers used open-ended boxes with the lower edges cut out like a rake. They would use this device to take the upper half off of the plant including the leaves, stems, and berries.[15]

In the winter, families depended on rice, berries, and maple sugar that they had preserved and stored. Charles Cleland has argued that wild rice and garden production were vital because they were the only foods that could be produced in great quantity and stored for later use.[16] Robert Keller also suggests that maple sugar ranked with wild rice as a staple but far surpassed wild rice in its variety of uses and sustained Ojibwes when there was a shortage of other resources.[17] In a like manner, berries sustained Ojibwe families and communities when other resources were thin. Frances Densmore recorded at least fourteen different kinds of berries and wild fruits that Ojibwes ate, and all of them could be dried and used for times when other foods were scarce.[18]

The social dynamics that surrounded gathering were just as important as the labor itself. While harvesting and processing wild rice, maple sugar, and berries, Ojibwe families lived together in camps. The numbers of families that occupied camps and the numbers camps located in a particular area varied depending on the abundance of these resources. For example, ricing camps were comprised of two to five extended families. A lake that had an abundance of rice beds could have several camps comprised of as many as fifteen to twenty families.[19] Berry picking drew large groups where many families and in some cases, communities, camped in areas where berries grew.[20] As was the case with ricing and sugaring camps, the numbers of people who congregated at berry camps depended on the quantity of berries available, which varied from year to year. Paul Buffalo remembered that his community sent out scouts to find berries and then "whoever wanted to go would go." The group encountered "other Indians." If they were newcomers to the particular berry field, he added, they "probably . . . were going to be invited to join in with them." He continued, "The tribe had much of the territory in those days and everybody pretty much used whatever area they wanted to, even though they most generally returned to the same places year after year."[21]

The camps served as places for social gathering where individuals and families renewed ties with one another or forged new ones. Vennum notes, for instance, that despite the work of harvesting and processing wild rice, camps were places in which people joked and horseplayed, told stories, formed romantic relationships, exchanged news, danced, sang, played games, and passed on knowledge of ricing to younger generations.[22] Similar activities took place in sugaring camps and berrying camps. Lorraine Wilson remembered that every evening, her family from Grand Portage and several other families "would congregate by one sugar bush, talk Indian, which was enjoyable, and make a big fire."[23] Paul Buffalo recalled that families in berry camps would "cooperate" as they set up the camps. "Strangers or no strangers, they worked together, and were in friendship," he remembered.[24]

The renewal of ties to the land and the spirits of the plants themselves were also an important part of the labor of harvesting and processing them. Ojibwes considered (and consider) wild rice a sacred plant, and they treated it as such. Wild rice featured prominently into the Ojibwe migration story, which explains how Ojibwes came to the Great Lakes from the Eastern Seaboard; according to the story, an important stopping place was the place where food grows on the water.[25] Wild rice, maple sugar, and berries were also feast foods, and Ojibwes placed them in offerings and considered them some of the most valuable foods of all.[26]

There were important ceremonies that were proscribed for harvesting these and other plants as way of establishing respect for and sustaining a good relationship with the natural world. Before harvesting any kind of plants, groups or individuals said prayers and put offerings out so as to honor the plant and to avoid causing offense.[27] Rules also outlined respectful behavior during the harvesting process. For example, women who were menstruating or individuals who were grieving were to refrain from harvesting wild rice.[28] Prior to eating any of the harvest, families or communities also made sure to honor the plant that had provided them with food, usually by holding a feast for the first harvest of the season.

Following contact with Europeans, Ojibwes traded or sold their surplus berries, rice, and maple sugar, adapting their subsistence strategies to the capitalist market. Integration into the capitalist economy meant that subsistence was defined not just in terms of sustenance but also in terms of the goods or cash generated from the products of an individual's labor.[29] This new kind of subsistence did not lead Ojibwes to discard the traditional meanings or purposes of these activities altogether. Whether harvesting resources for food or for cash, they continued to sustain the social activities associated with this labor and understood it as an important part of their identity.

Although the nineteenth and twentieth centuries were periods of great economic and political change, these transitions were not isolated from earlier contexts. Prior to the treaties, the activities that comprised gathering played an important role in the fur trade. Foods such as maple sugar and wild rice were crucial to the survival of traders stationed at fur posts and fueled the labor of the trade. Thomas Vennum writes that wild rice "was essential not only at posts (both within the rice district and those outside of it, mostly to the north and west), but also as sustenance for canoe brigades of voyageurs who transported furs east and trade goods west."[30]

Maple sugar was equally important because Ojibwes traded it with white merchants, other indigenous peoples, and settlers long before the treaties.[31] The records of fur traders reflected a continuous concern with supplies of resources such as wild rice and an extensive trade for a range of resources that included everything from cranberries to corn grown by Native women.[32] Ojibwes sold or traded deer, moose, whitefish, lake trout, passenger pigeon, turkey, geese and ducks, bark, pitch, cordage, skins, and many other natural resources with non-Indians.[33] "As the fur trade became less important after the 1830s," Charles Cleland has argued, "trade in wild rice, meat, fish and other natural resources became more important to Chippewa as these commodities took up the gap left by the collapse of the international fur market."[34] After the treaties, Ojibwes continued to trade these items informally with settlers, but they also sold them in the local market for cash.

Ojibwe relocation to reservations following the treaty of 1854 and land loss due to allotment made it more difficult to continue these livelihoods. Through allotment policy in the 1870s and 1880s, the federal government pressured Ojibwes to farm individual tracts of land, but in order for them to do so, the land had to be cleared of timber. During this period, little farming actually took place because Ojibwe men focused on harvesting timber from their allotments and demonstrated little interest in farming even if they had conceded to the Indian agents' wishes. Reservation lands were unsuitable for Euro-American agriculture. Resisting pressures to assimilate and dealing with a diminished land base, Ojibwes attempted to perform seasonal subsistence activities to the greatest extent possible and relied on their rights to hunt, fish, and gather off-reservation as a means of support, but by the 1880s, their efforts were stymied by growing numbers of non-Indian hunters and fishers as well competition with commercial sources of fish and game.[35]

Some Ojibwe women drew from their knowledge of plants to make a living as midwives and healers in the growing settlements in the region. Marceline Couture Champagne was born in Moose Lake Minnesota in 1868. Her father, John Couture, was French Canadian and her mother, Margaret Loonsfoot, was the daughter of Mangosid, a headman and medicine man from the Fond du Lac. While there is little information on Marceline's childhood, it is likely that she learned about Ojibwe ways of life through her mother, including the uses for various wild plants. In 1887, Marceline married a French Canadian man named Desire Champagne. They moved to the town of Duquette, Minnesota, where Desire farmed and Marceline worked as a midwife. She traveled from home to home in the area helping to deliver babies, and she likely drew on her knowledge of plants to assist with childbirths since a range of roots, barks, berries, leaves, and flowers were used for healing.[36] Tragically, Marceline lost one of her own children during childbirth. Due to the negligence of the physician, who did not tie her infant's umbilical cord, the baby bled to death. However, she went on to live a successful life and to continue her work. During World War I, she was elected the president of the local chapter of the Red Cross, and when she passed away in 1944, her friends remembered her fondly.[37]

Ojibwe women also sold a wide range of wild produce as well as crops from their gardens to settlers and residents of local towns. The kinds of commodities they sold depended on the success of specific crops and the abundance of resources during certain years, and also the kinds of produce that Euro-Americans were interested in purchasing. Patricia Shifferd has pointed out that there is less evidence of the sale of wild rice than other commodities in local newspapers and Indian agent reports for northern Wisconsin during the 1870s and 1880s and suggests that non-Indian newcomers to the area may have found this food less desirable than others or that Indians preferred to store it for protection against bad ricing years rather than sell it.[38] Vennum also suggests that wild rice served as a currency until the mid-nineteenth century but that it diminished during the reservation era because of a number of factors. He notes that by the turn of the century, non-Indian hunters were focused on cultivating wild rice to attract wildfowl.[39] By the twentieth century, wild rice and the ricing process increasingly fell under the control of non-Indians, who built their own mechanized processing plants and gained control of the market.[40] Moreover, the surplus production of wild rice dropped after the fur trade, as Ojibwe communities shifted from a food-based economy to a money-based economy and entered other forms of work.[41]

A sizable maple sugar industry existed in both the United States and Canada, but the market for maple sugar began to diminish in the 1890s when beet sugar and cane sugar replaced maple sugar in the mass market and elevated it to a luxury item, which fewer people purchased.[42] Moreover, the settlement of the region impacted the viability of selling maple sugar. Many non-Indians made sugar themselves. As Robert Keller explains, "a maple tree as lumber sold for thirty times its value in syrup."[43] Wild rice and maple sugar remained important to the Ojibwe economy and culture nevertheless.

Euro-American newcomers to the region readily purchased berries from Indians in order to vary their monotonous diet of bread, potatoes, salted or dried meat, and the limited amount of fruits and vegetables that the short growing season and rocky soils afforded. Like Ojibwes, many non-Indians picked berries and drew on the land for their sustenance.[44] Many non-Indians also purchased wild produce from Native peoples, especially the settlers who lived in the small but growing towns around Lake Superior. In some places, Ojibwes constituted a majority of the berry pickers. Robert E. Parker, an early Bayfield settler, remembered traveling with his father and a childhood friend to pick berries at Presque Isle Bay near Marquette, Michigan, in the early twentieth century. When they came to the bay they found a great number of other pickers who were friends of his father's. Most of them, Parker recalled, were "being of the true Native American race."[45]

The *Bayfield Press* announced in September of 1871: "[The cranberry crop] promises a splendid yield in this section and already large amounts have been picked by the Indians. They bring a fair price and find a ready market."[46] In July 1883, the *North Wisconsin News* reported, "A few blueberries have been brought into town this week, but all was purchased promptly by our citizens for home consumption, at a shilling a quart."[47] In August, the newspaper reported, "Blackberries are coming into market. They are selling for ten cents a quart."[48] In September, it announced that "the Indians brought about 100 bushels of cranberries this week, which our merchants purchased. The berries were very good considering the recent frost."[49]

Between 1875 and 1890, local Indian agents regularly commented on the conditions of berry crops in their annual reports to the commissioner of Indian affairs. In 1873, for example, agent Isaac L. Mahan listed "cranberries, &c., $8,500" under the yearly production figures for the Bad River reservation.[50] In 1875, Mahan noted that Bad River people had harvested 350 bushels of berries.[51] Likewise, in September of 1883, the inspector for the Indian Service explained that the schools on the Bad River reservation were not in session "occasioned from the fact that the Indians are all, both old and young, engaged in gathering their harvest of cranberries, and have been necessarily absent from the agency."[52] In 1876, a poor berry crop caused concern among Indian Service employees. That year, anticipating "suffering during the coming winter," the government farmer at Bad River requested that Ojibwes be allowed to cut timber on their allotments because there would "be no rice or hay on the rivers this season, and the cranberry crop will be a total failure."[53]

In November of 1884, J. A. Stack, the government farmer on the Fond du Lac reservation, reported to La Pointe agent M. A. Leahy that some Ojibwes who sold the timber on their allotments had "made a good beginning at having cleared fields ranging from five to twenty acres and have some stock and raise hay, potatoes, and garden tracts."[54] He found that they were "quite successful" when they lived on their claims, but he expressed dissatisfaction that "a greater number are collected in villages and depend on their labor picking berries, making canoes, and fancy articles of beadwork they chase up for a livelihood."[55] Stack's statement reveals the extent to which Fond du Lac Ojibwes derived an income from berrying. He saw berry picking and other forms of labor that Ojibwes performed as erratic. One might expect this perspective from a government farmer hired to teach Ojibwes the value of agriculture. Such attitudes were tempered by the fact that Ojibwes were still in the process of clearing timber from their lands, which the Indian Service saw as a necessary step preceding farming, but they reflected the notion that even when Ojibwes were engaged with the market economy, government officials continued to see any economic activity linked to subsistence as an invalid form of labor.

Ojibwe people described berrying not only in terms of an income but also in terms of the social relations that it entailed. Against the backdrop of reservation and assimilation policy, Ojibwe berrying can be understood as a subtle form of resistance to the colonial initiatives of the federal government. Ojibwe women often picked berries off-reservation in ceded territory, disregarding the artificial boundaries that the federal government imposed on them. Moreover, they continued to do so in camps or large groups, resisting the individualism emphasized by assimilation policy.

In July of 1894, John Anamosing, a leader at Fond du Lac, wrote to Agent W. A. Mercer requesting that he send police to protect Fond du Lac people from the harassment of outsiders while they were berrying. "A large number of my band are camped at a point known as Big Sand on the line of the N.P. [Northern Pacific] R.R. within the Reservation for the purpose of picking berries," he explained. "People come there from various parts. Some of them bring liquor and carouse and disturb the peace and quiet of the pickers and I request that a police [sic] be sent there to stay during the berry season for the protection of the peaceable population."[56] Berrying had clearly become imperative to the extent that large numbers of Ojibwes went berrying picking and needed to be protected.

Berrying was an especially important means of income for women. "The young men are found in the logging camps, sawmill, and on the railroads," wrote Agent Mahan in his 1878 annual report to the commissioner of Indian affairs. "The old men and women hunt, fish, and gather berries, and otherwise assist in providing foods. But few families live upon the reservations."[57] Similarly in 1889, Agent Leahy reported: "In the berry season, the women and children gather the fruit, which finds in neighboring towns a ready sale at remunerative prices."[58] Paul Buffalo indicated that "scouts" would find the best areas for berrying and then "reported to the families of womenfolks where they saw the most berries."[59]

Berrying and other forms of gathering provided an especially crucial source of income to women who did not have male relatives to contribute to the support of the household and to whom wage work was not readily available. In the 1880s, Qui-ka-ba-no-kwe, or Dawn Woman, of the Bad River reservation found herself in this situation after her husband, Ma-ne-go-osh Marksman, died. Refusing to give up her children to other relatives, she supported her family single-handedly through gardening and harvesting and selling wild produce. Qui-ka-ba-no-kwe's grandson, Jerome Arbuckle, noted: "Although the eldest of the children was only six or seven years of age and the youngest was still strapped in the di-ki-na-gun, or cradleboard, the mother was not deterred from participating in the harvesting of natural or wild crops. These crops were the edible roots, nuts, berries, and wild rice." Harvesting wild plants, including berries, was a livelihood that Qui-ka-ba-no-kwe could undertake while caring for her children. She could pick cranberries while keeping an eye on them. "After cautioning the children to remain in the canoe," Arbuckle explained, "Qui-ka-ba-no-kwe picked berries within the sight and sound of the children." While she picked berries, "the children played and slept in the craft the whole day, occasionally partaking of the food and drink left for them by their mother who also left her berry picking 'to see how they were' from time to time." Qui-ka-ba-no-kwe sold or bartered surplus wild crops to lumber camps or to merchants in Odanah and Ashland, Wisconsin. She later married John Diver from the Fond du Lac reservation, who worked as a day laborer in the lumber, fishing, and building industries in Wisconsin.[60]

Many Ojibwe stories of berrying also centered on family travel to areas where berries were growing. They attest to the continued mobility of Ojibwe people even after the creation of reservations, as well as the continued significance of berrying as a form of labor that linked Ojibwes throughout the region. John Condecon traveled with his family from Ontonagon, Michigan, to Eagle River, Michigan, to pick berries in the summer of 1872. His entire family traveled in birch-bark canoes to Eagle River, where they "joined other Indians living at the place." "Our occupation there was picking blueberries and huckleberries and selling them to procure the necessities of life," Condecon explained. From Eagle River, Condecon and his family moved twice more, to L'Anse, Michigan, for an annuity payment, and then back to Ontonagon by way of Houghton, Michigan. The next summer, Condecon and his family traveled to Bad River, where they "joined large numbers of Indians from Ashland and Odanah who were going to the prairie country to pick blueberries." They dried the berries for their own use "and sold the surplus to whites."[61] These memories speak to the common patterns of seasonal mobility that Ojibwes retained after the establishment of reservations as well as the importance of berrying as a source of revenue.

Decades later, in the early twentieth century, Ojibwes still shared these experiences of mobility. During her childhood, Maude Kegg traveled with her family from their home in Portage Lake, Minnesota, by canoe and wagon to pick berries on the shores of the Mississippi River. They then sold their berries in Brainerd, Minnesota. Berrying was the way that Ojibwes "made their living," according to Kegg. They sold berries to buy lard, flour, and sugar—"whatever they needed." Kegg concluded, "That's the only way the Indians made their living long ago, always working on their own."[62] Not only did Kegg's descriptions suggest the continuity of Ojibwe mobility to harvest berries, but she also placed berrying squarely in a cash economy and defined it in terms of its value as labor.

In addition, berrying, unlike hunting and fishing, appeared to be an aspect of treaty rights that was less likely to be criminalized by state regulations imposed as early as the 1880s and increasingly imposed after the 1890s.[63] Due to the political interests and influence of sportsmen, state governments mostly focused their regulatory efforts on hunting and fishing, though they occasionally harassed Ojibwes who were ricing and maple sugaring. Florina Denomie wrote of berrying in the 1930s, "You are assured good meals during the season, plus some real money, and large families often reap a substantial harvest, as in this occupation you are not hampered by state labor laws, and children may pick regardless of their ages."[64] Though Denomie described labor laws rather than treaty-related laws, her comments suggest that state conservation officials were not too concerned about berrying. As state opposition to hunting and fishing rights grew, then, berrying became an increasingly important industry.

THE FRUIT-GROWING INDUSTRY

At the turn of the century and in the decades following, devastating forest fires wreaked havoc on the region as a consequence of logging—namely, downed timber and cutover land on and off-reservation. The transformation in berrying intersected with the growth and decline of the regional lumber industry. From 1890 to 1909, Indian agents expressed concerns that if Ojibwes did not cut and sell the remaining timber on reservations, it would be lost to blow downs and forest fires.[65] These concerns also intersected with a desire to bolster the allotment process and to promote agricultural enterprise. From the view of the Indian Service, the sooner Ojibwe lands were devoid of timber, the sooner Ojibwes could turn their attention to farming rather than hunting, fishing, or gathering.

In 1890 and 1891, the Indian Service proposed two unsuccessful congressional bills calling for the harvest of the remaining timber on Ojibwe reservations under the jurisdiction of the La Pointe Agency. The agents' fears were realized; in 1896, fires ripped through the Red Cliff reservation, destroying 6,500,000 feet of white and Norwegian pine.[66] In the winter of 1894, multiple fires passed through the Bad River reservation, reducing the class of timber from prime green timber to dead and downed timber, and devastation by forest fires continued into the next year. Again, in 1900, from 1908 to 1909, and as late as 1917, the reservation experienced devastating fires fueled by downed timber. The entire Lake Superior region experienced an increasing number of forest fires. The worst of these was the fire of 1918, which ravaged large sections of the Fond du Lac reservation and surrounding areas.

Yet, despite the devastation that these fires caused—destroying homes, businesses, and farmlands—they bolstered blueberry and raspberry crops, which tend to thrive in burnt and cutover areas.[67] These conditions provided a new wealth of resources for berry pickers, who found the berries growing in greater abundance and size. Many Ojibwe families sought burnt and cutover areas for their rich berry crops. In the first decade of twentieth century, Marie Livingston, an Ojibwe woman from Bad River, took a berrying trip with her family to an area near Gordon, Wisconsin. Her father came across a patch of berries that was about "one mile square."[68] It had originally had been a part of a jack pine forest that had been destroyed by a major fire. The area was "a real Eldorado for berry seekers," Livingston recalled. "The berries were so large and thick that it was impossible to avoid stepping on them; the clusters looked like grapes."[69] Similarly, Florina Denomie was amazed at the size of the berries that grew in the berry fields near a campground in northern Michigan. "This is the one time I beheld blueberries growing on stems four to six inches long, in clusters like grapes," she recalled. The place where Denomie's family discovered the berries, she added, "probably constituted the first crop of the 'burnt over land.'"[70]

The long-term impact of the forest fires and cutover lands and the decline of the lumber industry altered the local economy and spurred a new agricultural movement. From the beginning of the twentieth century to the 1940s, agricultural experts encouraged settlers to farm cutover lands in northern Wisconsin.[71] The movement to farm the cutover was a product of the Progressive Era's country life movement. Government officials and reformers attempted to transform northern Wisconsin into an agricultural hub.[72] They promoted the industrialization of agriculture.[73] They believed that rural America needed to be transformed by more efficient institutions and practices, and they asserted that agriculture needed to be more productive in order to contribute to the success of the industrialized nation that the United States had become.[74]

On the southern shore of Lake Superior, the movement was manifested in fruit farming. The most well-known and perhaps most successful of these ventures was William Knight's fruit-growing enterprise in Bayfield. Knight, born in Delaware in 1843, as a young man, traveled to Wyoming, where he worked as a trader at Camp Washkee. At the age of twenty-six, he relocated to Bayfield to assist his brother, John H. Knight, with his work as the Indian agent at Bayfield. In 1870, William worked as the superintendent of the newly constructed sawmill at Red Cliff. In the following decades, he pursued a number of ventures that made him one of the wealthiest men in Bayfield. These included buying and selling fish, managing a brownstone quarry, running a logging company and sawmill, and founding a bank. Knight was also active in civic affairs, serving as a member of the town board and county clerk and running unsuccessfully for the Wisconsin state assembly in 1910.[75]

Around the turn of the century, Knight became interested in commercial fruit farming. After clearing the stumpage on his lands, he planted a substantial cherry and apple orchard. According to his daughter Eleanor Knight, his belief that "Bayfield's future in agriculture was great and that marketing was one of the first problems" led him to organize the Bayfield Fruit Association in 1910.[76] In 1912, the organization merged with the Bayfield Fruit Shippers Association to become the Bayfield Peninsula Fruit Association and continued to market fruit for Bayfield farmers. In the 1940s, the association became a cooperative. It was liquidated in 1953.[77] Knight promoted fruit-growing in Bayfield County and on Sand Island, marketing apples, strawberries, and raspberries with an interest in selling cutover lands and turning Bayfield into a prosperous agricultural community. For at least two decades, a substantial fruit-growing industry thrived in the Bayfield area.[78] In 1913 alone, Bayfield fruit farmers exported 17,500 crates of raspberries, 1,500 crates of blueberries, 888 crates of strawberries, 478 crates of blackberries, 170 crates of plums, and 78 crates of gooseberries.[79]

Indian agents' efforts to pressure Ojibwes to farm paralleled this movement, and allotment policy bolstered their endeavors. Although allotment had a far-reaching impact on Ojibwe communities, Red Cliff was most drastically affected. Ojibwes had farmed on a minimal scale on Red Cliff, but by 1923, all usable timber had been cleared from the reservation, and by 1929 all community members had been granted title or patent in fee to their allotments.[80] Anthony Godfrey suggests that many Red Cliff people sold their lands or sought other forms of income in order to survive because they cut all of the useable timber from their lands. He writes, "Landless, they supported themselves through jobs in local shops and factories, by raising strawberries on non-Indian farms, and/or through commercial fishing."[81] But it is not actually clear whether Ojibwe people were raising berries on non-Indian farms or their own. In 1905, agent S.W. Campbell reported that many Ojibwes used proceeds from their allotments to purchase farms located outside the boundaries of reservations.[82] Campbell's statement may explain why some Ojibwes raised berries on farms at the same time that the Indian Service considered their original lands alienated.

Ojibwes from the Bad River and Red Cliff reservations turned to farming in the early twentieth century in growing numbers. In 1904, Campbell reported, "While a majority of Indians on other reservations have good gardens, hay meadows, and pastures under cultivation, the Bad River and Red Cliff Indians have commenced farming operations on a larger scale."[83] Because of the federal government's policy that money from the sale of timber could be used only for "permanent improvements and in cases of necessity," Red Cliff and Bad River Ojibwes "ceased their importunities and commenced clearing their allotments."[84] However, it is more likely that the decline of timber resources and the lumber industry itself contributed to this development.

By the early 1910s, the superintendent of the Red Cliff reservation, J. W. Dady, endeavored to implement new farming ventures at Red Cliff. Dady's annual reports to the commissioner of Indian affairs indicated that there was a small but growing fruit industry on the Red Cliff reservation. In 1915, Dady reported that Red Cliff Ojibwes planted approximately 400 apple trees, 50 plum trees, and "a number of small bush fruits." He encouraged the cultivation of the "bush fruits" on the reservation because "the Indians will take good care of them as they yield good returns in the spring of the year which helps to carry the grower along through the rest of the growing season."[85]

Red Cliff's proximity to the town of Bayfield, as well as to a newly constructed highway, bolstered the community's farming ventures. Certainly William Knight's new agricultural movement provided Red Cliff farmers with opportunities to get their crops to market and to work cooperatively with other fruit farmers. Some reservation farmers became members of the Bayfield Fruit Growers Association. In 1922, the Indian agent at La Pointe wrote, "We have a Fruit Association of farmers in town [Bayfield] which the Indian farmers are members, in fact the Indians are encouraged to become members of all associations and lodges of the district." He added that the opportunities for marketing agricultural products were "excellent due to the presence of the Fruit Association which handles all farm products as well as fruit."[86]

In 1926, the agent explained that one could make a good living from farming and dairying at Red Cliff, but because farmers there held only small plots of land, "they have been giving more attention to gardening, truck farming, and the raising of berries and bush fruit than any other line of activity." There were connections between the agricultural movement surrounding Bayfield and the Red Cliff people's efforts to farm berries. "As the white people are following the fruit raising venture more than farming," the agent wrote, "the Indian is quite naturally following in the footsteps of his white neighbor." The lower startup costs of berry and fruit farming motivated many Ojibwes. A strawberry patch, for example, could "be set out without expending very much money in getting started." As members of the Bayfield Fruit Association, the agent added, Red Cliff Ojibwes "receive the same benefits and advantages from this that their white neighbors receive."[87]

Farming berries and other fruits for commercial purposes differed from traditional Ojibwe gathering practices or even the small-scale gardening that Ojibwe women did. Growing and harvesting blueberries entailed se-lecting particular plant varieties that would yield the biggest crop in the sandy and red clay soils of the region. Digging holes for crops could be done by hand or, more efficiently, with a tractor-mounted auger. For the most productive growth, blueberry bushes had to be planted five feet apart in rows that were eight to ten feet apart. Blueberry farmers then fertilized the plants, irrigated the soil, controlled pests, and protected the plants from frost.[88]

Commercial fruit farming did not necessarily undermine Ojibwe con-nections to the land; indeed, there is evidence that Ojibwes cultivated crops like corn or transplanted wild rice for future use.[89] In some instances, agriculturebecame a means to mitigate the loss of resources caused by al-lotment and to resist the anti-tribal policies of the federal government. The story of the Blackbird field on the Bad River reservation provides one such example. In 1858, Chief Keesh-ke-tow-wag (Cut Ear) invited all of the peo-ple of the community to his home for a feast. Once everyone was assem-bled, he told them that he needed their help "to clear land for a large com-munity garden." The community cleared and drained eighty acres of land and gardened there for twenty-five years. Between 1888 and 1890, Chief James Blackbird filed this community clearing under his allotment and it remained a center of community activity. The community today uses this site as their powwow grounds.[90]

This economic transition affected the gender dynamics surrounding berrying and other forms of gathering. Similar to the dynamics of wild rice harvesting, berrying, once a women's activity, became work shared by men and women during the Great Depression. As other opportunities for income available to Indian men declined in the early twentieth cen-tury, they became increasingly involved in labor that had traditionally been under the control of women.[91] The Indian Service's focus on imple-menting industrial farming on reservations compounded these changes. Indian agents encouraged Ojibwe men to pursue agricultural ventures in lieu of work in declining industries, such as lumber, while they encouraged Ojibwe women to focus on domestic labor and gardening.[92]

The decision to grow berries and orchard fruits was clearly influenced by a burgeoning fruit-growing industry in the region. Raising a crop that already grew wild in the area meant that these ventures were more likely to be successful. But Ojibwe gathering traditions also overlapped with this choice and explain why growing numbers of Ojibwes at Red Cliff turned to berry farming. Ojibwe farmers retained access to plants that had always been an important source of food. While farming berries for commercial purposes was clearly different than harvesting berries in the wild, berries still had to be picked in ordered to be taken to market. By cultivating and harvesting berries, Ojibwes could at least sustain some of the customary social and cultural connections associated with berrying.

What is most important about the transformation of berrying is that it illustrates how Ojibwes repurposed a traditional form of labor that was integral to their identity, ensuring its persistence even within the context of industrialized agriculture. Caroline Parker wrote that John Bear, a well-known Lacrosse player from the Red Cliff reservation, "found solace in gardening, raising strawberries, raspberries, apples, cherries, and grapes—and he found a good market for his products" in his old age.[93] That Bear found solace in farming in addition to making money from it indicates that this labor held some of its original meaning that was distinct to Ojibwe culture.

Ojibwe families did not allow the process of allotment and the privatization of land to prevent them from sharing resources with one another. They resisted the federal government's efforts to break up their communities through the allotment by sharing their resources. Paul Buffalo explained that blueberries were abundant and "even if a family privately owned only a small U.S. government allotment of land of forty acres they couldn't pick all of the berries on it anyway." If the Ojibwe families who held the allotments were picking berries and encountered a new group of berry pickers, Buffalo recalled, they would say: "We have this blueberry patch here, and a village up there. We work up there. It seems like you like to be alone, but you're welcome to our village. So if you want to come to our village, I'll tell the others there that you'll come, and we'll expect you." These families also hosted social gatherings, where, sitting around the campfires they "told their history of where they're from. They told one another about their life. They told their history of life, and who they are." In the process, the berry pickers discovered their connections to one another. "By their expression, by their words, and by them talking," Buffalo explained, "one from the first group would realize a visitor as his relation. . . . [They would say], 'I find, I understand, that you have the same blood as I have because this relation of mine went down and lived in your area, in the eastern part of our territory.'" From these conversations they "found out relationships from a-way back."[94] Buffalo's account demonstrates that picking renewed and drew ties between Ojibwe people and highlights how these ties were integral to their history and identity. Ojibwe communities did not allow the privatization of their lands to prevent them from sharing the resources located on them. In contrast to the aims of allotment policy, the act of inviting other Ojibwes to pick berries that grew on their lands enabled allotment holders to retain important community relationships.

Despite their initial success, the fruit-farming ventures at Red Cliff and in the surrounding area lasted only a few decades. Agriculture began to decline when it was curtailed by state officials and planners during the New Deal era. They recognized that northern Wisconsin would never become a thriving agricultural center. New Deal policy-makers favored the consolidation of agricultural operations. Even the regional farms that were commercially oriented were not large enough to benefit from the legislation that supported these aims.[95] Rather, federal and state governments turned greater attention to the reforestation and conservation of northern Wisconsin lands.[96] The Bayfield Fruit Association survived this era, in the 1940s becoming a co-op, which lasted until 1953.[97] Despite this decline, remnants of William Knight's original orchards exist in Bayfield, and the town holds an annual apple festival to celebrate its agricultural heritage.

There are no large apple orchards on the Red Cliff reservation that indicate that the reservation was once part of this short-lived industrial agricultural movement. However, the Red Cliff Band now operates a community garden under the supervision of the Red Cliff Health Department, which provides healthy food for band members and encourages them to grow their own foods. The garden features a range of food crops, including some blueberries and raspberries. Red Cliff sells some of the surplus produce at the Bayfield farmers' market.[98] This revival in small-scale agriculture benefits the community.

The decline of industrial agricultural operations in the early twentieth century, however, suggests that Red Cliff people's histories diverged from those of the non-Indians living near them. The decline of agriculture at Red Cliff was caused by the dispossession of tribal lands. By the early 1930s, Red Cliff people had lost most of their lands to allotment, and by 1933, the reservation was comprised of a few thousand acres of allotted land. The rest had been lost as a result of sales and the inability of those Indians who were deemed competent to pay taxes on their lands; 505 out of 600 Red Cliff Band members were landless as a result of "tax problems." One of the major focuses of Indian New Deal was actually to purchase land to add to the reservation land base.[99]

WORK IN THE BERRY FIELDS

Despite the dispossession of lands, Ojibwes continued to rely on berry picking as a source of seasonal income, and this labor grew in importance during the Great Depression when wage work or relief was not available. Traveling to berry fields and patches each summer, they picked berries for a wage or sold the berries they harvested to traders, dealers, or local grocers and bakeries. Ojibwes throughout Minnesota and Wisconsin also sold wild rice they harvested during the Great Depression, and, with federal support, they also established cooperatives on Minnesota reservations, such as White Earth and Mille Lacs.[100] The federal government also facilitated ricing in some communities. The Works Progress Administration, the Indian Division of the Civilian Conservation Corps, and the Minnesota State Forest established rice camps in an effort to revitalize Ojibwe economies in northern Wisconsin and Minnesota. However, state governments also undercut the economic benefits of these projects by issuing ricing licenses to increasing numbers of non-Indians during the same period.[101]

Ojibwes harvested and sold berries on a large scale during the Depression. The 1938 Economic Survey of the Consolidated Chippewa Jurisdiction of Minnesota estimated that Indians harvested $10,000 worth of blueberries annually and that the average Indian family picked twenty-four quarts of blueberries for sale daily. The survey also recognized the importance of this industry in larger regional and national markets. Among the customers who purchased berries from Ojibwe pickers were "several large bakeries which specialize in pastry." A Duluth bakery bought large amounts of blueberries from Ojibwes and marketed its products to a wide ranging area. Some companies that purchased "wild fruits" arranged to transport Ojibwe families to "berry producing lands" and provided "for the purchase of each day's harvest and the shipping of fruit to consumer centers."[102]

Berrying remained important for Ojibwes because it was a ready source of income when other work was scarce. Florina Denomie noted that Bad River Ojibwes turned to berrying in the absence of work relief: "A few days ago (July 15, 1938), those who were dependent upon the relief agencies for maintenance were notified that no further relief would be extended for some time, and advised to go to the berry fields. Of course, many would have gone regardless of this advice, as the Chippewas for centuries back have always looked forward to the berry season as a considerable source of income."[103]

Denomie's other comments speak to the social aspects of berrying and raise questions about the meaning of labor for Ojibwe people. They suggest that although Ojibwe labor came to be defined in terms of the income it generated, it also became the means through which they sustained their relationships to the land and built relationships with one another. "Besides berry picking affording a financial gain," Denomie wrote, "it also offers an opportunity for general recreating." Living in the berry camps was beneficial: "You are living in the open, where the children romp and play, and sleeping in a tent at night, you have the advantage of breathing only the purest air, as the ventilation of the tent is hard to equal. Thus the berry fields hold out to you improved health conditions, recreation for your children, and while you may come to the berry fields rather sun burn and a shade darker, you feel better in every way." Denomie described a berry-picking heaven, where working on the land was rejuvenating and improved one's health. Berrying brought together large groups of Ojibwes, who camped in the same location for years. "In the camping ground on the berry fields back of Washburn [Wisconsin]," Denomie wrote, "one observes a small tent city. The Indians have gone to the same camping grounds for decades past."[104] These camps were located near towns like Washburn, because the pickers could more easily sell their berries to non-Indian buyers.

While in berry camps, Ojibwes socialized not only with one another but also with other Native people from the region. Ojibwes interacted with Ho-Chunk (or Winnebago) people who traveled north to pick berries. A large group of Ho-Chunk people from Wisconsin Rapids, Wattenberg, and Eagle River, Wisconsin, picked berries in the same camps. Interjecting some humor about Ojibwe and Ho-chunk rivalry, Denomie wrote: "The Indians make it to the berry fields every summer and, perhaps, if the fires of hostility among the Indians had not been smothered, the possession of the berry fields would be the cause of another argument and war. The Winnebagos are friendly, however, and usually after the berry harvest they pay the Indians of Odanah a visit, and both unite in a general pow-wow." These interactions created a pleasant atmosphere in the camp. "In the camping grounds just referred to," Denomie commented, "the sound of the Indian drum is heard coming from the Winnebago group in the late hours of the evening." She added: "The valley in which the tents are located is filled with the sound of the radio in the evening, and while you are actually in a desert, you have the advantage of modern entertainment, if you prefer this to the drum and song of the Winnebagos."[105]

On August 7, 1938, Ojibwes and Ho-Chunks played a baseball game in the village of Odanah, perhaps during the same visit that Denomie described. Baseball games appear to have been common events during the berry season. In August 1933, the *Ashland Daily Press* reported that the "Odanah tribe of Chippewa Indians" and the "Winnebago tribe" would play against each other in a baseball game that had been put together as part of a "peace conference" organized by Ojibwes from Bad River.[106] It is likely that Bad River people organized the conference at a time when

Ojibwes and Ho-Chunks would have been picking berries together in the berry fields anyway. These events suggest that berrying was an intertribal activity, characterized not only by the labor that it entailed but also by large social gatherings and exchanges between Native people of the region where they built connections with one another.

Ojibwes who grew up during the Depression recalled experiences resembling those Denomie wrote about. Michael Morrison of Grand Portage recalled that when he was a boy, the blueberries and raspberries that his family picked "brought in a lot of income to our family." Morrison's father built wooden crates for the berries that held thirty-two quarts of berries. The Morrisons did not own a car so Morrison's father would hire a person to drive them to the woods and then pick them up five days later. "[The driver] would leave us there," Morrison explained, "and since we didn't have tents or anything to sleep in, we lived right out in the open, eating the berries we picked, the rabbits we snared and the bannock we cooked. All we brought with us was the bare necessities." Morrison recalled that his family picked a lot of berries: "Figure it out—there were four of us kids who were old enough to pick, plus my dad. Each of us had a crate. So there were five crates, each with thirty-two quarts. That's 164 quarts in all." The combined labor of the four children and the father allowed the family to earn more income than would a smaller family. Morrison reflected on the meaning of berrying: "Although I don't pick berries anymore—I guess I've been spoiled by the white man's ways—whenever I buy blueberries or raspberries now it reminds me of those days. And they were happy days."[107]

Similarly, Isabelle Whelan and her family traveled some distance from their home on the Fond du Lac reservation to pick berries. "We would pick blueberries in the summer," Whelan recalled. "Dad made what we called a blueberry box made of wood with leather straps. He carried it on his back. We went clear to Danielson's (about 3 miles west from our residence) to gather berries." In the 1940s, Whelan's family also derived some economic benefit from her father's eighty-acre berry farm, which the Bureau of Indian Affairs had purchased from a non-Indian family. According to Whelan, "The berries were plentiful." Many people came to the farm to pick berries, but Whelan's father "would only let some in," and her family picked the rest. Whelan's mother canned some for the winter, and they sold the rest. Whelan personally benefited from the berry harvest on the farm. "I remember my cousins and I sent for some school clothes with dollars we made from berries," she recalled. "A green dress and fancy shoes out of the Bell Hess catalog." "We spent many happy hours in the woods with the family," Whelan concluded. "To this day, I go picking berries and making jellies." Whelan's memories reflected the social connections associated with berrying, as well as its link to contemporary berry picking.[108]

The history of berrying exemplifies the changing meaning and purpose of Ojibwe labor associated with gathering, as well as the multiple meanings that this labor held for Native people. Berries had been a key form of sustenance both before and after the treaties. Harvesting berries was one of many gathering rights that Ojibwes exercised for their survival, but this activity changed over time and was defined by American economic expansion and imperialism. In the nineteenth century, berrying became a mechanized agricultural enterprise. The new techniques for growing and harvesting berries contradicted indigenous Ojibwe beliefs that harvesting plants was part of their reciprocal relationship with the land. However, whether Ojibwes picked berries for a wage on a farm or independently in the woods, meadows, and marshes of the region, they continued to draw on this labor to define their relationships with one another. In berry camps, Ojibwes built and sustained connections with one another in the face of allotment and assimilation policies focused on undermining them.

Berrying continues today. Ojibwes no longer perform this labor on as large a scale as they did during the late nineteenth and early twentieth centuries. The profitability of harvesting and growing berries diminished as they and other produce were shipped to supermarkets from states such as California, Washington, Oregon, and Florida as a result of even greater mechanization of agriculture after World War II. However, it is unlikely that berrying stories will disappear. As Thomas Peacock, a member of the Fond du Lac Band, has eloquently put it,

> Times change. The post–forest fire, clear-cut habitat that supported the lush blueberry picking areas no longer exists [*sic*]. Most of us now buy blueberries in the supermarket. Does that mean there will be no new blueberry- picking stories? Will our relationship to a plant our ancestors used as sustenance somehow become lost in the blueberry muffins sold in deli's or the individually wrapped fried pies sold in convenience stores? Have we become too distant from our earth to remember the sweet dance of the wind, rain, sunshine and earth in the making of these things? Have we forgotten that all things have a reason and purpose, and spirit?
>
> We think not.
>
> Our relationship with all of these things goes back many thousands of years. Our ancestors saw bears eating blueberries. Our grandchildren will do the same. We are part of a story that goes on forever.[109]

CHAPTER TWO

They Can't Arrest Me.
We Got Treaty Rights!

Criminalizing Hunting and Trapping

While berrying exemplified Ojibwe people's creative opposition to the federal government's efforts to undermine their social and cultural values, Ojibwe struggles to hunt and trap led to more overt forms of resistance. Under the restriction of state game laws, Ojibwes fought not only to retain the traditions connected to hunting and trapping but also to defend the livelihoods critical to their economies and their sovereignty. Walter Bresette, one of the most vocal Ojibwe treaty rights activists of the twentieth century, said his grandfather inspired his own activism in the 1990s. "I remember the story of grandpa . . . when he would show up at the house . . . and . . . pretty soon he'd start looking for the shot gun. And ma would say: 'What are you doing dad?' He said: 'Well I'm going to get some supper.'" "You can't do that," Bresette's mother would say. "They'll arrest you. It's against the law." But Bresette's grandfather would persist, exclaiming, "They can't arrest me. We got treaty rights!" Bresette continued: "My grandpa was there. He was there on Madeline Island when they signed that treaty. And he told me why they signed that treaty. Now, my grandpa wouldn't lie to me. If he says we got treaty rights. We got treaty rights." Bresette's grandfather would then go off to hunt rabbits. "Of course he'd get arrested," Bresette added. "They'd throw him in jail. They'd steal our supper. And sometimes we needed that supper."[1]

Walter Bresette died tragically from a heart attack in 1999, but local community members remember his dedication to Ojibwe treaty rights. Bresette's story illustrates how past generations' struggles to exercise treaty rights shape more recent Ojibwe political activism. It shows that hunting and Ojibwe struggles to exercise their sovereignty were interwoven;

something as simple as shooting rabbits for dinner could become a form of defiance against state policy.

Ojibwe headmen reserved the right to hunt and trap to provision for their people's survival and their sovereignty in the treaties of 1837 and 1842. Their foresight became increasingly valuable during the latter half of the nineteenth century. Ojibwes sought new opportunities for earning an income in the commercial markets for fur and meat. Selling these commodities enabled Ojibwe hunters and trappers to compete with non-Indian hunters and trappers who moved into their territory. However, in the late nineteenth century, the federal government pressured Ojibwes and other Native peoples to give up hunting and trapping for wage labor and farming. Federal policy-makers believed that Indian hunting and trapping practices anchored them to a primitive, savage state.[2] They thought that if they compelled Native people to give up hunting and trapping for what they considered valid forms of work, they could expedite their assimilation into American society. Wage labor and agricultural contributed to the growth of the U.S. economy and facilitated American Indian citizenship. Because hunting reinforced indigenous mobility and connections to the land, it fell outside the boundaries of what Euro-Americans considered appropriate labor. State governments also argued that assimilation and allotment rendered American Indians subject to state laws and that U.S. citizenship annulled treaty rights. They emphasized that Indian hunting and trapping practices were savage and wasteful, and they justified their efforts to extend control over Indian lands and resources by declaring that treaty rights afforded Native people unlimited and unfair access to game.

However, hunting and trapping remained vital to Ojibwe survival. From the turn of the century onward, Ojibwes challenged state and federal policy by hunting and trapping in violation of state game laws, taking state officials to court, and by demanding compensation. In the process, they demonstrated that hunting and trapping rights were an integral part of their nationhood. Citing the treaties, they insisted that they remained members of an autonomous tribal nation and that states did not have the power to restrict their rights to hunt and trap. Under the restrains of state and federal policy, treaty rights became a critical vehicle through which Ojibwes asserted their sovereignty and resisted colonialism.

HUNTING, TRAPPING, AND THE SEASONAL ECONOMY

As vital sources of food, clothing, and other necessities, hunting and trapping were essential to Ojibwe economies. Ojibwe men hunted year-round, and how often depended on family and community needs. They tracked and hunted a range of animals, including deer, moose, and elk, using bows and arrows to kill them. They trapped animals such as otters, beavers, martens, minks, fishers, bears, rabbits, and partridges using snares made of nettle or basswood fibers or traps in which a log was positioned to crush the animal when it tried to eat the bait beneath the trap. Hunters and trappers treated the animals they pursued with respect and regard, honoring those they killed with prayers and offerings. In Ojibwe culture, individuals had deeply personal and spiritual relationships with specific animals that would assist and provide them with guidance throughout their lives. These alliances came through dreams and encounters with animals as well as having a name or being part of a patrilineal clan associated with a particular animal.

Men were responsible for supplying families with game, and they gained prestige for their hunting skills, but women, who were largely responsible for butchering game as well as processing and distributing meat and furs, also hunted and trapped.[3] This cooperative relationship between men and women enabled communities to make use of game more efficiently. Large animals like bear and moose required a number of people to haul the carcass home and butcher and process the meat and hides, so it was more productive to work in groups to maximize the quantity of food.[4] Hunting and trapping linked family members and generations, as young people learned how to hunt, trap, and process meat or hides from older generations. Thus, hunting and trapping not only constituted an integral part of the seasonal round as an economic, social, and ceremonial activity but also linked humans and the natural world.

These livelihoods remained fundamental to Ojibwe economies after contact with Europeans. From the early seventeenth century until the mid-nineteenth century, Ojibwes hunted and trapped for trade using guns and metal traps supplied by Europeans. Their labor was critical to the fur trade. Ojibwes supplied both the furs and the labor that supported the transport of furs to economic centers and operated the fur-trading posts in areas that Euro-Americans still considered remote.[5] In addition, they provided food and other necessities to traders who were unable to obtain them through their own means. To maintain alliances with their Ojibwe trading partners, fur traders followed the protocols of gift-giving, reciprocity, and intermarriage. Bruce White likens the gift-giving practices of traders to those of modern-day car salesmen, who offer perks and discounts in order to draw customers away from their competitors.[6] Because of the dependency of traders, Ojibwes' engagement in the fur trade had important political dimensions. By supplying furs to and forming advantageous relationships with traders, Ojibwes exercised power over the political and diplomatic climate of the Lake Superior region for centuries.

During U.S. expansion in the mid-nineteenth century, the market for furs, hides, and meat changed. With the decline of some animals as a result of overhunting and overtopping, fur prices rose and furs became luxury items processed and utilized by the garment industries of North America and Europe.[7] The furniture-making industry grew with settlement as leather hides were used to cover chairs and chair seats and fur was used to stuff chairs, sofas, and pillows or to cover floors.[8] Ojibwe hunters and trappers supplied game to individuals, trading posts, and mercantile companies.[9] In some cases, they owned their own traps or guns and independently supplied furs or meat to these businesses. In other instances, they arranged for a company to supply items such as traps in exchange for furs. These arrangements resembled older fur-trade relationships, which indebted hunters and trappers to a specific company and eliminated competition from other businesses, but they were more frequently based on cash rather than trade goods.

Settlers moving into new areas and new developments in transportation shaped these transitions. The growth of the railroad and shipping industries made it easier for hunters and trappers to travel to areas where they could find game and to transport their furs to larger markets. They shipped game via the railroads to St. Paul, Minneapolis, and Duluth, to markets farther east, and to Canada.[10] At the same time, however, these developments led to the near extinction of some species, such as buffalo, and to increasing competition as more hunters had access to land and resources that had once been remote and largely inaccessible.[11]

Indian hunters and trappers filled a niche, delivering meat and produce in local communities lacking a butcher or grocer. Peter Beaver lived in Superior in the mid-nineteenth century and sold game and produce to local residents. John Bardon remarked that Peter Beaver "was an outstanding example of stolid but consistent friendship" to the settlers of Superior. Beaver's "main occupation in the community was to supply wild rice, maple sugar, ducks, venison, partridge and other game, in season." According to Bardon, Beaver knew how to "dress muskrats and cook them so that they would taste like chicken. Skunk was also on his bill of fare," and he was "absolutely punctual and reliable" in delivering these commodities.[12]

Similarly, Wau-beh-meh-shay-way, a healer who lived in the area during the same period, made a living through hunting and trapping. Over the course of a year, he traveled along the lake shore from Ontonagon,

Michigan, to Grand Portage and back again. According to Bardon, he hunted and fished as he traveled the area, "trading game and furs for tea, coffee, port, and other 'luxuries.'" Bardon described him as "a remarkable hunter and trapper. He could invariably get any game that might be in the neighborhood."[13] As the economy of the region began to shift from one based on industry to one based on tourism and sports hunting, Wau-beh-meh-shay-way pursued new opportunities. In addition to trading game and furs, he worked for the Bardon family as a hunting guide and used various wild plants to remedy the family's minor ailments while on the trail.

Indian agents expressed mixed opinions about the value of hunting and trapping in Ojibwe communities, particularly at Grand Portage, where the soil and climate made it nearly impossible for Ojibwes to farm. Grand Portage's proximity to Canada also meant that the community had access to the Canadian market for furs. In 1874, Indian agent Isaac Mahan reported that Grand Portage residents subsisted "entirely from their fishing, hunting, and trapping, and the little aid the agent is enabled to give them." The neighboring Ojibwe Bois Forte (Nett Lake) community were not on the reservation during the winter, Mahan explained, "but were hunting, trapping, and fishing in or near the Canadian line." They purchased pork and flour with the income generated from "the fruits of the summer's hunting."[14] Ojibwes from Grand Portage and Bois Forte traveled to locations where there was good hunting and trapping despite their containment on reservations. Mahan was concerned about their moving off-reservation, but he could not deny that hunting and trapping provided them with a much-needed income.

Unlike Mahan, most Indian agents in the nineteenth century did not recognize any economic value in hunting and trapping, and some perceived it as an outright challenge to their authority. Reporting on his efforts to convince Ojibwes to farm in 1881, Agent W. R. Durfee categorized hunting as a leisurely activity that clashed with "civilized" forms of work. "The maturity of the crop lies too far in the future to excite his cupidity or rouse him from his lethargy," he complained. "In his native state he plunged into the woods in the morning on his hunting expedition, and at night returned with his game. The ancient habit [is] still attached to him."[15] Similarly in 1890, Agent M. A. Leahy reported: "Little progress can be made in the work of civilizing the Indian until he has been taught to supply his physical wants in a civilized way. As long as he is compelled to seek a precarious existence by hunting and fishing he will continue a savage."[16]

Yet, despite their efforts to discourage hunting and trapping, Indian agents could not prevent Ojibwes from making a living from these activities.

Working within the larger seasonal economy of the area, Ojibwes combined wage labor with hunting, trapping, and fishing. This strategy enabled Ojibwe hunters and trappers both to continue to exercise their treaty rights and to diversify their economic actions; if wage labor was unavailable at a certain time or hunting and trapping was poor, they still had an income to rely on.[17] Ojibwe families diversified their livelihoods in order to adapt to fluctuations in the local seasonal economy as well as changes in the environment. For example, in 1875, Isaac Mahan commented that the annual wild rice crop was a source of concern to him and the communities under his jurisdiction because it was not only an important source of food but also "the resort of numerous wild fowl," an additional resource that Ojibwe people "either consumed at home or sold in the neighboring towns."[18]

Ojibwes found creative ways to hunt and trap in spite of Indian agents' efforts to stop them. Not only did they combine hunting and trapping with wage labor; they also divided these activities among community members. In 1878, Mahan reported that Ojibwes at Grand Portage were "living almost entirely without government aid; the old men and women at hunting, fishing, and trapping, the young men as packers and guides into the mining districts along both the American and Canadian lines."[19] It appears that as wage labor became available to young men from Grand Portage, older generations hunted, fished, and trapped.

The Beargrease family was particularly efficient at resisting confinement on a reservation and combining hunting and trapping with a range of new occupations. In 1854, Agent Selden Clark met with a community of ninety-seven Ojibwe people living at Prairie Lake, near Cloquet. Clark attempted to convince the community members to leave their lands for a new home on the Fond du Lac reservation, promising them agricultural tools and assistance. Some community members decided to accept Clark's offer and moved to Fond du Lac. However, Moquabimetem (whose name literally translates as "bear grease"), a prominent leader in the community, refused this offer.[20] He took his family to the north shore of Lake Superior to the village of Beaver Bay, where a small but growing community of Ojibwes and Germans had been established. Moquabimetem made a living primarily through hunting and trapping, but he also did wage labor, delivering mail along the northern and southern shores of Lake Superior and working on a schooner called *The Charley*.[21] The wage labor provided a secondary means of support, but the travel required for these jobs also allowed him to continue hunting, fishing, and trapping.

It was through Moquabimetem's occupation as a mail carrier and a crew member on *The Charley* that his son, John Beargrease, became acquainted with these forms of labor. At an early age, Beargrease worked with his father, assisting him on his mail- carrying routes and the schooner.[22] When Beargrease was in his teens, he worked on a number of passenger and freight ships on Lake Superior. In 1879, he began carrying mail on his own route along the north shore and, like his father before him, supplemented his income by trapping. His mail-carrying routes were located along the traplines that he and his brothers set every winter. As he traveled, Beargrease would gather the pelts from the animals that he had trapped and then pack them along with the mail. He also drew on social networks with other Ojibwes whose traplines were located nearby to collect pelts and trade.[23] Once Beargrease procured the pelts, he took them to the general store or trading post where he delivered the mail and sold the furs. This became a lucrative endeavor for Beargrease, enabling him to act as an intermediary between Ojibwes who trapped and hunted near his route and traders who purchased the furs in nearby towns. Beargrease became so well known for his work as mail carrier that local newspapers reported his activities on a weekly basis and publicized the speed and efficiency at which he carried the mail between the towns on the north shore.[24] Today, the John Beargrease Sled Dog Marathon, a popular race held every January between Grand Portage and Duluth, commemorates his life and work as a mail carrier.[25]

Despite the determination of Indian agents to discourage hunting, it remained a key source of income as well as a means to foster social and cultural connections. Ojibwe men frequently hunted and trapped together. Joe Thomas and a number of other men from Grand Portage trapped and hunted near Swamper Lake in northern Minnesota in the early twentieth century. Thomas's daughter recalled that only the men went to this place. They stayed there all winter and returned to Grand Portage in the spring.[26] Betty Gurno also recalled that her uncles spent time trapping together near the Fond du Lac reservation.[27]

The first time an individual killed an animal marked an important transition in his or her life. The Ojibwes recognized these events as turning points and honored them through feasts and invited community members to attend. In the early twentieth century, Bob Wilson's family acknowledged his early hunting accomplishments. Wilson remembers spending "many happy days" with his cousin Jack Couture "roaming the woods and fields of the Couture farm in quest of 'big game.'" After days of unsuccessful hunting, Wilson managed to shoot a small chickadee. He took the chickadee home and "proudly showed 'the kill'" to his mother, who was amused over his "big game." She dried and kept the chickadee for a future ceremony.[28]

At the age of ten, Wilson convinced his father to take him hunting, and he killed a bear. When they arrived home they found their friend Anton Kabec visiting. After Kabec learned that Wilson had killed the bear, "he immediately stated that the event should be celebrated in accordance with the Indian custom." Kabec invited a number of older men from the community for a feast. During the meal, John Diver "discovered" the chick-a-dee his mother dried in his dish "and promptly ate it." Putting the chicka-dee in the dish appears to have been a ceremonial gesture in honor of the first animal Diver killed. After the men ate, John Diver gave a speech, saying that Wilson would have good luck in his hunting.[29] The feast marked a key turning point in Wilson's life and honored the bear he had killed. By inviting community elders to the feast, Wilson's family ensured that the event would be remembered.

Florina Denomie described hunting as an important part of her identity as an Ojibwe woman. She killed a porcupine while she and her grandmother were working in the sugar bush one spring. They were out of meat and Denomie told her grandmother that she was going to hunt for something to eat. She engaged in the complex process of tracking and killing the animal. Once she had the porcupine, she was ready to celebrate her achievement: "I was happy because I was successful in getting something, and as I sighted the sugar camp I hollered, 'Grandma, I got a 'gog' [porcupine]. She came running to meet me, and picked up a long stick and was ready to strike it when I told her that it was already dead. To my surprise it was still alive, and instead of dragging the animal, I was actually leading it. Grandma had to finish the killing."[30] Denomie and her grandmother skinned and cooked the porcupine and then honored it in a ceremonial feast. The women eventually used the porcupine's quills to decorate birchbark baskets. For Denomie, hunting included the use of traditional skills and sometimes humorous experiences that taught her more about this activity. Hunting represented close, affectionate ties between her and her grandmother.

THE CRIMINALIZATION OF HUNTING AND TRAPPING

At the turn of the century, Ojibwes faced increasing constraints on their ability to hunt and trap as state governments imposed games laws targeting Indians, which made it more difficult for them to make a living and sustain the social and cultural traditions connected to this labor. States' focus on fish and game legislation accompanied the Progressive Era conservation movement, and it represented new shifts in public thinking about land use. State officials, recognizing the negative environmental impact of extractive industries like lumber, mining, and commercial fishing, were searching for new ways to reinvigorate the declining economies of the northern part of the region. Their remedy was to draw urban tourists to the region to enjoy the natural environment. One of the most popular activities among wealthy urban men was sports hunting, and many of them traveled to northern Minnesota and Wisconsin in search of game. The increasing popularity of this activity reflected a belief in the use of land for recreational purposes rather than for a livelihood.

State governments targeted treaty rights as way of asserting control over natural resources as well as indigenous livelihoods. The criminalization of Ojibwe hunters and trappers was a central part of fish and game policy. According to Bruce White, Ojibwes were "a negative example against which non-Indians could unite in their desire to preserve fish and game, a handy aid to building consensus in the white community about game and fish policy, and if all else failed, a scapegoat for declining game and fish populations."[31] State officials and sportsmen promoted popular ideologies about race and labor in order to justify pursuing Indian hunters and trappers. They expressed their values about land use in opposition to those of other races.[32] Indigenous hunting techniques provided fodder for their claims. Environmental reformers portrayed animals as innocent victims of Native hunters and trappers. Moreover, sports hunters emphasized the brutality and violence of Indian hunting and trapping practices that did not apply to activities like fishing.

In 1896, Samuel F. Fullerton, the head of the Minnesota Game and Fish Commission, argued that treaty rights had become obsolete because Ojibwe hunting techniques changed "If the right that these Indians claim was originally granted to them by treaty," he asserted, "it was at a time when there were no market interests whatever and no value in game other than what it was worth as food to the parties securing it, and the purpose for which they now kill game—simply for trade or barter—was not at all contemplated at the time."[33] State officials dismissed treaty rights as outdated privileges and argued that the commercial hunting was not a treaty right.

Sportsmen defined their practices as sophisticated and civilized in contrast to Indians'. They distinguished themselves from "common hunters" by following a sportsman's code. The code called for a studied view of the landscape and the habitat of game, extensive knowledge and precise use of guns and fishing rods, and a sense of pride and etiquette in killing an animal.[34] Sportsmen redefined hunting and fishing as leisurely pursuits that allowed them to express their masculinity and their sense of refinement in opposition to the savagery that they attributed to common hunting practices.[35] Euro-American efforts to hunt in this manner reflected an increasing preoccupation with the perceived threats to masculinity posed by urbanization and industrialism.[36]

Discrimination against specific groups based on race or ethnicity was not an uncommon strategy among conservationist and sports hunters and fishers. Karl Jacoby has argued that law and lawlessness constitute "the twin axes around which the history of conservation revolves." In the nineteenth and twentieth centuries, the activities of rural people, including Indians, were increasingly deemed illegal and in violation of conservation laws.[37] Racial and ethnic differences served as key basis for the designation of lawlessness and a means to control the activities of certain populations. In the postbellum South, white sportsmen prevented African Americans' mobility and access to key sources of food and income through fish and game laws, ultimately undermining their economic independence.[38] In the Midwest, elite sportsmen voiced concerns about the threats they believed Southern European immigrants posed to wildlife, reflecting American opposition to immigration at the time.[39] For example, White points out that William Hornaday, an opponent of commercial hunting in Minnesota, referred to Italian immigrants as "human mongoose" and advised Americans to "look out sharply for the bird-killing foreigner; for sooner or later, he will surely attack your wildlife."[40] This focus on race ultimately served the purpose of uniting white Americans against specific populations across class lines.[41]

State officials believed Indians and Euro-Americans were taking advantage of their lack of power over reservations to illegally engage in commercial hunting. In 1893, the Minnesota Game and Fish Commission's annual report focused on both Indians and non-Indians who resided on reservations and hunted for a living. The commission reported that a large quantity of game was "secured ostensibly on the Indian reservations; and by those who are professional market hunters, who are employed by dealers in that commodity, both in this and adjacent states." "[It is the] custom of these dealers," the report continued, "to employ Indians and irresponsible white men and half breeds, who reside on the reservation, [to] do the killing, and to bring the material to some convenient point for shipment to the dealers who reside in Chicago, or some other large city outside of the state."[42] In 1895, the president of the Minnesota Game and Fish Commission emphasized the allegedly wasteful practices of Indian hunters who were encouraged by "unscrupulous traders" who were only interested in reaping a profit. He wrote, "Once an Indian gets on the trail of a moose he never leaves him until he kills him; so that game has no chance with their method of hunting. Their favorite time is in the summer when they kill the deer for their hides alone, and afterwards leave the carcasses to rot."[43] Such descriptions were common and reflected attempts on the part of state officials to justify targeting Indians.

Local Indians and Euro-Americans resisted these laws because they continued to rely on game as a source of food and/or income. In some cases, the two groups even worked together to foil the efforts of game wardens. In 1891, a warden in Cloquet arrested two Ojibwe men for selling moose meat to a non-Indian. He complained that there was "no use in one man risking his life in the woods alone up here arresting Indians and others who kill and sell meat of moose and deer to white people, when the town officers won't do anything to punish them or stop it." He reported that it was "a common occurrence to see squaws selling out-of-season meat and white men selling netted and dynamited fish, all of which people buy openly, and the city officials know it and do nothing themselves nor allow me to try and stop it."[44] Such occurrences reflect local resistance to these policies across racial lines. The warden's use of a slur to describe Ojibwe women, moreover, reveals the racist attitudes of state officials who targeted Native people, whom they believed were at the root of illegal activity in local communities.

In 1892, a warden from Crow Wing County, Minnesota, reported the migration of moose along the Northern Pacific railroad, then added, "The Indians are shooting them every chance they get, and it [is] almost impossible to catch the red devils."[45] In another report from the same year, a warden from Hubbard County in north central Minnesota explained to the Game and Fish commissioner that "the enforcement of game law has been a decided benefit in this country. I have the full support of the [sic] most of the sportsmen and all of the citizens." But he declared that Indians were the "hardest to lot to contend with" and requested advice "in regard to stopping these red skins. . . . You can get no fine from them and the agents will not keep them on reservations."[46] The warden's comments suggest the state's ambiguous relationship to Ojibwe people. He clearly recognized that Ojibwes were not citizens. However, he did not mention Ojibwe treaty rights. Rather, he saw Indians as an annoying hindrance.

The most malicious example of state persecution of Ojibwe hunters was the murder of Chief Giishkitawag, or Joe White, near the Lac Courte Oreilles reservation. On December 13, 1894, a state game warden and law officer arrested Joe White at Long Lake, Wisconsin, for hunting deer out of season off-reservation. As White was being handcuffed, there was and fray and the game warden clubbed White in the head with his rifle. White attempted to flee, but the officer shot him from about thirty yards away. White died later that day. The Washburn County district attorney filed murder charges against the two men in the Wisconsin Circuit Court of Washburn County. In March 1895, an all-white jury determined that the warden and officer had been acting in self-defense and found them innocent.[47] The results of the trial illuminate the state's blatant violation of treaty rights. Not only did the court excuse state authorities' use of violence to enforce state laws, it also sanctioned the limitless enforcement of game laws against Ojibwes exercising their hunting rights off-reservation.

VIOLATING AND THE COURTS

Ojibwes defied state authorities by reshaping the culture and the expression of identity surrounding hunting and trapping. Larry Nesper writes that the term "violating" encapsulates this Ojibwe defiance of state laws. Violating became a way of life for Ojibwe people as well as an expression of their identity. "Violating is not only economically significant," argues Nesper, "but a very important step for Indian boys becoming men, and to a lesser extent, for girls becoming women." Ojibwe men admit to violating with "proud defiance" and see it as an integral part of their identity.[48] Betty Gurno recalled the lengths to which her father and uncles went in order to trap and snare rabbits for food while avoiding game wardens during this period. The men traveled southwest from Fond du Lac to a remote trapping camp near Strout, Minnesota, via a train they called the "short line."[49] It is likely that by taking the train to this location, they avoided attracting the attention of wardens who might be patrolling near the vicinity of the reservation. After trapping and snaring forty to fifty rabbits, the men returned home. They also brought home venison, which, according to Gurno, "was illegal to take, but if they dried some earlier, they could bring that home." To Gurno, these actions were "a matter of survival."[50]

Arguing for the legitimacy of treaty rights in state courts became an extension of Ojibwe resistance. Since the political climate of the time supported state interests, state and federal courts ruled in favor of state jurisdiction over Indian people unless it was expressly prohibited by federal law. This shift toward state jurisdiction accompanied U.S. efforts to assimilate American Indians and to erode their indigenous sovereignty. Against this backdrop, early treaty rights cases make clear how conflicts over hunting and trapping became central to Ojibwe struggles to exercise their autonomy in the early twentieth century.

Bruce White discusses several turn-of-the-century treaty cases in a report for the Mille Lac Band of Ojibwe. In 1897, for example, Minnesota game wardens arrested Albert Porter and John MacArthur, Ojibwes from the Fond du Lac reservation who hunted off-reservation, for having a saddle of venison and they were sentenced to sixty days in the Carlton County jail. Gustav Beaulieu, an attorney from White Earth took their case. An article in the *Minneapolis Journal* suggested that Beaulieu argued that the conviction of the two men was illegal because they retained the right to hunt and fish in ceded land under the provisions of the treaties of 1842 and 1854.[51] Edward O. Stringer, the U.S. district attorney then presented the case to the Minnesota Board of Pardons, asserting that the men had the right to hunt and fish off-reservation without interference from the state. He argued that the treaties were ratified by Congress and that only the president could abrogate them.[52] The Board of Pardons denied the appeal, citing the Supreme Court decision in the 1895 case *Ward v. Racehorse* that held that state game laws overrode Bannock Indian treaty rights and that the state had the authority to regulate the killing of game within its borders.[53]

But the story does not end here. On April 17, 1897, La Pointe Indian agent G. L. Scott reported to the commissioner of Indian affairs that Beaulieu had informed Fond du Lac Ojibwes that they had the "perfect right to kill game in violation of state law." Scott included a letter from Beaulieu and his associate in which they explained they believed that the Board of Pardon's reference to *Ward v. Racehorse* ruling did indicate that Indians were accountable to state laws but argued that the Bannock treaty differed from the treaties that Porter and McCarthy referenced in their appeal. But the commissioner of Indian affairs informed Scott that Indians had to follow state laws regardless of their treaty rights in order to avoid further conflict.[54] Although Beaulieu did not prevail, by contesting the Board of Pardon's ruling, he encouraged other Ojibwes to resist state authority.

Two cases involving an Ojibwe woman named Julia Selkirk reflected further efforts on the part of the state to enforce game laws off-reservation in the 1890s.[55] Selkirk obtained furs from Indians and took them to the nearest railway station, where they were then transported out of Minnesota. In 1897, a game warden arrested Selkirk on the White Earth reservation for illegally possessing and selling game. The Game and Fish Commission confiscated the game and then sold it. Selkirk sued for damages, arguing that the state did not have the power to arrest her for exercising treaty rights on the reservation. After a number of appeals, the case went to the Minnesota Supreme Court in 1898.[56] Justice Charles M. Start concluded that the case was not about whether Indians could be arrested on-reservation but rather about the status of game. He argued that the White Earth reservation was created after Minnesota statehood and, therefore, the state owned all game within its boundaries, including on the reservation. He asserted that that while state wardens could not arrest Indians for violating state laws on the reservation, which was under federal jurisdiction, the state had the right to determine what to do with game located there, including confiscating and selling it.[57]

The court's ruling did not deter Selkirk, however. In 1899, she was involved in *Minnesota v. Al Cooney*. The Game and Fish Commission charged that Cooney possessed game after the state season had closed. After the lower court overruled the state's case, the state appealed the case to the Minnesota Supreme Court. Selkirk, who intervened in the case when the plaintiff demurred, argued that the state seized the game unjustly on the White Earth reservation. She explained that she was an Indian by birth and that she had traded with other Indians for the deer that they had killed on the reservation during the state-designated deer season and had intended to provide the meat to the Indian school on the reservation.[58] The Minnesota Supreme Court held that while the state did not have the right to forbid Indians from hunting for subsistence, it could regulate commercial hunting off-reservation.[59] According to the court, the state had allowed the tribal government to be present within its borders for thirty years, and had complied with Ojibwe rights to hunt and fish on reservations. However, game that was killed and sold to non-Indians off-reservation was subject to seizure by state authorities. Justice Thomas Canty proclaimed: "Such game is not protected by the license of the Indians to hunt in their traditional manner and may be seized by the state authorities, whenever this case can be done without interfering with the person of the Indian in whose custody or possession the game may be even though it is seized on the reservation." It was up to the jury to decide whether or not this argument applied to the case.[60] The rulings in both cases indicated that the state could claim ownership over game even if it was located within the boundaries of reservations. The courts targeted commercial hunting in both instances, affirming that game should be hunted for sport; if Indians hunted for self-support, they could hunt only for subsistence, not cash.

In Minnesota in the early twentieth century, state officials focused on American Indian citizenship as the rationale for enforcing fish and game laws within reservation boundaries. Allotment policy provided new impetus for the state to expand authority to reservations. Citing the provisions of the General Allotment Act, or Dawes Act, of 1887, state officials argued that Indians who had taken allotments were U.S. citizens and therefore subject to the authority of the state government.[61] In 1913, the local game warden in Cloquet reported to H. A. Rider, the state game and fish commissioner, that G. W. Cross, the superintendent over Fond du Lac, told Indians that they could hunt on their allotments without a license. Cross told the warden that he had been authorized by the commissioner of Indian affairs to do so.[62] Rider responded that the commissioner of Indian affairs was not familiar with Minnesota laws and that Indians who took allotments were citizens of the United States.[63]

States' assertions of power presented challenges to federal authority over Indian affairs and it raised concerns among Indian Service employees. In 1920, Cross wrote to Thomas Savoy, a game warden in Grand Marais, expressing his concerned about the arrest of two Indians who hunted on the Grand Portage reservation. He informed Savoy that Ojibwes had the right to hunt on the reservation and that the state did not have the power to regulate treaty rights within reservation boundaries and requested that the fines that they were made to pay be refunded. Taking control, Carlos Avery, the state game and fish commissioner, argued that Grand Portage land passed from the control of the federal government to Minnesota when it was allotted or sold. Consequently, he concluded, the reservation no longer existed and Grand Portage Ojibwes no longer retained the rights to hunt and fish as designated by treaty. Rather, they were subject to the same laws as citizens of the state.[64] Cross argued that allotment did not deprive Ojibwes of their treaty rights and that Ojibwe rights to hunt and fish were guaranteed by treaty and that treaty rights had never been nor could they be abolished by state governments.[65] There is no existing response from Avery.[66] It appears that Cross's argument did not prevail since state officials continued to regard citizenship as the rationale for restricting Ojibwe treaty rights for most of the twentieth century.

Many Ojibwes asserted that they were members of tribal nations and not subject to state jurisdiction on reservations. Between April and August of 1928, James Sharlow wrote a series of letters to the Wisconsin Conservation Commission from his home on the Bad River reservation. Earlier that year, I. H. Boomer, a local game warden, confiscated a beaver skin from Sharlow after Sharlow applied for a permit to sell the skin through Indian agent A. L. Doan. Because Mr. Boomer did not explain why he took the beaver skin, Sharlow complained to the conservation commission and requested compensation. On April 30, Sharlow wrote, "I being a full blood Indian, I have the right to trap beaver on the reservation according to our treaties with the federal government," and he requested that the skin be returned.[67] But Sharlow did not get the skin back. In another letter written on August 13, Sharlow explained, "Mr. Boomer is not giving you a true and correct statement of this affair, and unless I receive $25.00 which I consider this skin worth that he took from Mr. Doan, I will put the matter in other hands for final settlement."[68] The assistant director of the conservation commission responded that he had received Sharlow's letter and that Boomer would contact him, but he also suggested that if Sharlow did not think that Mr. Boomer had the right to seize the skin, "it would be necessary for you, I believe, to take court action to see that it is returned."[69] It is unclear whether Sharlow was ever compensated for his loss or whether the skin was returned. However, his persistent correspondence suggests that the economic loss caused by the confiscation of game was considerable.

A few Indians became game wardens or warden-trappers in order to navigate state laws and still make a living. In 1909, Carlos Avery, the executive agent of the Minnesota Game and Fish Commission, noted that Star Bad Boy, from Mahnomen, Minnesota, was "the first Indian ever entrusted with the authority of a game warden in this state" and noted that he "has shown marked capabilities in apprehending offenders, though lacking somewhat in discretion"[70] Another report published in 1916 included two pictures of Ojibwes employed by the state to assist with controlling wolf populations in the Superior Game Refuge. Under the pictures was the caption: "Good Types of Indian Trappers and Hunters—Such Experienced Men Are Commissioned to Trap and Hunt Wolves in the Superior Game Refuge."[71]

John (Jack) Linklater, who worked as a game warden in northern Minnesota from 1923 to 1933, was remembered as a hero by local residents. Linklater was Dakota and married an Ojibwe woman from Winton, Minnesota, while he was making a living as a trapper in the area. He worked as a guide on Isle Royale for a time and then was hired as a warden because of his knowledge of the area and experience living in the outdoors. He was successful at his work, and he also added to his income by commercial fishing on Isle Royale in the summers. One man recalled that "Linklater was a colorful character; his fine qualities, like his friends, were legion." Through his work as warden, he added, Linklater "became an idealistic outdoor character to every white person who was ever privileged to travel the wide open spaces with him. . . . [He] was the personification of honesty and courtesy, loyal to his trust, a true conservationist [and] unsurpassed in woods lore and marksmanship."[72] Linklater's accomplishments were exceptional; few Native people became state wardens.

Most Ojibwes continued to hunt, fish, and trap in spite of state laws. State efforts to enforce game laws during the Great Depression, however, exacerbated the financial difficulties Ojibwes faced. Ojibwes during this decade were concerned not just about the restriction of their treaty rights but also about the threat that game laws posed to the income hunting and trapping generated, and thus challenged state initiatives based on the assertion that hunting and trapping constituted legitimate livelihoods and were the source of a much-needed income. They compared these livelihoods with the frivolity of Euro-Americans hunting for sport during difficult economic times.

In spite of the federal government's granting of tribal self-governance during the New Deal era, Ojibwe people continued to lose ground to state encroachment on their hunting rights. In 1933 and 1940, Thomas St. Germaine, an attorney from the Lac du Flambeau reservation, argued cases based on Ojibwe treaty rights on and off-reservation before the Wisconsin Supreme Court. The first case involved Frank Dakota Johnson, who had accidentally shot and killed Frank Gervais, a non-Indian, while hunting on the Bad River reservation.[73] The state had charged Johnson with fourth-degree manslaughter and with unlawfully hunting deer during the closed season. In *State v. Johnson* (1933) the question was whether the state had the jurisdiction to charge Johnson with manslaughter and also whether state game laws applied to Ojibwes hunting on reservations. St. Germaine argued that the state did not have the authority to try Johnson because the shooting had occurred within the boundaries of the reservation and, under the Major Crimes Act, was under the jurisdiction of the federal government.[74] "At the time of the making of these treaties," Germaine also asserted, "hunting and fishing was not to the Chippewa Indians 'a sport' but a means of living—in fact the sole means of living in the Lake Superior district."[75] St. Germaine maintained that these livelihoods should have been give greater consideration by the courts. However, the Wisconsin Supreme Court held that because the lands on which the shooting occurred had been patented via allotment, state laws applied to Ojibwes on reservations. The ruling gave the state the power to enforce fish and game laws within the boundaries of reservations on lands that had been sold to non-Indians.

The second case, *State v. La Barge* (1940), involved John La Barge, a resident of the Lac du Flambeau reservation who was charged with possessing a doe off-reservation and out of season.[76] La Barge pleaded guilty under the condition that the State Supreme Court would determine whether the state of Wisconsin had the jurisdiction to arrest him. In hindsight, the case seems likely to have failed from the beginning. The state court would have ruled against treaty rights in accordance with Wisconsin fish and game policy. However, it enabled La Barge and St. Germaine to publicly contest state policy. St. Germaine maintained that the treaties entitled Ojibwes to the right to hunt in ceded territory and that they could not be arrested for violating state game laws. He called for the court to review the treaties; citing the case *United States ex rel. Winans v. Seufert,* he maintained that treaties must be understood as Indians understood them and in favor of Indians and that Indians were not limited to using subsistence methods they had used before treaties to exercise treaty rights. Arguing that the method that La Barge used to hunt the doe was irrelevant, St. Germaine cited *United States ex rel. Winans v. Seufert* to demonstrate how treaties should be understood and to point out "how careful the Red man is to utilize all of the deer carcass as distinguished from the way of his Pale-faced brother does who utilizes only the choice tenderloin and hind quarters of the deer, leaving the rest of the deer carcass for the wolves and other predatory animals to devour."[77] The court ruled in favor of the state, arguing that Wisconsin's admittance into the Union gave the state the authority to regulate Ojibwe hunting off-reservation regardless of treaty rights. But St. Germaine's arguments struck at the heart of the issues that were really at play. Sportsmen were the true criminals, wasters of game, not Indians.

Outside of the courtroom, Ojibwe people also expressed the value of these rights in economic terms, and they reasserted indigenous values of conservation to counter state arguments. In their writing and public rhetoric they challenged states' violation of treaty rights while stressing that conservation was an important Ojibwe value. They underscored the economic and cultural importance of treaty rights as well as the legitimacy of the labor they entailed. Ojibwes countered the state's arguments for criminalizing Indian hunters and trappers by describing in great detail the ways in which they performed this labor and by placing it within the larger context of their distinct relationship to the land as indigenous people and their history.

Daniel Morrison, for example, argued that the state of Wisconsin's hunting season did not apply to Bad River people. "One of the prized privileges of the Indians of the Bad River reservation is the right granted to them by treaty to hunt deer and other game with no restriction as to number or time," he stated. While game laws of the state of Wisconsin allowed "fifteen days, or so, in which to get your buck," he explained, the law was "not binding on members of the Reservation who are privileged to hunt at any time." Ojibwe hunters used "very good judgment as to the season for killing deer," because they had a "conservative mind" and they observed "the slogan: 'Do not take all today; reserve some for tomorrow.'" The right to hunt was critical to Bad River's economy, according to Morrison. Bad River Ojibwes killed several hundred deer each year on the reservation and the venison and hides were "an important factor in the maintenance of many Indian homes." They preserved venison for future use by canning it, salting it, and smoking it, and they utilized hides for items like "moccasins, jackets of various types, [and] costumes and [for] many other useful articles."[78]

Similarly, Jerome Arbuckle described the abundant populations of muskrat, beaver, otter, and mink in the Kakagon Sloughs on the Bad River reservation. The wildlife made the location "a favorite spot for the trapper." He believed that the preservation of this wildlife was necessary to ensure that hunting, trapping, and fishing could continue into the future. "Since the Kakagon country is an ideal place for the hunter and fisherman as well as the trapper," he said, "each should 'do his bit' towards the conservation of its native game for future generations."[79] Arbuckle discussed the types of waterfowl drawn to the Kakagon Sloughs and complained that many people disregarded the importance of conservation. "There are both white and Indian hunters who disregard the Conservation Laws," he wrote. "The writer has knowledge of a hundred and sixty-five ducks killed at one time by one hunter! Think about the future! Shooting from fast motor boats and the use of high-powered repeating guns is a highly destructive practice."[80] The Kakagon Sloughs had long been an important site on the reservation for hunting and trapping, as well as wild ricing, and Arbuckle was in favor of protecting this place. Though Arbuckle addressed Euro-Americans *and* Indians who wasted resources, the fact that he presented himself as an Ojibwe who was concerned about conservation suggests he was countering the opinion of the state and the non-Indian public that all Indians were wasteful and reasserting traditional Ojibwe beliefs about respectful land use.

Hunting and trapping had always been central to Ojibwe economies as means of sustenance, but this labor gained political importance as Ojibwes navigated the transformations that accompanied European and American expansion into their homelands. The federal government attempted to discourage Ojibwes from hunting and trapping because they stood in the way of assimilation. Federal officials believed that as Indians became integrated into the capitalist economy, farming and wage labor would eventually replace what they saw as uncivilized livelihoods. However, it was state game laws that presented the greatest challenge to Ojibwe livelihoods and their autonomy. State officials attempted not only to restrict the activities of Ojibwe hunters and trappers but to also undermine Ojibwe sovereignty.

Treaty rights stood in the way of state control over all natural resources within state borders. Drawing from earlier Euro-Americans' ideas about the savagery of Indian hunting practices, they focused attention on criminalizing Ojibwe hunters and trappers. State governments capitalized on federal efforts to incorporate Ojibwes into Euro-American society in order to bring reservations under state jurisdiction.

It was under these conditions that hunting and trapping came to represent for Ojibwes something more than economic survival. In the process of resisting the criminalization of activities that they had depended on for centuries, Ojibwes came to understand this labor as a marker of their nationhood and their struggles with colonialism. By contesting their arrests and the confiscation of game in state courts or in their daily encounters with wardens, Ojibwes like Walter Bresette's grandfather, Gustav Beaulieu, Julia Selkirk, Thomas St. Germaine, and many others defined hunting and trapping as fundamental political rights. Their actions illustrate how Ojibwe livelihoods came to be at the front and center of their struggles to exercise their sovereignty in the midst of state encroachment and the threat of assimilation.

CHAPTER THREE

Capital and Commercialization

The Struggle to Fish

At the same time that Ojibwe families began hunting and trapping for cash income, many also turned to commercial fishing to make a living. Mary Jane Hendrickson remembered her father as a commercial fisherman and "an Indian without a reservation." He was born in Michigan in the late nineteenth century, but the Indian Service would not recognize him as a member of an Ojibwe band because his family moved to Wisconsin when he was young. Hendrickson's father "never got anything from the Indian Department." He was even turned away from the Indian hospital in Cloquet, though he had a severe case of pneumonia. However, he eventually made Grand Portage his home. Like many other men living at Grand Portage during the early twentieth century, he plied the waters of Lake Superior for herring. In September and October each year, Hendrickson and her family moved to their fishing shack on Reservation Bay to take advantage of the herring season.[1]

At the age of eight, Hendrickson began helping her father in his fish house. "I'd do all the cleaning," she remembered. She also accompanied her father on his fishing trips helping him to split herring. Hendrickson looked back at these days with her father as valuable experiences: "When I think about it now, I'm glad I worked there, because I wasn't afraid to work. And whenever he went anywhere in the boat I was with him."[2] Hendrickson's story illustrates the extent to which fishing had become a key source of income for Ojibwe families in the early twentieth century. Hendrickson's father found a way to support his family despite the fact that the Indian Service refused to assist him. In the process, he taught his daughter about the value of hard work and persistence while spending treasured time with her.

The colonial relationship between Ojibwes and the United States shaped the transformation of fishing, an economic activity that families like the Hendricksons depended on. Ojibwes saw access to waterways and traditional fishing grounds as a critical part of their territorial and political jurisdiction. They were well aware of the shift taking place from the fur trade to the industrial economy when they reserved fishing rights in the treaties of 1837 and 1842. The United States defined these rights according to Euro-American demarcations of territory. For example, Article 2 of the treaty of 1854 set aside "two hundred acres on the northern extremity of Madeline Island, for a fishing ground" for the La Pointe Band, defining narrow boundaries of ownership in an area where they once had access to the Chequamegon Bay, all of its islands, and the lake beyond.[3]

The treaties opened the rich fisheries of Lake Superior to the development of the Great Lakes fishing industry. As the populations of local towns grew, Euro-Americans made a living selling fish to local residents. The growth of industrial centers and the expansion of railroads and shipping in the late nineteenth century generated larger markets for fish from the Great Lakes. Independent fishers and large fishing firms made a profit from Lake Superior's vast quantities of fish by netting, spearing, and angling. They plied the lake for unlimited quantities of fish and unlimited possibilities for wealth generated by the cession of Indian lands.

Like their non-Indian neighbors, Ojibwes made a living as fishers. Fishing rights enabled them to fish off-reservation and to engage in the commercial fishing boom. Despite the fact that commercial fishing was oriented around the extraction of resources for the capitalist market, many Ojibwes saw this work as an extension of older fishing practices. They also depended on commercial fishing to weather the federal government's efforts to transform their livelihoods. Federal officials' attitudes toward hunting and trapping and their attitudes toward fishing differed. They clearly saw hunting and trapping as leisurely pursuits (for both Indians and Euro-Americans) that interfered with the federal government's efforts to turn Ojibwe people into sedentary farmers. Unlike hunting and trapping, many Indian agents viewed commercial fishing as an acceptable occupation and noted commercial fishing as evidence that Ojibwes were successfully assimilating into American society. It was a form of labor that facilitated Ojibwe incorporation into the capitalist economy. They could not deny the economic importance of fishing because of the immense commercial fishing industry that engulfed the entire region.

Fishing would have remained a productive means for Ojibwes to retain economic independence had it not been for the expansion of large fishing monopolies that undermined the business of independent fishers. In response to state calls for conservation at the turn of the century, these large fishing firms worked closely with state governments to create legislation that targeted Indian fishers, shaping conservation efforts in Minnesota and Wisconsin to their advantage. Much of the time, wardens targeted independent Ojibwe fishers, who struggled to engage in a livelihood that had sustained them for thousands of years. The conflict over fishing continued well into the twentieth century, even after the decline of the Great Lakes commercial fishing industry.

OJIBWE INVOLVEMENT IN THE COMMERCIAL FISHING INDUSTRY

Ojibwe fishing methods were based on the spawning seasons of fish. Because of the depth and the cold temperatures of Lake Superior, as well as the long winter months, fish were only abundant in the spring and fall.[4] Beginning in April or May, as the water warmed, fish, such as lake sturgeon, walleye pike, and white suckers, migrated to the shallow water near lake shores or streams or rivers to spawn.[5] From September until mid-December, lake trout and various kinds of white fish spawned on the shallow shoals and reefs of the lake.[6] The availability of fish at different times of the year influenced the economic cycles, the development of technology, and the social organization of Native peoples living in the Great Lakes. Fishing techniques varied according to the season and weather conditions. While Ojibwes caught the largest volume of fish in the fall and spring, they developed technologies for fishing year-round. In addition to netting fish, they speared them at night by torchlight in the spring or through holes the ice in the winter. They also trapped fish and trolled for fish.[7]

Ojibwes considered fish and the underwater world from which they came powerful and dangerous and believed they should be treated with great respect. Fishers offered thanks to the water and fish before they began fishing in order to ensure their abundance in the future. They ascribed special powers to fish. Several traditional stories suggest that eating certain species of fish or too much fish could have transformative powers over a person.[8] One of the most powerful of fish in Ojibwe beliefs is the sturgeon (called *name*); it is also referred to as the king or peer of fish. Writing about Ojibwe communities on Lake Superior in 1855, the German travel writer Johann Georg Kohl observed: "A variety of herring is also found in the large shoals in this lake. The Indians, however, consider the sturgeon 'the king of fish' and it plays a very devilish part in their legends."[9] Ojibwe beliefs about the powers of the sturgeon endured into the twentieth century. Florina Denomie wrote that Ojibwe fishers suspended sturgeon from the ceiling of their homes as "wind predictors," believing that the sturgeon's nose would point the direction of the wind.[10] These beliefs persist today; in recent times, a number of communities have devoted attention to protecting and revitalizing the sturgeon populations of regional lakes and rivers.[11]

Ojibwes began to work in the commercial fishing industry between 1836 and 1842 as part of the American Fur Company's short-lived fishing venture on Lake Superior. The company's fishing activities were part of an economic experiment generated by new shipping technologies to transport furs and provisions. In 1834, company president Ramsey Crooks decided to replace the mackinaw boats the company used to transport furs and trade goods with schooners, which were more efficient and required fewer individuals to run.[12] But the use of the new boats would free the up labor of a great number of employees who were normally needed to paddle the boats, so Crooks decided to employ them as fishers instead. This defrayed the company's costs in constructing the new schooners and enabled it to supply additional provisions to its posts farther east.[13] Between 1835 and 1839, Crooks explored the northern and southern shores of the lake and established major fishing posts at Grand Portage (in 1836), Isle Royale (in 1837) and La Pointe (in 1839). He also established minor fishing posts near Fond du Lac, Keweenaw Point, Grand Island, and Sault Sainte Marie.[14]

Ojibwe and Métis men ran fishing stations, fished for the company, or worked as coopers, supplying the barrels that the company used to ship the fish to markets farther east.[15] At Grand Portage, the company hired twenty Indian fishers, providing them with salt, nets, and barrels, and paying them three dollars per barrel of fish in 1836.[16] The men working at the fishing stations engaged in contractual labor arrangements that would come to define the relationship between fishers and fishing companies for most of the nineteenth century.[17] Fishers employed by the American Fur Company were equipped with supplies in return for the catch and were paid from $100 to $200 a year, while fishers who fished "on their own account" were paid only for the barrels of fish they supplied.

The American Fur Company attempted to market and sell fish as far away as New York and New Orleans.[18] It had a fairly successful start. In 1836, the company shipped 1,103 barrels of fish from La Pointe, and in 1837, it shipped 2,600 barrels from the Lake Superior region.[19] By 1839, the yields from fishing exceeded 5,000 barrels.[20] Lucius Lyons, an agent of the American Fur Company, reported to the commissioner of Indian affairs in 1839 that "the Indians are encouraged to exertion in this branch of business, by the offer of a fair price for all the fish they can catch, payable on the delivery of fish at the different Store houses built to receive them."[21]

The American Fur Company's fishing operation, however, was short-lived since it coincided with a severe economic depression. The company supplied provisions to its employees, but there was no demand for fish in the larger national market. The national market, then became overwhelmed with food products, which were sold at low prices. By 1841, the American Fur Company had aborted its attempts to sell fish, and the next year, the company itself failed.[22]

The American Fur Company's venture foreshadowed the rapid expansion of the commercial fishing industry in the late nineteenth century. In 1926, historian Grace Lee Nute observed, "The history of the American Fur Company is so little known—especially its uniqueness as an example of Big Business half a century before the monopolistic and large-scale tendencies are popularly supposed to have originated in the United States—that an interesting and significant episode in its development has been overlooked."[23] More recently, Margaret Beatty Bogue has categorized the 1830s and the 1840s as a period of experimentation and growth for the Great Lakes fishing industry: It revealed, in hindsight, "the many characteristics of the industry in its heyday in the late nineteenth century."[24] Ojibwe fishers made these early fishing ventures possible. They became acquainted with commercial fishing years before it dominated the economy of the Great Lakes, and they adopted commercial fishing practices to make a living in the nineteenth century.

From the 1870s to 1890s, the commercial fishing industry on Lake Superior went through a period of rapid growth and record harvests that had never been witnessed before. In 1872 alone, fishers pulled 39,300,000 pounds of fish from the lake. By 1889, at the peak of the commercial fishing industry, the annual catch had expanded to 146,284,000 pounds.[25] Many Ojibwes worked as commercial fishers during this period. Indeed in 1887, it was estimated that a quarter of fishers in the region were "Indians or part Indian.[26] However, the conditions that led them to take on commercial fishing were not the same. The dispossession of lands as a result of the treaties and pressure by Indian agents on Ojibwes to embrace the cash economy led many of them into this work.

Despite confinement on reservations, Ojibwe families continued to travel to fishing grounds off-reservation. Bad River elder John Condecon recalled the abundance of fish in Lake Superior in the 1870s and traveling to areas where fish were plentiful, and he described fishing using a range of techniques. Condecon's family began their fishing trips at Ontonagon,

Michigan, and paddled along the lake shore catching fish as they went. The lake "held an almost inexhaustible supply of fish," and Condecon's father "always carried a net in the boat." A short time after setting his net, Condecon's father filled his boat with "the finest whitefish and trout" and "plenty of suckers," which, though a source of food, were of little commercial value, so Condecon's father released them.[27]

In 1872, Condecon and his entire family paddled in birch-bark canoes from Ontonagon to Eagle River, Michigan, where they "joined other Indians living at that place." From there, the family traveled to L'Anse, Michigan, and then returned to Ontonagon through Houghton, Michigan. Along the way, Condecon's father caught great quantities of fish, which Condecon's mother and sister dried and boxed. Many kinds of fish could be found in the Ontonagon River, and "all of the different families of Indians had their own boats or fishing grounds" along the river, Condecon recalled. They "caught all the fish they wanted to eat and sell." Ojibwe families fished for pike and later in the season, sturgeon. They trapped the sturgeon by constructing fences from one side of the bank to the other. When the fish swam downriver, they were trapped by the fences. The families then boxed and dried the sturgeon to consume later.[28]

The development of new fishing technologies and competition from Euro-American fishers in the late nineteenth century led Ojibwes to focus more heavily on netting fish. The kinds of nets fishers used depended how much money they had. Steamboats, net lifters, and new net materials made fishing more efficient and enabled fishers to catch greater quantities of fish. Pound nets, which were set in fixed locations and attached to posts in shallower water, were more reliable but required a greater investment.[29] Using pound nets was also labor intensive; it took three individuals to post and tend three to five nets.[30] Large fishing firms used these nets because they could afford them and had the labor available to tend to them.

Independent fishers tended to use gill nets, which required less capital and could be used anywhere on the lake. Fishers dropped the nets into the lake and several days later retrieved the nets filled with. On average, fishers owned fifteen to twenty gill nets, which two or three men could bring in via a small mackinaw boat or sailboat. Gill netting also had a longer season than pound netting. Fishers set gill nets from April to November but could also place them in holes in the ice during the winter. They could only set pound nets from May until the end of autumn.[31] After fishing, they pulled the gill nets and pound nets from the water, dried them on large reels, and stored them in net boxes. After 1890, fishers treated nets with various chemicals to prevent them from rotting, allowing them to eliminate the drying process.

Some fishers worked for wages using a fish dealer's equipment. Others bought equipment from the dealer and gave him two-fifths to one-half of their catch for the fishing season. Another set of fishers worked independently, owning their equipment and selling their catch to whomever offered the best price.[32] There were advantages and disadvantages to these arrangements for Ojibwe fishers in particular. Fishing independently enabled Ojibwe men to take advantage of the freedom that commercial fishing afforded. They fished beyond the boundaries of the reservation and retained some control over their livelihoods. They could also add commercial fishing to the seasonal round and could fish alongside a number of other forms of labor. However, fishing was also a risky business venture whether a person labored independently or under contract. It was subject to fluctuations in the market, and there were good and bad fishing seasons. Large fishing firms, whose access to labor and capital enabled them to weather these shifts more easily, often undercut small, independent fishing operations. And fishers who worked under contract may have spent less money on fishing equipment, but they could find themselves indebted to their supplier if their venture was unsuccessful.

Many Ojibwe men were willing to endure these risks in order to make a living. Indeed, fishing became critical to the economies of Bad River, Red Cliff, Fond du Lac, and Grand Portage because of their proximity to Lake Superior. In 1875, Indian agent Isaac Mahan wrote that Red Cliff Band members "made 1,000 fish barrels, and 15 boats have been built. . . . They have caught 150 tons of fish, 50 tons being caught during the cold winter months, and sold to parties for shipment south and west."[33] As this account suggests, a substantial number of Red Cliff fishers worked independently and sold their catch to fish dealers. In 1896, an inspector for the Indian Service observed that, through fishing, Red Cliff people "practically care for themselves." They "fished with nets along the bay joining their reservation, packing and shipping their fish in kegs." Several Red Cliff people informed the inspector that "3 or 4 families joining together have made between them during the fishing season from $1200 to $1100 yearly."[34]

Ojibwes living on the north shore of Lake Superior also caught great quantities of fish. In 1896, the local agent reported that Fond du Lac Ojibwes caught four tons of fish that they shipped to markets in Duluth and St. Paul and sold for five cents per pound.[35] In 1925, the Indian agent reported that the primary way Fond du Lac Ojibwes made a living was by "fishing during the open season and trapping [animals] during the winter."[36] At Grand Portage, Ojibwes also turned to commercial fishing for an income. At the beginning of the twentieth century, M. D. Archiquette, the reservation superintendent, acknowledged that the soil on the reservation was unsuitable for agriculture and that they could more easily make a living through fishing.[37] In 1916, he wrote that both the Indian and non-Indian inhabitants of the area earned 75 percent of their living through fishing, and he requested that the Indian Service supply the community with $900 for the development of fishing outfits. He also remarked that Grand Portage fishers fished to the same extent as their white neighbors and that they sold their catch to the same buyers.[38]

One of the benefits of commercial fishing was that it offered an alternative to government-run agricultural programs. In his memoir, *Crazy Dave*, Anishinaabe author Basil Johnston explains that this was one of the primary reasons his people began fishing on the Cape Croker reserve in Ontario. Johnston tells the story of a man named Budeese, "who was the only man who didn't believe that his life would be transformed from rags to riches by taking up a trade or tilling the soil, as Indian Affairs and the church had promised." Instead Budeese "continued to live as his ancestors had done, by fishing."[39] Budeese became even more successful when he turned to commercial fishing and sold his catch to an entrepreneur named Tom Jones who sold fish to buyers off of the reserve. Other Indians on the reservation also turned to fishing after they observed Budeese's success. Johnston points out the continuities between fishing for subsistence and fishing in a cash economy: "Fishing was a duty. It had always been regarded as such, as was hunting and harvesting; like hunting, harvesting, and keeping watch, it was a constituent of the word for 'work,' 'annokeewin' something that had to be performed to survive." Despite the different purposes of fishing for subsistence and fishing for cash, Cape Croker people saw connections between the two. Fishing allowed them to exercise self-determination. "When the people of the Cape took up fishing," Johnston writes, "they were resuming a duty they had not exercised for some time." Fishing gave them "some freedom from want and debt, and some control over their lives."[40]

Expansion of large fishing firms in the early twentieth century presented additional opportunities for work and more stability, but the labor arrangements these operations entailed severely curtailed Ojibwe autonomy. From the mid-1880s until World War II, commercial fishing was increasingly defined by vast, unregulated monopolies and immense exploitation of Lake Superior's fishing grounds. Fishing firms invested enormous amounts of capital in the industry in order to gain control of fisheries in the western Great Lakes. In 1880 alone, $1.5 million was invested in Great Lakes waters. It increased to $5.9 million in 1890. The number of fishers working on the Great Lakes also grew during this period and peaked at approximately 13,000 fishers in 1885.[41] A number of factors, such as the development of new technologies like refrigeration, as well as a larger workforce and more extensive units of production, bolstered these changes.[42]

Commercial fishing firms tapped Native communities for labor. Ojibwes worked as hired fishers or as hired hands in packing houses. In the 1890s in Sault Sainte Marie, the Canadian firm Ainsworth and Gainley purchased fish from and supplied Indians with gill nets, offering employment to "any Indian on the North Shore who wishes to work."[43] However, at the same time, the large amounts of money, political power, and territory these companies drew on enabled them to undercut small, independent fishing ventures. By 1885, roughly ninety fishing dealers controlled the Great Lakes catch.[44] These numbers diminished as large firms absorbed smaller ventures that could not compete.

The wages fishers earned depended on the location and type and level of operations an individual participated in, so it is difficult to gain a clear sense of the income generated from this labor. An 1885 study produced by the United States Commission of Fish and Fisheries provides some information on the wages hired fishers earned in the Great Lakes region. During this year, fishers earned from $20 to $35 per month in addition to their board, which was $50 at maximum. These wages increased if an individual was a captain or an engineer on a fishing tug; captain's wages ranged from $50 to $100 a month, and engineers made between $75 and $85, while crewmen working on such boats earned $25 to $50. In some parts of the Great Lakes, hired fishers earned $2 a day, which was an amount similar to the wages of an industrial worker.[45]

As a result of overfishing, the whitefish population on Lake Superior began to decline in the latter half of the nineteenth century. Therefore, fishing ventures increasingly depended on other species. The shift from fishing for whitefish to lake trout and herring changed the kind of labor workers performed in the fishing industry. The new focus on herring fishing not only changed fishing techniques, but it also changed the scale and methods of fish processing. Fishers brought in larger catches of herring and could use new fishing technologies to do so.[46] The fishers hauled their fish-filled nets to the docks, where hired hands picked them.[47] Once the hired hands pulled the herring from the nets, they took them to local packinghouses, where workers cleaned and packed the fish.

Larger catches and expanding packing operations required more labor. In the twentieth century, fish dealers hired hundreds of extra workers during the herring season, providing new opportunities for local communities.[48]

During the herring season in Bayfield, for example, men, women, and children crowded the docks of the town to pull herring from the nets. As late as 1944, John Chapple observed that the activity during the herring season at Bayfield was at such a pitch that "it makes you giddy." Four hundred men and women gathered at the docks, "working desperately trying to keep up with the fish as they are being piled upon the Bayfield docks." Chapple reported that "practically all high school boys and girls of Bayfield have forsaken their studies for the time being, with parental and community consent, to pick herring from the nets or fill other jobs."[49]

Ojibwes from Red Cliff traveled to Bayfield to pick herring. In 1922, the agent at Red Cliff wrote that the fall herring season offset periods when labor was not available. During the herring season, a man was "able to earn as much in three weeks as he can ordinarily earn in two months, as a reasonably skilled man can earn from $6.00 to $12.00 a day in cleaning fish, and from $5.00 to $3.00 a day working as a hand on fishing boats." In 1926, the Indian agent wrote, "Lake Superior in certain seasons furnishes an opportunity for commercial fishing which brings in quite large revenues to those engaged in it." He remarked, "The Indians are good fishermen and are expert sailors. . . . Bayfield has two or three commercial fish warehouses and in the fall of the year a good many Indian families are employed in cleaning, packing and storing fish for commercial use."[50] However, he did not acknowledge that many of the Red Cliff people who worked for the company had turned to this labor because shifts in the fishing industry had made it more difficult for them to make a living as independent fishers. Conditions only grew more difficult for Ojibwes as the fishing companies and state governments worked together to control fishing on Lake Superior.

FISHING MONOPOLIES AND FISHING REGULATION

By the turn of the century, commercial fishing on Lake Superior had become so extensive that several fish species were endangered. In response, Wisconsin and Minnesota, as well as the U.S. and Canadian governments, began to monitor and regulate fishing. State fishing policy reflected a new devotion to a modern regulatory government that would enable the states to monitor and manage natural resources scientifically. For example, in 1879, the Wisconsin legislature implemented laws regulating the minimum weight of the commercial sale of fish to three-quarters of a pound and banning nets with mesh that was less than 3 inches wide.[51] In addition, Wisconsin focused new efforts on creating fish hatcheries to replenish these species. It also hired more wardens to enforce conservation laws. Between 1897 and 1899, the number of fish and game wardens working in Wisconsin increased from five to thirty.

To some extent, state efforts to protect fish were fueled by public concern about the decline of regional fisheries. State governments focused on preserving fish populations for sports fishing by wealthy tourists. They frequently depicted commercial fishing as a threat to the natural environment and called for greater regulation. However, they could not ignore Great Lakes fishing firms' political power, influence, and capital. Though it would appear on the surface that the state government's goals would be at odds with those of the fishing firms, the two entities saw the presence of independent fishers and tribal treaty rights as threats. Thus the companies worked closely with state conservation officials to implement legislation that restricted Ojibwe rights to fish and to ensure their monopoly over the commercial fishing industry.

In public, state and federal officials emphasized the importance of supervising large fishing monopolies that had gone unchecked for far too long. In reality, large fishing companies had great influence over state and federal policy because they had close connections to members of the Canadian and American governments. They invested large amounts of money into the Great Lakes economy and, in some cases, contributed to fish hatcheries and stocking programs.[52] This influence was widespread, and it affected fishing in much of North America. Daniel Boxberger has demonstrated, for example, that corporate involvement in salmon fishing interfered with Lummi access to the resources in the state of Washington. He argues that as the fishing industry came to be dominated by fishing companies, the state government worked to restrict Indian fishing in the interest of big business.[53]

The A. Booth and Sons Company benefited the most from fishing regulations on the Great Lakes. The corporation, the largest fishing firm in the region, was worth $5.5 million in 1898 and was. The company began its fishing ventures on Lake Superior in 1885 in Bayfield and the surrounding area. In 1886, it extended commercial operations to Duluth and the north shore of Lake Superior. During the 1890s, it took over several fishing firms that had failed after the economic panic of 1893. By 1898, the company had consolidated all of the key fisheries on the Great Lakes in both Canada and the United States.[54]

The company capitalized on state regulation as a means of impeding competing fishing operations in the United States.[55] In 1894, company representatives urged the Wisconsin government to suspend pound-net fishing along the south shore of Lake Superior for five years to give smaller fish a chance to mature and reproduce.[56] The company pushed for these measures not because it was concerned about conservation but because of the productivity of its extensive gill-net operations.[57] C. W. Turner, the western manager for the Booth Company's packing operations, expressed these interests in a letter to the Wisconsin Fish Commission in 1893: "Now this is getting to be a serious question with us. We have invested over $200,000 in the state of Wisconsin at Bayfield and Ashland and would therefore ask protection from the fish commissioners, as something must certainly be done to protect our industry, as we are not there for today, but we are there for the future. . . . Now certainly some stringent measure must (or should) be taken immediately to offer us some protection, also to protect the fishing grounds, otherwise there will not be any white fish on the south shore of Lake Superior."[58] Turner reminded the commission of the extent to which the regional economy relied on the company's investments.[59] He believed the company's interests in retaining its monopoly could be met through the protection of the fishing grounds.

Closed seasons were especially beneficial to large fishing firms; they gave them time to market frozen fish while preventing other fish from reaching the market.[60] This strategy was especially detrimental to Ojibwes. In the process of enforcing seasons, state governments disregarded Ojibwe rights to fish in ceded territory and targeted Ojibwe fishers. From the mid-1880s to the mid-1890s, the Wisconsin legislature strictly regulated netting on the Chequamegon Bay in order to prevent the further collapse of the whitefish population in the region while giving larger fishing firms an advantage. Ojibwe commercial fishers bore the brunt of this policy since they depended on gill netting in order to make a living.

In 1895, an inspector for the Indian Service pointed out the connections between the state's seasonal regulations and Booth Company interests. He reported that Red Cliff Ojibwes had informed him that state laws prevented them from fishing and that several of them had been arrested for doing so. They told him that the treaty of 1854 "provided they should be allowed to fish and that [illegible] as the state forbid it, such revenue was gone, and they knew not what to do to obtain a living."[61] Advocating for Red Cliff Ojibwes, the inspector recommended that "it be ascertained if the state of Wisconsin has authority to change existing treaty provisions regarding Indians fishing." He went on to explain, "I fail to see wherein their fishing injures others except A. Booth & Sons, who have fishing stations on various islands in the vicinity with the shipping station in Bayfield. And in whose interests it is represented the recent state law was passed prohibiting fishing on the Bay."[62] He recognized that A. Booth and Son's benefited from this legislation and acknowledged the effects of closed seasons on Ojibwe economies.[63]

Wisconsin fishing laws also focused on restricting the size or location of Ojibwes' nets. Large firms could easily adjust to these regulations because of the amount of capital they held, but they made fishing more difficult for independent fishers, who could not always afford purchasing new equipment. In 1887, the Wisconsin legislature prohibited the use of all types of nets on the Chequamegon Bay, and in 1889, it employed the first wardens to monitor fishing on Lake Superior. In the same year, wardens arrested Red Cliff Band members for placing nets offshore the reservation, claimed that they were in violation of newly passed state regulation, which prohibited fishing on or near the shore.[64] The men who were arrested argued that "it has been customary from time immemorial for many of the Chippewa to obtain the major part of their subsistence from that source."[65]

In 1894, Wisconsin wardens prohibited Red Cliff Ojibwes from using their nets because they did not comply with the required mesh size. Red Cliff people disputed the validity of these laws based on their treaty rights. Indian agent W. A. Mercer commented, "The Indians feel they are entitled to hunt and fish as they may choose and that the treaty with the Government granting this privilege has never been changed."[66] The Indian agent consulted Wisconsin attorney general W. H. Mylrea about the matter. Mylrea responded that the federal government had not specifically reserved the right to manage wildlife when Wisconsin had become a state in 1849; therefore, the state held jurisdiction over fish and game. He concluded that "the Indians are amenable to state laws" and that "the power of the state to regulate and control the taking of fish and game is unquestioned." The state was at liberty to "punish Indians as well as others for the violation of fish and game laws."[67]

In 1896, Wisconsin game wardens arrested Antoine Buffalo and Michael DePerry and confiscated their nets because they were fishing on Lake Superior off the shore of the Red Cliff reservation. The men complained to Indian agent Mercer, who reported that "their nets have been removed from the water and their fishing suspended at the height of the fishing season and . . . they are being put to great inconvenience thereby, as it is at this period that they cure the fish, for their own use during the wintertime."[68] Red Cliff Ojibwes also informed the inspector of Indian affairs that state fishing laws had led to the arrest of several band members despite the fact that the treaty of 1854 stipulated their rights to fish.

Agent Mercer wrote to H. E. Briggs, the U.S. district attorney in Madison, Wisconsin, requesting that Briggs take immediate action regarding the "question of the rights of Indians to hunt and fish in ceded territory."[69] Briggs forwarded Mercer's request to the state attorney general, who replied to the letter in a matter of weeks, indicating that state boundaries were approved by Congress when Wisconsin was admitted into the Union and that the jurisdiction of the state "extends to the middle of Lake Superior" and thus included the shores of the Red Cliff reservation.[70] Neither constitution nor any act of Congress relative to the state of Wisconsin, he added, "withheld from the state the right to regulate and control the catching of fish and game within its borders."[71]

BLACKBIRD AND MORRIN: TWO EXAMPLES OF RESISTANCE AND RESTRICTION

As was the case with hunting, the activism surrounding fishing began in the early twentieth century and developed over the course of a number of decades. Citing their treaty rights, Ojibwes maintained that they had the right to fish on- and off-reservation using techniques they deemed appropriate and they protested state encroachment on their resources and their sovereignty. Local representatives of the federal government, including Indian agents, inspectors for the Indian Service, and federal judges also questioned and challenged the extension of state power over Ojibwes. However, the federal governments' broader focus on assimilation and allotment supported state jurisdiction. The Dawes Act bestowed U.S. citizenship to Indians who took allotments and bolstered state arguments that treaty rights were no longer valid and that Indians fell under the jurisdiction of state governments once they became citizens.

In the early twentieth century, two seminal cases in Wisconsin surrounding Ojibwe netting illuminate both how Ojibwes (and their allies) contested state fishing laws and how these issues culminated in state efforts to claim further jurisdiction. On April 23, 1901, Bert McLaughlin, a state fish and game warden, arrested John Blackbird, a member of the Bad River Band, for setting fishing nets in Bear Trap Creek, which was located within the boundaries of the reservation. The *Ashland Daily Press* remarked that one of the nets was very large, "extending twice across the creek."[72] McLaughlin confiscated Blackbird's nets, and Blackbird stood on trial in the Ashland municipal court for the alleged violations. The court convicted Blackbird for violating the state game laws and fined him $25.00 and additional costs amounting to $11.75. Because Blackbird was impoverished and could not afford to pay these fines, the court sentenced him to imprisonment and hard labor for thirty days.

Two attorneys for the federal government, William G. Wheeler and Henry Sheldon, appealed the court's decision as a test case to challenge the state's authority to convict and imprison Indians for netting on reservations.[73] Citing the Seven Major Crimes Act of 1885, which designated federal jurisdiction over specific crimes committed on reservations, Wheeler and Sheldon argued before the federal district court in Madison that the state did not have the jurisdiction to enforce fish and game laws on reservations.[74] They also argued that the state of Wisconsin did not have the power to add crimes to those designated by Congress or to try Indians in state courts for these crimes.[75]

Judge Romanzo Bunn, who had served as a professor of federal jurisprudence at the University of Wisconsin Madison from 1879 to 1885 and backed federal jurisdiction, heard the case and ruled in favor of Blackbird, concluding that the Seven Major Crimes Act gave Congress exclusive jurisdiction over reservations for certain criminal offenses. In addition, Bunn commented on what he saw as the moral wrongs that the state committed by infringing on Ojibwe treaty rights. He stated that after having taken large portions of land from Ojibwes in Minnesota and Wisconsin, setting aside reservations, and stipulating that Ojibwes would always have the right to hunt and fish in ceded territory, "it would be adding insult as well as injustice now to deprive them of the poor privilege of fishing with a seine of suckers in a little red marsh-water stream upon their own reservation." Bunn maintained that the kinds of fish that Ojibwes caught differed from the fish that white sportsmen or commercial fishers were interested in, remarking, "It is well known that these fish cannot be taken with hook and line, but only spears and nets. They are a fish that white men will hardly ever eat, though it is a matter of common knowledge that Indians prize them quite as highly as brook trout." He added, "When an Indian cannot get a morsel of pork and white flower, a red horse or sucker from some stream where brook trout would never abide, boiled or roasted by a camp fire, is sometimes a luxury, to deprive him of which would be ungrateful in the extreme." Bunn held that the state warden had been overzealous in his efforts to arrest Blackbird and ordered that "the prisoner," Blackbird, be released.[76]

The state of Wisconsin refused to abide by Bunn's ruling and continued to arrest Ojibwes. Just a few years later, *State v. Morrin*, which was heard in the Wisconsin Supreme Court, would provide the basis for states officials to claim that the state government held jurisdiction over all resources in the state. In 1908, a state game warden arrested an Ojibwe man named Michael Morrin and arrested him for fishing with gill nets on Red Cliff Bay on Lake Superior.[77] At the time of his arrest, Morrin had lived in Bayfield for over five years and had become a citizen of the United States under the provisions of the Dawes Act.[78] Morrin appealed the conviction, arguing that the provision in the 1854 treaty allowed him to fish in ceded territory. The Wisconsin Supreme Court utilized Morrin's appeal in order to reassert state authority, maintaining that the state's admittance into the United States by Congress in 1848 effectively eliminated Ojibwe rights to hunt and fish.[79] However, Congress had never delegated power to the state to enforce these laws, nor did it expressly eliminate Chippewa treaty rights under Wisconsin statehood.[80]

The differences between *Re Blackbird* and the *State v. Morrin* reveal how federal and state officials perceived and policed Ojibwe labor. The ruling in *Re Blackbird* was a unique case in that few judges ruled in favor of Ojibwe treaty rights at this time. Blackbird's case was heard in federal district court, and Bunn specialized in federal jurisprudence. But another significant element in the decision was Bunn's perception of Blackbird's identity. Bunn categorized Blackbird as a "full blood Chippewa." Blackbird was also fishing on the Bad River reservation rather than in ceded territory.[81] Bunn believed that Ojibwes fished for species that were undesirable to non-Indians and deemed John Blackbird's fishing acceptable because it did not threaten the desires of sports fishers.

In contrast, Michael Morrin deviated from the expectations of white officials who may have been ambivalent about Morrin's Indian identity based on his lifestyle. Not only was he of mixed Ojibwe and white ancestry, but he also resided in and owned property in the town of Bayfield. Thus he may have been perceived to be more prosperous than other Native people in the area. He also fished with a gill net on Lake Superior for commercial income. Moreover, he challenged his own arrest in state court.[82]

In the years following the *Morrin* decision, the state government drew from many of the arguments presented in the case, specifically those pertaining to citizenship and the loss of treaty rights, to extend its jurisdiction over tribal communities. Following larger trends in policy, the federal government largely accepted state claims that under the provisions of the Dawes Act Native people who had taken allotments were subject to the civil and criminal laws of the states in which they resided.[83] Both the federal government and federal courts equated allotment as well as citizenship with the erosion of tribal sovereignty. Charles Cleland points out that the federal government developed a standard reply which it gave to Indians who wrote to the government in protest of state violation of their treaty rights or in order to affirm them.[84] Federal officials told Native peoples that they were subject to court precedent, especially the supreme court decision in *Ward v. Racehorse* and later in *Kennedy v. Becker* as well as local court decisions in Michigan, Wisconsin, and Minnesota.[85] These cases supported state jurisdiction over treaty rights; states could charge Indians with the violation of conservation laws regardless of Indians' exclusive relationship with the federal government.

State governments continued to argue well into the twentieth century that citizenship eliminated treaty rights. Following the 1924 Indian Citizenship Act, Wisconsin and Minnesota asserted that all Indians were subject to state fish and game laws despite a provision that stated that the act would not affect the rights of any Indian tribes.[86] In the 1920s, the federal government reviewed the power of states to impose fish and game regulations on Indian peoples. In 1925, E. B. Merritt, the assistant commissioner of Indian affairs, wrote that the Citizenship Act did not abolish treaty rights and that no revocations of the treaty rights occurred under the 1854 treaty.[87] That same year, with the support of their agent, Ojibwe leaders from Bad River sent the commissioner an explanation of their view of the treaty rights designated in the 1837, 1842, and 1854 treaties.[88]

However, the Wisconsin and Minnesota state governments ignored these efforts. In 1932, H. W. MacKenzie, the chief warden of the Wisconsin Conservation Commission, complained about commercial fishers from Bad River. For years, Ojibwes from the Bad River reservation had set nets on the river for game and fish. MacKenzie asserted that they took "these fish, which primarily belong to the state, in great quantities, and have sold them right and left for any price they would bring, wherever they could find a market." He added, "You will understand these fish come out of state waters and are in reality state fish that we are trying to protect during the closed season." MacKenzie stated that legislation enacted in 1931 prohibited the removal of any protected wildlife and fish from the reservation without the permission of the Conservation Department. The state legislature passed the law "with the idea in view of stopping the wholesale slaughter of fish and game by Indians for the purpose of this sale." MacKenzie reasserted that the state had jurisdiction over all resources located within its boundaries regardless of whether they were on the reservation.[89]

Although the Minnesota and Wisconsin state governments devoted much attention to conservation in the early twentieth century, they were not able to prevent the deterioration of the Lake Superior fisheries. Independent fishers and large fishing firms both suffered from the effects of this decline. The Booth Fisheries Company flourished until 1933, when it abandoned its Great Lakes holdings in the face of bankruptcy. A number of smaller firms then acquired the company's holdings. The decline of the company marked the end of the commercial fishing on the Great Lakes.[90] Because of continual overfishing and damage to habitat, fish populations diminished even further. The invasion of sea lamprey also took a devastating toll on fish populations and continues be an environmental problem today.[91] Fishers also struggled with falling prices caused by the Great Depression. These factors eventually combined to make fishing an unprofitable endeavor for both large fishing firms and independent fishers.[92]

Bad River elder Joe Stoddard witnessed the dramatic economic and environmental changes that transformed the Lake Superior region in the late nineteenth and early twentieth centuries. He commented that the changes brought about by the settlement of the area were "both amazing and saddening." In particular, Stoddard was outraged by Euro-American efforts to "extinguish the privilege of the Chippewa to exercise the rights granted to him as a birthright and from the treaties with the United States government." He claimed that Euro-American arguments that Ojibwe slaughtered wildlife were inaccurate. Rather, "the arrival of the white man in this region marked the decline of the wildlife of the forests and waters and the virtual and complete extinction of many species."[93]

Stoddard contrasted Ojibwe fishing practices with those of Euro-Americans as proof of his argument. White commercial fishers "came with their pound nets and set them in Chequamegon Bay and along the shores of Lake Superior." After a day's catch, the fishers "removed thousands of pounds of sturgeon and threw them upon the beach to rot." The sturgeon, "which were considered by the Chippewa to be the peer of all fish, are now practically extinct. This is due to the methods of early white fishermen." After the fishers had rid the nets of sturgeon, he continued, they scooped white fish that they sought "into boats in immense numbers." He found the waste of fish by white fishers "appalling," adding, "The excuse offered by the fishermen for not liberating the sturgeon was that they would only catch them again. Therefore, they removed them forever, and a good job they made of it."[94]

"There were times, especially during the summer," Stoddard recalled, "when every Chippewa from all parts of this region would gather along the shore of Lake Superior, particularly between the mouth of the Bad River and Madeline Island." They would "cast their nets and take only what fish they could attend to" and "liberate" the rest "for some future time." Bad River Ojibwes would also travel to the locations where fishers dumped sturgeon and salvage some of the fresher fish for food "in attempt to mitigate the deplorable waste, although they could have taken the same species in the rivers at their doors with less effort."[95] Stoddard emphasized the role that the Euro-American fishers (as well as commercial fishing firms) played in the destruction of the Chequamegon Bay fishery and challenged their unjust accusations against Ojibwe fishers.

Jerome Arbuckle commented on the decline of the fisheries as well. Like Stoddard, Arbuckle discussed the impacts of commercial fishing on sturgeon and the importance of this fish to Bad River. He noted that the fisheries in the area were abundant and that Indian fishers could catch all of the fish that they needed. Commercial fishers disposed of large amounts of sturgeon because they had no market value, "and also because of their great size and weight they were a menace."[96] However, Ojibwe fishers did not waste sturgeon just because they were not commercially valuable. Rather, they gave the fish to families or individuals in need, a continuation of a traditional practice that enabled them to support the community. Through such generosity, Arbuckle's own grandmother and her children were able to survive after her husband's death left her without a means of income.

Arbuckle believed that Bad River people adhered to the values of conservation even during periods of unemployment when they relied on fishing for subsistence: "The wild life of the reservation maintained their numbers, despite the fact that they were legal prey at any time for approximately two thousand Indians." Left to their own devices, without state interference, Ojibwes respected the wildlife populations of the reservation. However, as Arbuckle put it, there came a time when Euro-American looked with "envious eyes" at the resources on the reservation and began to restrict Ojibwe treaty rights. "White commercial fishermen also find it profitable to set their nets in waters considered reservation waters," he wrote; "each year, this further depletes the number of fish in reservation waters."[97]

Roughly forty years passed before the state and federal courts recognized Ojibwe rights to fish. Ojibwe resistance to state laws in the 1970s and 1980s, however, was strikingly similar to the activism of earlier generations. In the 1971 test cases *State v. Gurnoe et al.* and *State v. Connors et al.*, the state of Wisconsin charged Ojibwes from Red Cliff and Bad River with violating gill-net regulations and fishing without a license on Lake Superior. The Supreme Court of Wisconsin affirmed that Ojibwes had the rights to fish since the 1854 treaty established their reservations on Lake Superior's shores.[98]

In 1974, brothers Fred and Mike Tribble of the Lac Courte Oreilles Band tested the legality of state jurisdiction when they speared fish off-reservation.[99] The state charged them and found them guilty of possessing a spear, for taking fish off-reservation, and for occupying a fish shanty without a legitimate tag. The charges against the Tribble brothers led the Lac Courte Oreilles Band to file suit in *Lac Courte Oreilles Band of Chippewa Indians v. State of Wisconsin* against state warden Lester Voigt in 1974, which resulted in the 1983 *Voigt* decision, which confirmed Ojibwe treaty rights in ceded territory.[100] The litigation surrounding the decision lasted until 1991, when Judge Barbara Crabb upheld Ojibwe treaty rights but also gave the state some regulatory power in ceded territory.[101] In the 1980s and 1990s, Ojibwes experienced anti-Indian backlash as a result of the *Voigt* decision, but fishing remained a key form of resistance. Today, the term "walleye warriors" refers to Ojibwes who, with resilience and tenacity, chose to spearfish in the midst of these challenges.[102] However, this activism did not simply materialize in the late twentieth century. It emerged from the sustained efforts of earlier generations of Ojibwes to make a living and to exercise their rights to fish amid state, federal, and corporate expansion—contexts shaped in full by decades of negotiation, erosion, and assertion of treaty rights.

Ojibwe blueberry pickers at Namakan Lake, Minnesota, ca. 1918.
Courtesy of the National Park Service, Voyageurs National Park.

Ojibwe men fishing near Sault Sainte Marie, Michigan, ca. 1898.
Image no. WHi-6911, courtesy of the Wisconsin Historical Society.

Ojibwe lumberjacks Edwin Matrious (left) and George Matrious,
Pansy, Wisconsin, ca. 1910. Courtesy of the Minnesota Historical Society.

(opposite) Postcard featuring John Smith (Ka-be-na-gwe-wes), age 112, ca. 1896.
Courtesy of the Minnesota Historical Society.

(JOHN SMITH)
KA·BE·NA·GWE·WES AGE 112

CHAPTER FOUR

From Landlords to Laborers

Work in the Lumber Industry

Unlike the history of livelihoods designated as treaty rights, the story of Ojibwe wage labor in the lumber industry is more difficult to trace because it has not been associated with Ojibwe labor traditions. This history surfaces in fragments, sentences, and paragraphs strewn throughout local memoirs, and it receives only passing mention in more recent scholarship concerned primarily with treaty rights. Still, delving deeper into the historical record presents a rich and complex picture of Ojibwe work in the lumber industry and what it meant in the midst of the swift dispossession of their lands after the treaties. In the 1940s, for example, Cloquet resident Walter O'Meara wrote in his memoir on his childhood there about his Ojibwe neighbors who had come to the town to find work in the lumber industry. He remembered exciting adventures with his boyhood friend, William "Nidji" Cadreau, whose father, Antoine Cadreau, came from the Fond du Lac reservation to work in one of the town's numerous sawmills. Nidji eventually became a pitcher for the Chicago White Sox in 1910 but then returned to the lumber town to work as a laborer much like his father had.[1]

O'Meara also described Susy Posey, an elderly woman from the Fond du Lac reservation who worked as a washerwoman in the town and likely made her living mostly by scrubbing the dirt and sweat out of the clothing worn by the town's lumberjacks and mill workers: "I still have a vivid memory of her hanging out the sheets on a windy day, a very small woman with a battered black hat on her head and a corn cob pipe in her mouth." O'Meara also wrote about the La Prairie brothers, Henry and John, who were well-known rivermen and burlers (log rollers), as well as Mike Houle, who was also a riverman who played on the Cloquet baseball team. After writing briefly about these individuals, however, O'Meara simply brushed their stories aside, concluding, "After the Indians came the loggers."[2]

Even though local settlers like O'Meara interacted with Ojibwe people on a daily basis, they could not recognize the contributions of Indians living in lumber towns and working in the lumber industry. Although Indian agents made concerted efforts to transform Native people into farmers and industrial workers as part of assimilation, few Euro-Americans truly embraced the idea that Indians could learn the skills required to work in an industrial capitalist economy. For the most part, Euro-Americans saw Indians as unreliable and unskilled workers who belonged on reservations.

Moreover, indigenous labor in the lumber industry contradicted popular beliefs about frontier development. Euro-Americans believed that Ojibwes were one with the forests that were being logged and that as the forests disappeared, so too would Ojibwes. In O'Meara's view, lumberjacks replaced Indians as the region progressed from the wilderness to civilized settlements. Euro-Americans rarely took stock of Indians who became lumberjacks or mill workers and who contributed to development. In their narratives about the lumber industry, few settlers mentioned Indians. If they did mention Indians, it was in passing, and they presented them as unique characters who added flavor to local lore. They saw Indian lumberjacks and mill workers as unique or as "Indians in unexpected places."[3]

Nevertheless, substantial numbers of Ojibwes, like Antoine and Nidji Cadreau, Suzy Posey, Henry and John La Prairie, and Mike Houle made a living in the lumber industry. Some Ojibwes wrote vivid accounts of this labor with a great sense of pride. The importance of this work in Ojibwes communities raises questions about what led them to engage in this work and what it ultimately meant to them. The answers are complicated and were shaped by Ojibwe efforts to exercise autonomy in the face of U.S. expansion.

The growth of the lumber industry depended on the cession of Ojibwe lands, and acquisition of timber was one of the primary motivations behind the negotiation of the treaties. Henry Dodge, the territorial governor of Wisconsin and commissioner of the 1837 Treaty, remarked that the land he sought through the treaty contained "from nine to ten million acres of land, and abounding in Pine Timber" and that this land was "of first importance to people of the States of Illinois, Missouri, and the Territory of Wisconsin for its Pine Timber."[4] The lumber industry's rapid growth was based the availability of thousands of acres of timber that Ojibwes relinquished in 1837, 1842, and 1854. In only a few decades, lumber barons like William

Vilas and Justus Smith Stearns purchased vast quantities of property in the Great Lakes and established logging industry empires worth hundreds of thousands of dollars. Settlers built sawmills, blacksmith shops, and furniture companies, and lumber towns, such as Cloquet and Ashland, sprang up around lumber mills. Moreover, hundreds of immigrant and migrant workers poured into the region to work in lumber camps and to cut the immense stands of pine timber, which was transported to growing cities in the South and the industrial centers of the Northeast.

In the face of these dramatic transitions, Ojibwes had little choice but to harvest and sell timber on reservation lands in order to make a living. In 1875, Lake Superior bands received the final annuity payment set aside under the treaty of 1854, which compounded their economic difficulties. Indian agents urged Ojibwe men to cut and sell timber in the interest of clearing land for farming and turning them into civilized, enterprising individuals. The Supreme Court reinforced these efforts in 1873 in *United States v. Cook*, in which it held that Indians had no individual right to cut and sell timber on reservation lands unless they intended to farm them.[5] While tribal members generally looked unfavorably on cutting and selling timber, many of them had little choice because it provided the best opportunity to make a living under difficult economic circumstances.

A number of Great Lakes tribes made a living from the lumber industry. For example, the neighboring Menominee tribe established successful lumber operations on their reservation that sustained their community until the mid-1950s.[6] The Menominees lobbied the Indian Office and Congress to authorize regulations and funding that would allow them to retain a hold over reservation timber, and they continued to cut and sell their own timber. In 1890, Congress passed legislation that affirmed the tribe's right to cut and market timber, funded the Menominee enterprise, regulated the tribe's annual harvest, and provisioned for the distribution of the earnings from logging among tribe members.[7]

Unlike the Menominees, Ojibwes did not gain protection or support for their logging operations from the federal government, and timber quickly slipped out of their hands.[8] Corrupt Indian agents and predatory lumber companies took advantage of the arrangements established by *United States v. Cook* to obtain timber from Ojibwe lands for little or no payment. The allotment of reservation lands in the 1870s and 1880s speeded up this process of dispossession, enabling logging companies to seize or purchase most remaining Ojibwe lands. By the 1930s, Ojibwe people held only a small percentage of the lands that had originally been set aside for reservations in the 1854 treaty.[9]

Ojibwe men responded to the increasing difficulties of living on reservation lands by taking up wage labor in the lumber industry. They incorporated wage labor into the seasonal round in a manner that allowed them to exercise treaty rights while compensating for the loss of resources and land. Many of them saw the skills they gained in the industry as a means to adjust to industrial capitalism and as a way to retain independence from the federal government.[10] Because the lumber industry grew out of colonization and dispossession of Ojibwe lands, it placed Ojibwe workers in the unique position of being laborers on lands that they once held. Ojibwes retained their connections to the land and also exercised their autonomy through this labor.

Settler expansion certainly undermined these connections. However, Ojibwes found ways to sustain relationships to their homelands and to exercise economic agency even when dispossessed of their lands. Though the lumber industry was heavily extractive and conflicted with Ojibwes' traditional relationships with the land, it still involved the process of "knowing nature through labor."[11] Much of the labor of felling trees, cutting lumber sections so that it could be hauled out of the wood, and then transporting it down rivers not only required knowledge of the landscape but also took place in Ojibwe homelands in the forest and on the waterways that had always been central to their livelihoods. It was against this backdrop that some Ojibwe men forged new expressions of identity and asserted their self-determination through their labor. Their position as indigenous people working on dispossessed lands rendered the meaning of their labor different from that of Euro-American workers.

EARLY LOGGING OPERATIONS AND THE LOSS OF TRIBAL CONTROL

One of the earliest tribal logging operations began on the Red Cliff reservation. Between 1870 and 1873, the government established a sawmill on the reservation placed it under the supervision of Indian agent and lumber baron John H. Knight. Under Knight, Red Cliff men cut and supplied lumber to the sawmill. After Knight left his post, agent Selden Clark, bolstered the reservation's lumber operations by building a seventy-foot dock and a harbor boom that could hold 50 million feet of logs, as well as a cooper and carpenter shop and a boardinghouse for the workers.[12] In 1873, Clark encouraged tribal members to cut and sell lumber from the reservation.[13] They "chopped and hauled nearly a thousand cords of wood, about 10,000 rails and fence posts, and nearly 300,000 feet of logs" for the government sawmill in Bayfield. He supplemented monetary wages for Red Cliff workers with government provisions as a replacement for treaty annuities. Clark used the timber Ojibwes supplied to the mill to pay for its operation costs, and he provided lumber to Red Cliff and Bad River Ojibwes to build houses.[14]

As part of these operations, Red Cliff people also sold timber to local businesses. In 1871, John Buffalo, a prominent member of the Red Cliff community, made a contract with a St. Paul tannery in which he would receive $3.75 for 100 cords of bark, which he transported by steamer to Duluth and then south to St. Paul.[15] Clark optimistically reported that operations on the reservation employed a number of Red Cliff Ojibwes and noted that, "as all the business was transacted by them, they were deservedly proud of their successes."[16] Like Buffalo, many Ojibwes survived the engulfment by the lumber industry by cutting and selling timber and by working at the reservation sawmill.

Joseph Bell, a Red Cliff elder, described work in the reservation sawmill in the 1870s. In the mid-nineteenth century, Bell and his family were forced to move from the St. Croix River to the Red Cliff reservation when the lumber companies moved into their territory to take advantage of the river for transporting timber and the valuable stands of pine timber surrounding its banks.[17]

As a young man, Bell worked in the Red Cliff sawmill, learning how to measure and cut the timber into boards. "One early spring," he recalled, "a white man came to prepare the mill for its spring cutting of the logs that had been cut and hauled during the winter by the Indians. The white man had trained one Indian, Frank Chingway, to run the saw. It was not long before this Indian had full charge of the sawing." While Chingway learned how to use the saw, Bell worked behind the saw collecting the slabs of wood and putting them into a pile. Once Chingway learned his position, Bell was promoted to work at the carriage of the saw, where he spun the gear that regulated the thickness of timber to be cut. Bell "received $2.00 per day" and "a grocery order of $7.00," which could be used in stores in Bayfield. "Many piles of lumber were made," Bell recalled, "and the Indians were delighted by the thought that they would soon have houses to live in." The Indian Service operated the mill to furnish labor for reservation projects and to instruct Ojibwes in the values of wage labor and capitalism. But Bell also saw this labor as a much needed opportunity to take care of his family: "Even at my young age, I was kept busy continuously, urged on by necessity, since I was the key support of my mother and sister."[18]

Antoine Day, a carpenter and boat builder at Red Cliff, convinced the agent to set aside some piles of timber left over from the sawmill operations to build homes for community members. After waiting several years for the lumber promised by the agent, Bell's "dream" of building his mother a house came to fruition. Whenever the timber was available, Day cut it and took it to the site where Bell built the house. After Bell finished the house, he felt that he had provided for his mother and could pursue other opportunities off-reservation. "Seeing that my mother had a home at last and that work was scarce since the closing of the Indian-owned sawmill," Bell explained, "I decided that I wanted to see some of the world." Bell left home to join a party of surveyors and worked as an axman, clearing downed timber littering the roads of northern Wisconsin.[19]

Had the allotment of reservation lands not accelerated the sale of reservation timber, some timber might have remained in Ojibwe hands. Allotment also left tribal communities increasingly vulnerable to the corruption of Indian agents as well as legislation designed to grant Euro-Americans increasing access to Indian lands. Article 3 of the treaty of 1854 provisioned for the division of Ojibwe lands. Allotment began for Ojibwes at Red Cliff and Bad River reservations in the mid-1870s and ended in the early 1880s.[20] Ojibwe lands on the Grand Portage and Fond du Lac reservations were not allotted until the 1880s. As part of allotment, Indian agent W. R. Durfee devised a plan to regulate lumber operations and individual lumber sales in 1882.[21] Durfee believed that the plan would enable Ojibwes under his jurisdiction to clear their allotments for farming and that it would provide them with an "opportunity to acquire the habits of transacting business."[22] At first, this strategy was successful in generating an income for tribal members. In the second year of the plan, for example, five members of the Red Cliff Band made a profit of $3,108 in lumber sales.[23] In the same year, twenty five members of the Bad River Band made a profit of $18,000 in lumber sales.[24]

However, any further economic benefit these communities would have derived from Durfee's plan was cut short by a change of hands. In 1885, James T. Gregory replaced him as the Indian agent at La Pointe. Prior to becoming an Indian agent, Gregory had worked for John H. Knight and William Vilas, the most prominent lumber barons in northern Wisconsin, and Vilas used his political influence to get Gregory's appointment.[25] Gregory's primary aim was to make timber accessible to lumber interests and to undermine the monopoly that Ojibwe held over this resource. As soon as Gregory took his position, he began to complain that Ojibwe abused Durfee's system. He claimed that since the system required that contractors hire Indians, Ojibwe worked sporadically and were able to manipulate the conditions of their labor. In 1886, Gregory complained that because Ojibwe workers from the Fond du Lac, Lac Courte Oreilles, and "Red River" (i.e., Red Cliff) reservations knew that lumber contractors were required to hire them, they worked for only short periods and left after they were paid for their lumber. He also complained that they forced contractors to pay higher wages than they would normally pay white workers.[26] Claiming that he could not find Ojibwe workers to cut lumber each season, Gregory hired white lumberman to cut timber on the Ojibwe reservations under his jurisdiction. He also lowered the price of contracts and allowed timber to be cut at an accelerated rate.[27]

Under Gregory's watch, white contractors extracted enormous amounts of timber from Ojibwe lands within the span of only a few years. While information on the impact of this policy on all four reservations is scant, the amount of timber that contractors harvested from the Bad River reservation clearly demonstrates its devastating impact. In 1887, contractors harvested 23,202,972 feet of timber, more than had ever been harvested in a season. Although the timber was worth $135,735, contractors paid Bad River people only $42,913. In 1888, the rate at which contractors were harvesting timber from these reservations drew the attention of the U.S. Senate Committee on Indian Traders.[28] After an investigation, the committee concluded that by 1888, half of the commercial timber had been extracted from Ojibwe lands under the La Pointe agency.[29] The committee reported that under Gregory's tenure, Durfee's original plan "had been perverted into a system under which greedy contractors have rushed upon the reservation," concluding that Gregory "brought in swarms of white men . . . [who] have already denuded the finest timber tracts, and are stripping the allotments so rapidly, that it is probable that within two or three years the pine timber of the reservations will all be gone."[30] The federal government removed Gregory from his post, but it did not compensate Ojibwe communities for the loss of timber or profits from the timber sales under his jurisdiction.

In the wake of this investigation, the Indian Service implemented the "La Pointe plan." The plan stipulated that Ojibwes were to sell their to lumber to a company assigned to each reservation. The companies were required to erect mills on each reservation, all timber cut on the reservation had to be manufactured on the reservation, and Indians were to be given preferential employment. The Indian Service chose contractors who would pay the most for Ojibwe timber. While this plan made it easier for the federal government to monitor lumber operations on reservations, it also allowed large lumber companies to hold monopolies over Ojibwe timber and labor.[31]

The J. S. Stearns Lumber Company ran one of the largest operations under the La Pointe plan. From 1894 to 1922, the company dominated the economy of the Bad River reservation, employing hundreds of Indians and non-Indians alike.[32] The company advertised "Indian Reservation Soft Pine and Norway Lumber" on its official letterhead, which also featured an illustration of two Indians wearing blankets standing in front of a teepee.[33] The illustration romanticized and to some extent advertised the company's operations, but it hardly reflected the realities of life on the Bad River reservation. Although Ojibwe men earned decent wages in the sawmill, Bad River people as a whole were not receiving the market price for their timber. The company took advantage of the La Pointe plan, basing payments for timber on prices negotiated in 1893. The Indian Service continued to receive higher bids from other companies until 1903, but it always gave the contract to J. S. Stearns.[34]

In Minnesota, federal legislation compounded the detrimental impact of allotment in Ojibwe communities. Melissa Meyer writes that the implementation of allotment on the White Earth reservation in northern Minnesota "paralleled a national trend in which Congress allowed local interests to determine Indian policy."[35] In 1889, the Nelson Act prevented the allotment of pinelands on Minnesota reservations because they were of greater value than other lands and thus could not be divided equally. However, under the terms of the act, each band was forced to cede the remaining trust lands that were allotted. The federal government then sold these lands to lumber interests, giving them access to prime timber, and deposited the proceeds in a permanent fund that earned 5 percent interest annually. The act stipulated that fifty years after allotment, three-quarters of the money was to be distributed in per capita payments, and the rest was set aside in interest funds to be spent on Ojibwe education. However, Ojibwe communities received nothing from the sale of their timber, and within forty years of the act, the United States had pilfered all of the money in the permanent and interest funds.[36]

Congressional legislation made it even easier for non-Indians to obtain access to reservation timber in Minnesota in the early twentieth century. In 1904, the Steenerson Act allotted an additional eighty acres to tribal members deemed worthy by the federal government, and the Clapp Rider attached to the act, authorized them to sell timber on their allotments. In combination, this legislation allowed a few tribal members to sell large quantities of land, and it opened additional lands to logging.[37] Although it is unclear how this legislation directly affected Fond du Lac and Grand Portage in specific terms. It appears that the loss of land and timber that these communities experienced was similar to those of the White Earth Ojibwes.[38] By the early twentieth century, the extent to which logging and allotment contributed to the dispossession of tribal lands in the Lake Superior region was clear. In 1900, 11,567 acres of land on the Red Cliff reservation had been allotted, and by 1934, 92 percent of it had been alienated. By 1919, 115,968 acres had been allotted on the Bad River reservation, and by 1934, 48 percent of it had been alienated. In the same years, 24,191 acres had been allotted on the Grand Portage reservation and 56 percent acres of that had been alienated, and 37,121 acres had been allotted on the Fond du Lac reservation and 42 percent alienated.[39]

WORK IN THE LUMBER INDUSTRY

The history of allotment in reservation communities and its intersection with the growth of the lumber industry illustrates a tragic cycle of land and timber loss due to the corrupt practices of Indian agents and the encroachment of lumber interests. Although the federal government attempted to address some of these problems through reforms like the La Pointe plan, its efforts to regulate lumber sales on reservations weakened rather than protected Ojibwe control over reservation timber. The federal government's allotment policy and its mismanagement of lumber operations on reservations transformed Ojibwes from land holders to wage laborers. However, Ojibwes interests diverged politically from non-indigenous workers, who sought economic citizenship. In the midst of the loss of land and resources, there was little choice for Ojibwes other than to seek out new livelihoods. Although the federal government implemented allotment to foster Indian incorporation into Euro-American society, most Ojibwes utilized wage labor as a means to exercise their economic autonomy rather than to assimilate into American society.

Although there is an absence of specific figures, the annual reports of Indian agents and inspectors of the Office of Indian Affairs as well as the accounts of Ojibwes themselves suggest that by the late nineteenth century substantial numbers of men from Bad River, Red Cliff, Grand Portage, and Fond du Lac made a living by working in area lumber camps or sawmills. In 1882, Agent Durfee reported, "The young men are industrious workers and find, when not engaged for themselves, ready and remunerative employment in the saw-mills, lumber-camps, and other industries in the vicinity of the [Bad River] reservation."[40] Durfee's successors echoed these words until the Great Depression.

Men could do a number of different jobs in a logging operation based on their skills. There was also flexibility in some occupations that allowed individuals to learn new skills and work their way into higher-paying positions. However, the majority of the workers were lumberjacks who ranked at the bottom of the workforce. Some of these workers were local men who became lumberjacks intending to learn the occupation and move through the ranks, but most were migrant workers who intended to earn their pay and move on.[41] As the lumber season began in the fall, large numbers of men swarmed into logging camps and lumber towns to pick up work. In November of 1906, the *Bayfield Press* announced: "It is estimated that close on to 2,000 men have arrived in Bayfield this fall to work in surrounding country."[42]

Generally, the timber was cut by three-man crews consisting of two sawyers and an "under cutter," who was in charge of the crew. The under cutter had the difficult task of picking out the sound trees and determining which direction each was to be cut, and the sawyers then felled the trees. An axman then was responsible for measuring and marking where the logs were to be cut at the sawmill. A second axman was responsible for cutting a road so that the logs could be hauled on enormous sleighs powered by draft horse teams to the main lumber road and then onto a nearby waterway. Another person employed as a "road monkey" kept the lumber roads clear, and an individual employed as the "top loader" packed the sleigh. This work required the skills to determine the most efficient way to load the logs so that they would not tumble off the sleigh as the horses dragged them along the bumpy roads.

Once the timber reached the waterway, lumberjacks drove it downstream by burling the logs (that is, standing on the logs and rolling them to move them to specific points in the water). This work took place in the spring when the water was at its highest. At the start of the lumber industry, contractors chose land along waterways for the efficiency of hauling logs to nearby sawmills. As railroads began to run through the region in 1880s and 1890s, trains became the most efficient way to transport lumber to sawmills. The railroads also enabled logging to expand to areas less accessible to water and accelerated the pace of timber extraction.

The extent to which Ojibwe men worked in the lumber industry depended on individual needs and interests. Engaging in many different occupations within the industry or combining it with other forms of wage labor afforded Ojibwe men some economic flexibility, as well as skills to make a living when other forms of income were scarce. In 1879, at the age of seventeen, John Condecon began work as a lumber cruiser, hiring his skills out to a number of different parties, surveying and estimating the value of timber in northern Michigan. He and his family members took allotments on the Bad River reservation in 1884, but he continued to work off-reservation. Between 1886 and 1921, Condecon worked as a time keeper, foreman, grader, scaler, contractor, and cruiser in the lumber industry. As a contractor, he shipped 60 to 100 railroad cars of cedar, spruce, and balsam annually from Bad River. As a foreman, he managed a logging camp of 75 to 150 men. Like many other men from the Bad River, Condecon also worked for J. S. Stearns loading timber on the banks of the Bad, White, and Vaughn Rivers.[43] When the lumber industry began to decline, Condecon combined this work with work in the growing tourism and recreation industry as hunting and fishing guide for the Cochran family.[44]

Antoine Dennis, also from Bad River, worked in the lumber industry for a number of years but combined this work with many other kinds of labor. In 1928, a local newspaper featured an article on Dennis's life because he was being considered as a guide for President Calvin Coolidge on one of the president's famous vacations in Wisconsin. "To the forest Dennis owes his existence," the reporter proclaimed. "From it he has eked a living since boyhood, trapping, fishing, logging, and as a licensed guide." The writer went on to describe the various seasonal occupations from which Dennis made a living. In the spring, Dennis worked as a log burler (or roller). With "the aptitude of a true woodsman," he wrote. "[Dennis] became an expert driving logs downstream." His "squirrel-like skill in keeping his footing on the slippery tree trunks" was notable. In the summer, Dennis carried mail on foot, and in the winter, he hauled the mail by dogsled "from Superior and Bayfield, Ashland and the copper country beyond." He "also learned the culinary arts" and worked as a cook for gangs of lumber cruisers and timber estimators.[45]

Ojibwe men had different reasons for becoming lumberjacks, but many were motivated by a desire to maintain their autonomy. Some men attached this labor to their sense of masculinity as well as their responsibility to help take care of their families. In the mid-nineteenth century, George Starr was forced to support himself and his family at Bad River after his father's death. (The elder Starr had been arrested and imprisoned by local authorities after a conflict between him and "some half-breeds" and died in a fire that burned the jail down.) "Being left without a father in these tender years," Starr explained, "I grew up to young manhood, realizing that it was up to me to stand on my own two feet."[46] He took up work clearing timber for the roads of the town of Ashland and later for the railroad that crossed the town.

New opportunities opened up as the town of Ashland grew in the 1870s and 1880s. As a young man, Starr witnessed the regional lumber boom, with the growing number of sawmills running to support the settlement of Ashland and the surge of non-Indians drawn by the economic opportunities the boom provided. Starr described the major transformations in the regional economy, as well as those in his own life, that led him to seek work in the lumber industry. "I followed the lumber industry for quite a long time in preference to fishing and trapping," Starr explained, "because the latter occupation was very hard in those days. My home at that time was a wigwam, but as I was employed in Ashland in the sawmills, I purchased lumber through my labor and built a house in the mill town."[47] His memories demonstrate how Ojibwe men found a means of retaining independence while engaging with the forces of settlement and industry. In this case, Starr chose to replace traditional forms of subsistence with logging because it was a more efficient way to make a living.

Paul Buffalo's decision to become a lumberjack was influenced by the same regional transitions Starr faced, but his motivations differed. He aspired to work in the lumber industry out of the admiration for the lumberjacks he watched as a child. Buffalo recalled that the lumber camps had large bunk houses with bunks made of lumber and that "the lumberjacks with whiskers—and tobacco juice running down their whiskers—worked the whole day." In the early morning, "all the lumberjacks got an axe and went rushing off for timber." Buffalo was fascinated by this work: "When I was a little boy, I was standing there watching them. I was wishing I was able, someday, to join them. Every time I'd take hold of some can-hook, or learn how to spin a can-hook and grab a log, I thought that was slick. How they would handle those tools!" As a lumberjack, Buffalo had the opportunity to learn a range of skills. Indians became loggers by "learning from the whites and using their tools," he said. "[Ojibwe lumberjacks] got along just fine."[48] For Buffalo, work in the lumber industry exemplified Indian adaptability and persistence. Ojibwe men learned a trade that would allow them to prosper in the north woods under the changing circumstances of the late nineteenth and early twentieth centuries.

More broadly, although logging was done on- and off-reservation, work off-reservation afforded a large measure of freedom Ojibwes could not find on reservations. Though Ojibwe men might work under the direction of a lumber foreman in a lumber camp or sawmill, it was not like working under the surveillance of an Indian agent or within the confined space of a reservation.[49] If the conditions of a camp were bad or a foreman was troublesome, a worker could move on to another camp or another labor opportunity. An Indian agent could hardly protest Ojibwe men working in the lumber industry because it mirrored the kinds of work that non-Indians performed. Many agents saw this work as evidence that Ojibwes were adopting the trappings of civilization. Indian agent Isaac L. Mahan wrote that over half of Red Cliff Band members were "engaged outside of the reserve in logging camps, cutting wood, and other civilized occupations." The lumber industry, he added, took many young men from Grand Portage to "distant parts of Canada, working in mines, lumbering, wood chopping, &c."[50] In some cases, entire families relocated to towns near lumber camps or sawmills. An inspector for the Indian Service noted in 1881 that with "the inducements of high wages the able bodied men are leaving [the Bad River] Reservation and moving their families to Ashland into lumber camps."[51]

Lumber camps varied in size, but they usually consisted of a kitchen or dining hall, a building for a blacksmith, a horse barn, a store, or "wanigan," and bunk houses for the workers. The camps, which were usually located deep in the woods, far from families or the comforts of society, were not pleasant places to live. While some men moved families near lumber camps, it was more common for them to travel alone. A few women worked as cooks or cook's assistants in the camps, but most camps were staffed entirely by men. Living in lumber camps was a different experience from living in Ojibwe harvesting camps. In harvesting camps, Ojibwe families camped in well-ventilated tents and wigwams or slept in the open air. Women and children worked together to maintain the camps and to keep them clean and comfortable. Lumberjacks, on the other hand, lived in shanties built of roughly hewn logs built low to the ground, with moss and mud filling the chinks between the logs. There were no windows; the only light source came from a skylight above the fireplace and kerosene lamps and lanterns hung throughout the building. The thin walls of these shanties hardly kept the below-zero chill out during the winter, and the only warm place was close to the stove. Lumber camps were also more crowded than Ojibwe harvesting camps. Men crammed into wooden bunks with hemlock boughs or straw for cushioning, a scratchy wool blanket for warmth, and whatever they could use as a pillow.[52] Despite the fact that lumberjacks were supposed to boil their clothing and bathe each week, usually on Sundays, they had a difficult time preventing the spread of lice in such close quarters.[53]

Living in the close quarters and the isolation of the camps forced lumberjacks to get along or at least to tolerate one another. Many of them expressed a sense of cooperation with their fellow workers. Paul Buffalo felt that lumber companies treated Indian and white workers equally and that the men got along relatively well. "In the logging camps they hired Indians and whites both," he explained. "It didn't make any difference. There was no discrimination. No. All worked together. All worked happily."[54] In reality, lumber camps were backdrops for violence and discrimination against certain groups of workers. But Buffalo's perspective suggests that some Ojibwe men might have found life in a lumber camp a welcome change from reservation life or the racism they faced working in the towns bordering reservations.[55]

Life in the camps also facilitated cultural exchange and expression among the men. Men of many nationalities and backgrounds worked in the camps, and they spoke a range of languages. For example, Polish and Ojibwe were the predominant languages spoken in some lumber camps in northern Minnesota.[56] Exposure to workers from different nationalities and cultures on a daily basis appears to have encouraged the expression of distinct identities. Ola Johnson, a Norwegian immigrant who worked in lumber camps in northern Wisconsin between 1860 and 1880, recalled, "There were many nationalities in the camp—Yankees, German, Frenchmen, Irishmen, and we three Norwegians." He went on to describe singing contests that the men in the camp organized in the evenings for entertainment. Men belted out "their national songs," and the camp determined which man was the best singer.[57] At time when federal government focused on eradicating indigenous cultures and languages, these circumstances must have seemed liberating to at least a few Ojibwe workers.

Cultural differences stood out in the lumberjacks' clothing. Most men wore leather, lace-up boots, flannel shirts, wool pants, wool socks, long underwear, and felt hats, but there were some distinctions in the ways that they dressed.[58] In his book on the lumber industry in Wisconsin, Malcolm Rosholt noted that most men came to the woods wearing their old clothes no matter what color or style they were.[59] He pointed out the uniqueness of the dress of Ojibwe lumberjacks in particular. In one photograph, a young Ojibwe man standing on pile of lumber wears what appear to be beaded leggings over his wool pants and a cap on which brass buttons have been sewn in a distinctive pattern.[60] In two more pictures, an Ojibwe lumberjack wears a wool coat covered with brass buttons sewn on in similar patterns.[61]

Ojibwe men also forged a sense of distinctiveness based on the difficulty of the work they performed in the lumber industry.[62] These occupations were some of the most difficult and dangerous, and workers who performed them were quite dispensable. Bayfield resident Eleanor Knight wrote, "There are countless graves of unknown lumberjacks in this part of the country. They came and went leaving only one great mark that they had been here—the disappearance of the timber."[63] Lumberjacks who were particularly skilled at a dangerous jobs often achieved local notoriety. The riskiness of these jobs suggested how critical it was to learn and retain these skills. The wrong cut by a sawyer could send a tree falling in an unpredictable direction and severely injure or kill crew members. Logs could tumble from sleighs and crush men behind them, and burlers could easily slip from the logs be crushed and drowned in the icy undercurrent of a river. According to Paul Buffalo, lumberjacks "always look for safety in the woods. . . . You can get killed very easy in the woods, if you don't know the woods."[64]

Buffalo recalled that Indians and Finns took on the most breakneck jobs in the industry. In the late nineteenth century, Americans saw Finnish immigrants and Indians as racial others. Many Americans believed that Finns were "Mongolians" and thus were not as smart as whites. American society also looked down on both Finns and Indians because they were reluctant integrate into mainstream American culture and to stop speaking their native language. Employers thus gave them some of the most dangerous jobs in the lumber industry. But, according to Buffalo, Ojibwes and Finns performed these jobs well; the acquisition of these skills, despite the dangers that came with them, was an indispensable opportunity to make a living in the capitalist market.[65]

The most well-known workers in the lumber industry were the log burlers, who, with graceful quick steps and arms extended, balanced on large churning logs, though if they lost their balance they would be killed. So risky and yet breathtaking was this work that it inspired log-rolling contests that spectators watched in nearby towns. In August of 1908, thousands of spectators came to watch one such contest at the White City, an amusement park in Duluth named after the White City in Chicago.[66] Competitions centering on labor were not uncommon during the nineteenth century. Plowing or mowing, breaking or drilling rocks, cutting trees, and laying bricks or rails could all be turned into competitive activities. Such competitions gave workers the opportunity to advertise their skills and capabilities to employers and boosted workers' productivity.[67]

In log-burling competitions, two men stood on a twelve- to sixteen-foot-long log that was at least fourteen inches in diameter. The competitors wore caulked boots with steel pegs or spikes on the bottoms so that they could grip the logs with their feet. Using their arms to balance they began by slowly rolling the log until it was spinning at a fast pace. The object of the competition was to remain on the log until one of the men fell off. The winner was the person who made the best two rounds of staying on the logs out of three tries or the best three rounds out five tries. They were usually awarded a significant amount of money.[68]

Ojibwe burlers from the Fond du Lac reservation gained renown for their abilities to win these contests. Lumber cruiser Louis La Prairie, lumberjack Henry La Prairie, river driver John La Prairie, boom man John Houle, and lumberjack John Matrious were all known for competing in these contests. In 1905, the *Cloquet Pine Knot* proclaimed that "the La Prairie Boys (John and Henry) are undoubtedly the best log rollers in Northern Minnesota."[69]

Logging became a significant part of these men's identities because of their local fame. Observers noted the Indian identity of log burlers. On August 18, 1906, the *Duluth News Tribune* referenced Ojibwe log burlers in the headline, "Indians Look Like Winners—Log Rolling Card Proves to Be One of the Best Features of the Season at the White City." Henry La Prairie, John La Prairie, Joseph Matrious, and John Houle all won prize money in the log-rolling competition that day.[70]

These men also entertained crowds outside of the competition. The *Duluth News Tribune* reported: "The Chippewa Indian boys [i.e., Henry and John La Prairie, John Houle, and Joseph Matrious] will also give an exhibition of three men on a log. The contest has drawn crowds to the White City and is considered by the management to be the best attraction of the season." They also performed with "Mrs. Ka-ta-toa," a man wearing a dress, a peekaboo blouse, and a short skirt and holding a parasol. She impressed onlookers with her expertise at log rolling and made them roar with laughter when she sent one of the men flying into the water.[71]

Henry La Prairie was one of the most famous of Ojibwe burlers. The fact that he was an Indian captured the attention of local people. Superior resident John Bardon wrote: "Henry La Prairie is a French and Chippewa half-breed, originally from the Fond du Lac reservation. Like many of his kind he became an expert woodsman and incidentally used to drive logs on the streams in this vicinity." Bardon attributed La Prairie's agility to his Indianness, suggesting that this was what made La Prairie an exceptional burler. As the railroad expanded into the region, Bardon related, La Prairie followed "the same general line of work except that the railroads now bring logs to the mill instead of being driven down the streams." But La Prairie continued to take great pride in his abilities. "He carries his caulked boots among his immediate possessions," Bardon wrote; "[whether La Prairie is] drunk or sober, they are cherished and watched with unfailing care. They are yet his one infallible—but faiding [sic] resource."[72]

In addition to working in lumber camps, many Ojibwe men made a living working in local sawmills and as carpenters, coopers, black smiths, and boat builders. Work in the lumber mills enabled Ojibwe men to learn yet more skills that they could rely on to support themselves in the midst of the lumber boom and Euro-American settlement. The growing towns of the region required lumber for new homes and other buildings and furniture. In the late nineteenth century, businesses like the Bayfield Woodenware Company manufactured and boxes, staves, and decorative woodwork to local homeowners. Other prominent industries, like commercial fishing and shipping, also depended on boat builders and coopers to construct barrels to store fish. Sawmills and furniture factories needed increasing numbers of workers to keep up with demand.

In 1878, Isaac Mahan reported, "Many of the males are found at Ashland, and other white settlements, employed in the mills, sash and door factories, cooper, blacksmith, and carpenter shops, or earning their daily bread at other kinds of educated labor."[73] Similarly, Captain R. D. Pike, the owner of one of Bayfield's first and largest lumber mills, recalled that Joe La Pointe, who was from an Ojibwe family in the area, "was the only man recognized as being capable of running a mill [since he] could do his own filing and sawing."[74]

The La Pointe plan encouraged lumber companies to establish sawmills on reservations, and to hire Ojibwe men as well. Indian agents, who saw this labor as a yet another opportunity to turn Indians into civilized industrial workers, recruited Ojibwe men. On the other hand, the skills Ojibwe men learned in reservation sawmills would eventually help them acquire work elsewhere. Observing the economic conditions of reservations under the La Pointe agency in 1896 (and exaggerating the economic opportunities available to Indians at the time), Indian agent W. A. Mercer wrote: "Employment is afforded all able-bodied Indians who will work in the reservation sawmills, and many are so employed. Others are learning the blacksmith and carpenter trade."[75]

THE DECLINE OF THE LUMBER INDUSTRY

Under the La Pointe plan, lumber companies expanded their operations, eventually holding monopolies over all areas of production. They purchased timber stands and operated lumber camps in order to assure a steady supply of lumber. They operated mills in local cities such as Duluth, Superior, Bayfield, Washburn, and Ashland, making all of them prominent lumber towns. However, the federal government bolstered this process on reservations by stipulating that only one lumber company was allowed to operate on a reservation. Reservations resembled company towns. The J. S. Stearns Lumber Company dominated business in the town of Odanah on the Bad River reservation between 1894 and 1922, employing Indians and non-Indians alike. The sawmill employed so many people from Bad River and the surrounding area that when it closed in 1922, around 1,000 non-Indian residents vacated the reservation and a large number of Ojibwes were left unemployed.[76]

Once the lumber companies removed all the valuable timber from the region, they moved to the Pacific Northwest, where timber was still abundant. Logging permanently altered the regional environment, rendering what were once dense forests into a landscape splintered with stumpage and cutover lands. The downed timber that remained after clear-cutting fueled forest fires, which destroyed any remaining timber and rendered the cutover land useless. Reflecting on this devastation, Jerome Arbuckle wrote: "The [Bad River] reservation at one time was blanketed with a magnificent stand of virgin white and Norway pine. This timber was indiscriminately slashed down until the entire reservation which comprises seven townships was denuded of larger timber." Once logging operations were no longer profitable, he added, "the logging and timber company packed up of and moved out, leaving a group of unemployed Indians upon a barren reservation."[77] However, an unexpected outcome of forest fires was the growth of berries; on the cutover land, the berry industry thrived.

Despite the diminishment of timber, the Indian Service continued to encourage lumber contractors on reservations to cut timber to encourage Ojibwes to farm.[78] While some land could support a few hardy crops, farming was still an incredibly difficult task. The rocky soil, marshlands, and short growing season on the north shore of Lake Superior in particular made agriculture a thankless endeavor. In her history of Grand Portage, Carolyn Gilman writes: "What an Ojibway was to do with 160 acres of inaccessible, rocky cutover land was a mystery. Few ever lived on their allotments; many sold them to land speculators and timber interests."[79]

The combination of the federal government's lack of insight and the environmental devastation caused by clear-cutting and fires rendered much of the land in tribal communities uninhabitable. When faced with the high cost of transforming cutover land, poor growing conditions, and paying taxes, many Ojibwe sold or abandoned remaining allotments. The sale of lands was part of the process of allotment that had begun earlier. But it was accelerated by the federal government's push to harvest most reservation timber and the declining economic and environmental conditions that followed. As indicated in Chapter 1, Red Cliff was one of the reservations hardest hit by these conditions. According to one historian's estimates, by 1929, when Red Cliff Band members had been granted title to or patent-in-fee for their allotments, 95 percent had already been alienated.[80] So extreme was the sale of land at Red Cliff that in 1929, U.S. Congress held hearings on the conditions of Indians in the United States. When asked about the volume of land sales on the Red Cliff reservation, the government farmer explained that the land was useless and that it was simply more beneficial to sell it.[81]

In the 1930s, during the Great Depression, the federal government shifted attention to conservation and forestry initiatives that coincided with work relief programs. The federal government stepped up forestry conservation programs that had full bearing on the reservation timber and lands. The Civil Works Administration (CWA), the Works Progress Administration (WPA), the Indian Emergency Conservation Work Program (IECW), and later the Indian Division of the Civilian Conservation Corps (CCC-ID) provided employment to tribal members and focused on implementing an array of forestry programs. At Grand Portage, Fond du Lac, Red Cliff, and Bad River, Ojibwes worked in a number of forestry projects, including reforestation, timber stand improvement, disease and insect control, timber surveys, and fire protection.[82] Moreover, the provisions of the 1934 Indian Reorganization Act promoted tribal self-determination and made it possible for tribal communities to purchase lands.[83] Despite this initiative, the federal government undermined Ojibwe self-determination by leaving forestry management in the hands of the Bureau of Indian Affairs with little input from tribal members.

It was against the backdrop of the federal government's new focus on creating jobs and implementing forestry programs on reservations that Ojibwes began to reflect on their work in the lumber industry. They remembered the tremendous changes that it brought to their lives and communities, as well as the forces of expansion and colonialism that it represented. These perspectives were as diverse as Ojibwe economic choices themselves. In some cases, Ojibwes recalled the devastation caused by lumbering, as well as the role that the lumber industry played in the dispossession of tribal lands and resources. In other instances, they took pride in their work in the lumber industry.

Bad River elder James La Fernier, who was born in 1851 and came of age when the lumber industry was at its peak, looked back on his work in the lumber industry in the 1930s. Alluding to the paternal attitude of the federal government regarding the so-called Indian problem, La Fernier challenged the idea that it was based on the primitive state of Native people. Rather, he said, the notion that "the Indian was a 'problem' was only the condition of the mind of those who were appointed his guardians, and, as a matter of fact, he needed no guardian to look after him." He stated that "the removal of timber from the forest caused the migration of game to more remote parts" and that game laws restricted Ojibwe abilities to hunt where they pleased. La Fernier stressed the importance of wage labor to Ojibwe survival and noted that Indian skills and abilities equaled those of non-Indians. Despite the difficulties they faced, he asserted, each Ojibwe worker was "able to stand up with his white brother and earn his bread by the sweat of his brow" when "conditions were equal."[84]

La Fernier noted the damaging effects of the lumber industry, but he also expressed pride in Ojibwe participation in the lumber industry as evidence of their sufficiency and hard work. "As I look back," he said, "I can vision Indians leading surveys, operating logging camps, many working in sawmills, and others working in other lines of industry; the Indian youth was shown how to work in the formative period of his life and the gospel of its necessity was clearly and indelibly impressed on his mind." He concluded, "The Indian was self-supporting in primitive days; and today all that he asks for is an opportunity to work to make himself self-sustaining."[85] La Fernier drew from a longer history of Ojibwe labor to highlight the importance of Ojibwe self-determination and survival.

Looking back on this work in his old age, Paul Buffalo suggested that Ojibwe loggers were some of the most desired workers in the industry. One logger was ready to offer Buffalo work, but he had some doubts about the reliability of Indian workers, saying that Indians were undependable and did not know " 'the value of money.' " Buffalo responded to this critique: "I've talked to the loggers and they say that, but, ya, they couldn't turn the Indian down because the White loggers like the Indians' work. I never was turned down. I think there's very few Indians that were turned down in a logging camp—in my days anyway. They always hired us." By emphasizing the abilities of Indian workers, Buffalo hinted that they had qualities that were indeed unique and set them apart. When faced with an employer's prejudice, he stressed that being Indian actually made him a desirable worker. Buffalo went even further to suggest that workers of certain backgrounds were better equipped for labor in the lumber industry. He asserted: "All nationalities can learn logging. As I say, anybody can make a practice of it, and can soon learn how to if they are at all interested when they get in the woods." But some nationalities were better at this work than others: "Finlanders and Indians work together very well. They get along very good. They work together like a team of horses, and they look good in the woods."[86]

Daniel Morrison grew up off-reservation near Iron River, Wisconsin, at the turn of the century. In the early twentieth century, his family took allotments on the Bad River reservation. Morrison's father, John, attempted to obtain federal aid when J. S. Stearns Lumber Company swindled timber money and then sold the timber at inflated prices.[87] Yet Morrison also saw some positive aspects of Ojibwe work in the lumber industry. Like Buffalo, he tied the success of Ojibwe lumber workers to their Indianness, suggesting that it made them distinctive and contributed to their skillfulness. "The American Indian has proved by actual results that he is entitled to recognition among our most skilled workmen, and in some lines he is shown that he is superior to his white brother and has been given the preference," Morrison wrote. He went on to discuss Ojibwe work in the lumber industry: "In the early days, as well as present time one will find Indians engaged in all kinds of labor, skilled and unskilled. In the logging days much work requiring skill and experience was done by Indians. Indians were found slucing [sic] and driving logs down the river; they were engaged in logging operations, a work, which required skill, experience, and knowledge, such as the intelligent running of lines, intelligent reading of maps, estimating timber, scaling, and decking and loading of logs." By comparing Indian and Euro-American workers, Morrison boldly emphasized the abilities of Ojibwes. But Morrison went even further to suggest that Ojibwe workers were better than non-Indian workers because of their difference. He explained: "In the earlier days these skilled positions were filled by whites, in the later days, Indians, [who] being naturally expert woodsmen, proved themselves adept for these lines, and in the last days of the operation of the Stearns mill, at Odanah, Indians filled these positions almost entirely."[88] Morrison indicated that these qualities were innate to a people who had made their living off of their lands. While Morrison's descriptions echoed Euro-American racial stereotypes, he also suggested that Indian workers possessed certain skills based on their indigeneity.

The dispossession of lands and resources as well as settler expansion shaped the experiences of Indian and non-Indian workers. But for Indian workers, work in the lumber industry presented a unique set of challenges based on the conditions of colonialism they were subject to. Ojibwe workers pointed to their labor as evidence of their perseverance and industriousness. This discourse served not only to distinguish Ojibwes from Euro-Americans but also to stress the importance of self-determination. The federal government focused on eroding Ojibwe sovereignty as well as their ownership of lands and resources through the treaties. It was precisely because of this that Ojibwe labor in the lumber industry was different from that of non-Indians; Ojibwes made a living on lands that had once been their own.

Although the federal government pressured Ojibwes to engage in livelihoods that facilitated their assimilation into Euro-American society, it could not influence the meaning Ojibwes connected to their labor or ultimately the purpose it served them. Despite the dangerous and difficult nature of labor in the lumber industry, it became a vehicle through which Ojibwe men forged distinct identities as Indian workers. They saw this work as a means to reassert their connections to the land as indigenous people even though they had lost ownership. Ultimately, it was through these assertions that Ojibwe workers challenged Euro-American assumptions about the assimilation and disappearance of Indians following the growth of the lumber industry and affirmed their distinct presence through wage labor. Ojibwes continued to exercise creative forms of agency as they capitalized on new economic opportunities left in the wake of the lumber industry.

CHAPTER FIVE

Tourist Colonialism

Reinventing the Wilderness and Redefining Labor

Between the 1880s and World War II, the tourist industry filled the economic gap left by the decline of the commercial fishing and lumber industries. During this period, tourism came to dominate the economy and environment in northern Wisconsin and Minnesota. The growth of tourism led to the transformation of cutover environment that had been ravaged by the lumber industry into a wilderness oriented toward the recreation of summer visitors. This new industry required that the region that had been dramatically altered by the extractive forces of industrial capitalism and settler colonialism throughout most of the nineteenth century reshape its public image, environment, and economy for vacationers. In his recent study of the Apostle Islands in northern Wisconsin, James Feldman uses the term "rewilding" to describe the process through which tourism transformed what had become an environmental wasteland into a wilderness.[1] He argues that "the meaning of wilderness has changed over time, especially in its relationship to consumerism and commercialization of nature."[2]

Tourism transformed Ojibwe labor just as settler colonialism and the processes of cutting over and extracting resources did in the late nineteenth century. In the early twentieth century, tourism offered new opportunities for wage work and commodity production that fused Ojibwe labor with the performance of Indianness. However, efforts to restore the wilderness for recreational consumption led to further restrictions on Ojibwe rights to hunt, fish, and gather. The tensions surrounding the opportunities and limitations that tourism entailed surfaced in the daily lives and actions of Ojibwe working in the industry. The efforts of tourists and the state to redefine land use and indigenous labor in the Lake Superior region was a form of tourist colonialism. Mari Yoshihara writes that although tourism is distinct from other forms of travel because of its focus on leisure and entertainment, it "plays a significant role in both reinforcing and reconfiguring national, racial, regional, class, and gender hegemony." Tourism, she explains, "reshapes and renegotiates the notions of the 'familiar' and the 'exotic,' 'culture' and 'nature,' 'modernity' and 'authenticity,' 'labor' and 'leisure,' according to the interests of not only the tourist industry but also of tourists themselves who carry diverse cultural and socioeconomic baggage as well as the hosting 'natives' whose relationships to and stakes in tourism are equally diverse and complex."[3] The various desires of tourists, state governments, and Ojibwe people shaped the tensions surrounding Ojibwe work in the tourist industry. Ultimately, these tensions centered on Ojibwe struggles to exercise autonomy over their lives and their labor in the face of tourists' efforts to redefine them.

Tourists began traveling to the western Great Lakes just prior to the Civil War. They were fascinated by the rugged natural environment inhabited primarily by Native Americans.[4] They traveled north to escape the noise, congestion, and pace of urban life in cities like Chicago, Milwaukee, the Twin Cities, Cleveland, St. Louis, and Lincoln.[5] The development of railroads in the 1870s made the region more accessible to vacationers and contributed to the emergence of a tourist industry in the early twentieth century.[6] Rail travel was costly, so vacationers who traveled to the region prior to World War I were largely wealthy urbanites.[7] Between the wars, the automobile replaced the railroad as the primary mode of travel, which enabled increasing numbers of middle- and working-class tourists from midwestern cities to journey to the north woods.[8]

By the early twentieth century, the region's landscape had been dramatically transformed by the lumber industry. In fact, one would think that the landscape of northern Wisconsin would have held out little appeal to vacationers and tourists at this time. After decades of logging, what was once heavily forested land was cutover and covered in stumps and downed timber.[9] The forest fires that blazed across the landscape added to its desolation.[10] Moreover, the waste from local sawmills muddied streams and rivers, leading to the decline in the water quality and threatening fish species.[11] Feldman notes that when landscape architect Henry Kelsey visited the region in the 1930s, he observed, "The hand of man has mercilessly and in a measure irrevocably destroyed" the "virgin" beauty of the Apostle Islands, which he believed would become "a smoldering and desolate waste."[12]

Despite these conditions the region became one of the most popular destinations in the Midwest.[13] Tourists traveled to northern Wisconsin and

Minnesota for sports fishing and hunting. Wealthy men who vacationed on the Brule River organized fraternities, such as the Gitche Gumee Club, and built clubhouses for sports fishermen.[14] Area business owners built large resorts, such as the Hotel Chequamegon in Ashland and the Island View Hotel in Bayfield, as well as cottages or cabins to attract middle- and working-class vacationers.[15] They canoed on local waterways like the Brule River and St. Croix Rivers and yachted on Lake Superior.[16] They picnicked at local landmarks, such as the lighthouses on the Apostle Islands, and visited sites of historical significance like the Old Mission Inn on Madeline Island, which had once been a Protestant mission for Ojibwes living there.[17]

The allotment of Ojibwe reservations in the 1880s and 1890s freed up land on which vacationers from urban areas and wealthy locals built homes, compounds, and camps to get away from cities and the stress of modern life. These were not quaint cabins one would associate with roughing it but rather palatial estates built on several acres of land that had several bedrooms and many modern amenities like electricity and running water.[18] According to historian Hamilton Nelson Ross, Colonel Frederick M. Woods of Lincoln, Nebraska, even "satisfied his longing" for a bowling alley by building one in his large summer home located on Nebraska Row on Madeline Island.[19]

Wealthy summer residents were the most actively involved in the movement to restore and reshape the region's environment and economy. Many of them were politically influential or were themselves members of the state government. Joseph Cullon writes that the Winneboujou Sportsmen's Club "literally transported St. Paul elite social life to the banks of the Brule in the summer." The mayor of the city and the governor of Minnesota regularly visited the clubhouse.[20] Though they largely came from urban areas, a majority of wealthy summer residents had familial ties to the region and to the settlers who had shaped its history. Many of them were key political figures in Minnesota and Wisconsin. One of the founders of the Winneboujou club, Christopher O'Brien, was a well-known Minnesota politician and lawyer who served as the mayor of St. Paul from 1883 to 1885. In the mid-1900s, he joined forces with other residents on the Brule River to lobby the Wisconsin legislature to establish a state forest on the land surrounding their estates. O'Brien came from a family involved in state politics and the promotion of settlement. O'Brien's brother Thomas was also a lawyer and served in a number of state and city appointments, including the justice of the Minnesota Supreme Court. O'Brien's father, Dillon O'Brien, was a novelist and worked as a teacher among Ojibwes at La Pointe. In 1863, he settled in St. Paul and worked with Archbishop John Ireland to establish Irish colonies in Minnesota as a solution to Ireland's land problem.[21]

John H. Knight was the first person to build a summer home on the Brule River, and he played a strong political role in the Chequamegon Bay region. Between 1870 and 1873, he was served as the Indian agent at La Pointe.[22] He also served two terms as the mayor of Ashland and for four years as chairman of the Democratic State Central Committee. Knight's interests were not strictly relegated to conservation since he also made his fortune as the founder of the Superior Lumber Company.[23] One newspaper credited Knight with establishing the Brule River as a vacation area, reporting ironically that "it was on the Brule that Colonel John H. Knight planned and carried out a greater Ashland, cleared the forest and made northern Wisconsin not only a playground, but a rich and prosperous country." Knight invited a number of politicians to visit him in northern Wisconsin to enjoy this "wonderland." These men included Colonel William F. Vilas, Senator William Spooner, Edward Wall, Senator John Kingston, Wisconsin Supreme Court justice John B. Winslow, Senator George Merrill, and Senator William Rust, all of Wisconsin, and Governor Samuel Van Sant and Senator Cush Davies of Minnesota. According to the paper, it was around the campfire that these men planned the economic development of Wisconsin and Minnesota.[24] This was, of course, the same economic development that had transformed the landscape into cutover.

Given these entanglements, it is not surprising that vacationers turned to the state governments of Wisconsin and Minnesota to shift and control land use in the north woods. In the process of enacting conservation policy, these individuals pressed the state government to restrict economic activities of local residents who relied on natural resources for their subsistence or to make a living in commercial markets. They believed that extractive land use was detrimental to the environment. As a result, they lobbied for a complex web of regulation that enabled state officials to monitor and supervise land and resource use and that would protect land for vacationers' exclusive use.

What is more, the money spent by tourists motivated state officials to enforce conservation laws with vigor. In 1895, the Minnesota game and fish commissioner claimed that "if the game and fish which the state was capable of maintaining was preserved, it would be worth $1,000,000 to the citizens of the state." He also reported, "We think that this year alone, at least $500,000 has been left in the state by citizens of other states coming here to spend their vacation, and of course, spend their money." He went on to declare that these initiatives furthered the interests of all citizens of the state and that individuals who violated regulations were essentially stealing the state's resources.[25]

The redefinition of the landscape and land use had a unique impact on Ojibwe livelihoods. Tourists were drawn to Native peoples based on what they perceived as their primitive qualities and their closeness to nature. Indians created an ambience that enhanced tourists' experiences in the wilderness, so wealthy vacationers hired Ojibwes. This interest presented new opportunities for Ojibwes to make a living in jobs that were not open to local whites. Yet, despite the economic opportunities tourism presented, it also transformed their lives. The tourist industry relegated Indians to labor that non-Indians associated with Indian identity, while preventing them from entering jobs that did not fit within that mold.[26]

While tourism privileged labor associated with Indianness, non-Indian efforts to redefine Indian labor were certainly not a new dimension of colonialism. Assimilation policy and allotment also focused on transforming Native livelihoods and enabled Euro-Americans to appropriate and control land and resources. Vacationers worked with the Wisconsin and Minnesota state governments to restrict Ojibwe livelihoods through fish and game laws.[27] They believed that Ojibwe treaty rights to hunt, fish, and gather in ceded territory stood in the way of the states' ability to protect all resources within their borders.[28] There was a great deal of overlap between settler colonialism and tourist colonialism. Indeed, both Knight's and O'Brien's backgrounds demonstrate that some wealthy vacationers were quite familiar with the nineteenth-century projects of settler colonialism and federal Indian policy.

An important dimension of this history is how Ojibwe people responded to tourism and exercised agency through their work. A number of scholars have demonstrated that although it was colonial in nature, tourism provided opportunities for Native peoples to invigorate their identity and culture. Larry Nesper, Grant Arndt, Clyde Ellis, and John Troutman have illuminated how Indian performances for non-Indian audiences facilitated both cultural survival and the reimagination of identity.[29] Paige Raibmon has demonstrated how Native people of the Northwest coast both collaborated in and challenged white notions of authenticity through performances and labor, such as hop picking, for their own economic, political, and social ends.[30] Jessica Cattelino has shown how Seminole enterprises such as commercial craft production and alligator wrestling enabled Seminole people to maintain cultural and political autonomy.[31] Tina Loo reveals how Indian guides in British Columbia subtly resisted and undermined the control and condescension of sportsmen employers in their daily interactions with them.[32] And Melissa Rohde examines how Lac du Flambeau Ojibwes asserted their connection to homelands and sustained the reservation community by working as guides and engaging with the tourist industry more broadly.[33]

This chapter outlines the many ways in which Ojibwe people made a living in the tourist industry and its importance to their economic and cultural survival, but it also charts a new direction by examining the impact of tourism on Ojibwe sovereignty and activism. As part of their efforts to reinvigorate and experience the wilderness, tourists were not only fascinated observers but also individuals actively engaged in the project of restricting and reshaping Indian labor to fit their vision of the wilderness. These efforts not only led to the enactment of conservation policy that restricted treaty rights but also shaped the individual interactions between Ojibwes employees and tourist employers. Ojibwes took advantage of the opportunities that this work afforded to sustain their culture and identity, and they utilized their interactions with tourists to contest tourist desires as well as state policy.

Ojibwes made a living in the tourist industry as performers, domestic servants, and guides as well as through the production and sale of commodities. The idea that Indians were exotic, close to nature, and part of a primitive culture made them valuable to employers. Tourists believed that the presence of Indians enhanced their experiences in the wilderness.[34] Travel literature often recommended hiring only Indians as guides since they were perceived to have an inherent understanding of nature or a connection to the wilderness that white guides did not.[35] The presence of Native people figured prominently into tourists' memories of their vacations. Writing about a family picnic in 1891, Arthur Tenney Holbrook recalled the presence of Indian servants: The "scene" of the picnic was "unforgettable with the dark figures of the Indians moving in the background, the blazing fires, the reflections in the lake, and the sparks flying upwards to join the stars."[36] Similarly, Rebekah Knight Cochran, John Knight's daughter, wrote that her first memory of the Brule River "was being poled up-river from Winnebojou in a birch-bark canoe by an Indian guide."[37]

PERFORMANCE AND PAGEANTRY

Large numbers of Ojibwes performed in pageants, exhibitions, and dances for tourists. Aside from earning an income, Ojibwes were motivated to do this work for other reasons. Clyde Ellis suggests that although dancing in Wild West shows subjected Native peoples to degrading or exploitative conditions, such as the derogatory attitudes of tourists or the corruption of managers, it also provided an opportunity to escape the poverty and the control of Indian agents on reservations.[38] Similarly, Larry Nesper has shown that performing at the Lac du Flambeau Indian Bowl allowed Ojibwes to "re-imagine" and express a distinct sense of identity as Lac du Flambeau people.[39]

Businessmen hired Ojibwes to perform in dances and pageants off-reservation as a means of drawing money to local towns. In the 1880s and 1890s, the Hotel Chequamegon in Ashland hired Bad River people to perform dances for visitors in front of the hotel. In 1896, Indian agent William Mercer and Buffalo Bill Cody arranged a meeting between Bad River leaders and Dakota and possibly Lakota leaders employed by Cody to sign a "peace treaty" on the hotel grounds.[40] The drama of this event was based on the history of conflicts between Ojibwes and Dakotas over the territory that Ojibwes eventually occupied; a peace treaty signed by the two tribes would have been an exciting and memorable event indeed to the non-Indian observers and the approximately 900 Ojibwes who attended the event. Eric Olmanson notes that so many Ojibwes attended the event that the Indian agent arranged to have them fed and sheltered at the Hotel Chequamegon, "instead of allowing them to roam about without restraint." The large number of Ojibwes staying at the hotel in turn drew crowds of curious white onlookers eager to see them.[41]

Pageants were another kind of show that featured Ojibwes in a combination of scripted drama, music, dance, and displays. In 1924, businessmen from south shore of Lake Superior sponsored the Apostle Island Indian Pageant, which drew thousands of people to the area. The pageant, comprised of thirty-five scenes played by more than 400 actors and running over the course of three days, portrayed the early history of the area up to the 1854 treaty. It depicted Euro-American history in the region and events that loosely related to Ojibwe history. "Mokadjiwens," an Ojibwe "brave" narrated the story, which followed the progression of Euro-American civilization in the region and celebrated settler colonialism. Organizers revived the pageant in 1925 and 1926, but they decided not to continue after that because interest in the event had dwindled.[42]

The pageant employed at least 400 Ojibwes who worked as crew members or actors.[43] They came not only from the nearby communities of Red Cliff and Bad River but also from communities located farther away, such as Lac Courte Oreilles. In addition to earning $8.00 for their participation in the event, it is probable that many individuals saw the pageant as a means to reconnect to each other and work together.[44] Evidence suggests that some Ojibwes saw their participation in the pageant as a positive experience. The historical significance of the pageant persists today. The Legendary Waters Casino at Red Cliff displays pictures of the pageant. In one picture, Ojibwe women stand in a line posing in bathing suits, in others Ojibwe men wear regalia beaded in traditional floral patterns and feathered headdresses. And at a recent storytelling event in Ashland, Wisconsin, a woman from Red Cliff mentioned that her relative had participated in the pageant.[45]

Ojibwe communities and neighboring tribes also hosted events to draw tourists to reservations. Events held in their own communities enabled Native people to retain control over the income they generated and to manage the impact of tourism on their communities.[46] Grant Arndt suggests that Ho-Chunk powwows became increasingly commercialized when Ho-Chunk Indians began to charge admission to white audiences attending their dances in the early twentieth century.[47] Ojibwes in northern Wisconsin adopted similar practices. Daniel Morrison recalled the celebration that Bad River member John Two Birds sponsored in 1904 to commemorate the signing of the treaty of 1854, which led to the creation of the reservation. As part of the celebration, Bad River members put together an exhibit "portraying the habits of early Indian life, with performers in full Indian costumes." According to Morrison, the celebration "attracted people from all parts of the state" and "the people who witnessed the performance voiced their satisfaction enthusiastically." He regretted that events like this were not more frequent because they generated a sense of "pride in the history of the Chippewa people, their folklore, and their customs."[48] The event was important because it allowed Ojibwes to commemorate an important political event in their history and to draw attention to the treaty at the same time the state of Wisconsin sought to restrict treaty rights.

Another dimension of performance and the tourist industry was photography. Photographs of Ojibwe people wearing regalia and situated in romanticized poses, gazing off into the distance, holding cradleboards or standing beside non-Indians were popular among tourists, and many of these were turned into postcards. Like performing in dances or pageants, posing in photographs exposed Ojibwes to stereotype and the predatory gaze of tourists. In their study of postcards of Ojibwe people, Patricia Albers and William James analyzed early-twentieth-century photographs of Native people in Minnesota and Wisconsin that were sold for public consumption and presented romanticized or degrading images of Native people.[49] For example, one postcard in the book features the image of an Ojibwe woman wearing late-nineteenth-century clothing with a child in a cradleboard on her back; the caption reads, "Had lots of fun with this native girl."[50] Albers and James note that the picture is degrading because it implies that the man sending the card engaged in sexual activity with the young woman in the picture. Images like this illustrate how photography contributed to the distorted perceptions of Native women as promiscuous and as objects of Euro-American desire.

However, as Bruce White points out, the nature and meaning of a photograph also depended on the context in which it was taken and the relationship between the photographer and the subject: A number of factors influenced photographs' meaning, for example, whether they were taken by a private individual and or by a professional photographer in a studio, whether the photographer was Ojibwe or non-Indian, and how Ojibwes themselves understood and used these images.[51] Some Ojibwes used photography to make a living. John Smith, an Ojibwe elder from Cass Lake, Minnesota, for example, posed in photographs for tourists as means to make a living and to travel around Minnesota to visit friends and family. Smith lived at Division Point, where the Great Northern Railroad Company had a turntable, making rail travel easily accessible to him. In his old age, Smith was known as "Grandpa John," "Chief John Smith," or "Gah-bi-nag-wii-i-wiss" (meaning "Wrinkled Meat") because his face was so wrinkled.[52] Smith became popular among local non-Indians because of his friendliness and storytelling abilities, as well as his age and resilience, and was considered a character of note. Local newspapers featured articles describing his appearance, reporting on his activities, or quoting entertaining things that he said. As result, he obtained free transportation to any destination he wished. "A lot of White people respected him," Paul Buffalo recalled. "He got on the first 'passengers,' the first passenger trains, and he got on the steamboats, and automatically he had a passport. That was just the way he lived. He didn't have to pay. It didn't cost him anything on the train. It didn't cost him anything on boats. It didn't cost him anything on wagons, trail wagons. It didn't cost him anything." When Smith died in 1922, a local newspaper claimed that he had died at 137 years of age.[53]

Smith utilized the attention he received to his advantage. Buffalo noted that Smith "used to have a lot of pictures and he'd get on the 'passenger train'" with them. "[He] would get on anywhere, Bemidji, Grand Rapids. They'd let 'im ride free. He'd get on the train, sit down, and dig in his pack. They took his picture, and they gave him a whole bunch of pictures for his extra pennies or nickels. He'd get up and walk down the isle of the train and holler, '*Wolf*. Tickets. Tickets.'" Smith sold his pictures for a nickel each, and that was how he "got by." He also attracted prospective passengers to the trains. "When you ride the train," the conductor said, "everybody wants to ride, John."[54] Smith was also offered the best hotel rooms in Duluth, Minnesota, because "he was a well-known old man," and a businessman in Cass Lake built a wigwam in his store for Smith to live in while he visited town.[55]

Smith became one of the most photographed Indians in early twentieth century Minnesota. The photographs show him dressed either in a feathered headdress or roach and regalia beaded with woodland designs or in regular clothes.[56] The photographs include captions such as "*Ka-be-nah-gwey-wence* (John Smith), age one hundred and thirty five" and "*Kahbe nagwi wens*: The man who lived in 3 Centuries."[57] Smith's story and his photographs present an intriguing example of how the combination of railroad travel and non-Indian fascination provided unique opportunities for this Ojibwe elder. Drawing on his age, appearance, and charm, Smith was able to generate an income and to traverse most of northern Minnesota.

MATERIAL CULTURE AND TOURISM

The sale and production of commodities to tourists also became an important means of income. Ojibwe women sold items such as articles of clothing and bags embroidered with elaborate beadwork, as well as beaded jewelry and charms, dolls, and birch-bark baskets, picture frames, and birdhouses to tourists. They also sold natural commodities like maple sugar, berries, and wild rice. Some individuals constructed and sold birch-bark canoes that vacationers purchased to display in their summer homes or to use on area rivers and lakes.[58] John La Rock, an Ojibwe guide, built a birch-bark canoe for President Calvin Coolidge to use when he vacationed on the Brule River in the summer of 1928.[59] Arthur Tenney Holbrook noted that birch-bark canoes, as well as photographs of Indians making the canoes were treasured items among wealthy vacationers in the area.[60]

The production of many of these items had been an important activity before tourism emerged and it remained part of the seasonal round. Individuals could produce them in their spare time or during the winter months. Obtaining the materials to create these items was relatively easy, since they were readily available in the natural environment, or, in the case of beadwork supplies, fairly affordable. Selling these items could be an extremely profitable venture that provided much-needed supplemental income. In 1895, the La Pointe Indian agent reported to the commissioner of Indian affairs that Ojibwes from Bad River and Lac du Flambeau took part in a carnival in Milwaukee where they generated a lot of attention. "The Indian exhibit provided one of the chief attractions of the carnival," he wrote, due to the public's interest in their handwork. Ojibwes, he added sold "articles of beadwork, birch-bark work, etc., which found ready purchasers."[61] It is difficult to trace the amount of income generated from the sale of these commodities because many transactions took place informally between individuals. However, in the 1940s, Carrie Lyford, the supervisor of Indian education for the Bureau of Indian Affairs, acknowledged that "a good steady market for the best Indian work has never been established, though many of the traders handle hundreds of dollars-worth of Indian-made goods each year."[62]

As was customary, Ojibwe women made their families clothing and items like baskets that they used in day-to-day life. Ojibwe women continued to do beadwork, make baskets, and sew clothing within the domestic contexts to which Indian agents, field matrons, and other government officials relegated them as part of assimilation.[63] Indeed, Jane Simonsen suggests that some field matrons even saw the production of traditional arts and crafts as something of a cottage industry that under their supervision would introduce a systematic work routine.[64]

In 1905, La Pointe Indian agent S. W. Campbell remarked that Ojibwes were "noted for their bead and birch-bark work. . . . They make and dispose of great quantities of [it], which forms one of the principal industries among the women of the tribe."[65] Additional examples suggest the continued importance of these activities over the following decades. Between 1920 and 1922 federal officials examined Ojibwe households on the Lac du Flambeau reservation to measure the extent to which assimilation policy transformed Ojibwe society. In addition to noting the quality of their housekeeping skills, the surveyors listed a range of items that women made. These included traditional crafts, such as beadwork, tanned hides, moccasins, baskets, reed mats, and woven bags, which they sold to tourists. They also sold wild rice, maple, sugar, and berries.[66] The sheer number of items produced by women, evident in late-nineteenth and early-twentieth-century written records and photographs, shows that this labor was central to Ojibwe household economies.[67]

Ojibwe women sold their handwork at pageants, exhibits, powwows, tribal cooperatives, and, later, roadside stands. Ojibwes also sold handcrafted items for resale to local merchants, who displayed them in windows and cases of their stores. As the tourist industry grew and more and more people traveled to the region via automobiles, Ojibwes enjoyed the economic benefits. In fact, this aspect of the tourist industry became so widespread that in 1943, Lyford reported: "During the summer months Indian homes in Old Village, on the Lac du Flambeau Reservation in Wisconsin, present a busy scene with the women working at their crafts.

The roadside displays of finished work are attractive to the ever increasing number of tourists. Around Mille Lacs Lake in Minnesota for miles the roadside stands display birch-bark work, moccasins and other beaded pieces, with the Indian craftsmen fashioning additional articles nearby. Scattered throughout the lake country evidences of the perpetuation of crafts are found, a single stand sometimes appearing on a little traveled road."[68] As Lyford suggested, the growing numbers of tourists who visited the north woods generated a growing market for Indian handwork and a new source of income for Ojibwe women.

GUIDES AND DOMESTIC SERVANTS

Ojibwes who worked for wealthy vacationers also benefitted from a new source of income. For a wage of between one and two dollars day Ojibwe guides led eager sports fishermen to areas where game or fish was abundant, and situated them in the perfect place to catch game or fish.[69] In some instances, they helped sportsmen to aim guns and net fish.[70] They also purchased groceries and provisions, prepared meals, set up camp for overnight trips, transported baggage, and chopped wood.[71] Some guides gained a reputation for their excellent cooking abilities, as did John La Rock, the Brule River's "premiere chef al fresco," for the way he cooked game.[72]

Sportsmen were heavily dependent on Indian guides, though they did not always give them credit for a successful hunt or kill. Although Arthur Tenney Holbrook took full credit for killing his first deer, he described how his Ojibwe guide, Joe Gheen, helped him. One evening, Gheen led Holbrook to a location where he would likely find a deer. After a great deal of waiting, Gheen signaled to Holbrook that a deer was coming.[73] Using a jacklight to spot the glow of the deer's eyes, Gheen told him when to aim his gun and when to shoot. Holbrook continued to rely on Indian guides as an adult. He described catching a prize fish on the Brule River with the help of his guide, Ed Dennis, who maneuvered their canoe so that he could reel the fish in.[74] As Holbrook shouted orders, Dennis paddled the canoe to where the fish was thrashing in the water so that Holbrook could net it and pull it into the boat.[75]

Some wealthy summer vacationers built cabins for guides or allowed them to camp on their lands. Ojibwe women (who were often family members of guides) lived and worked in the households of these vacationers or at local resorts cooking, cleaning, and doing laundry. Eliza Morrison and Mary Bouskey cooked and took care of the children in the camp of the Gray and Purcell families near the St. Croix River.[76] Other women tanned hides for sports hunters who visited to Brule River to display in their cabins dens or lodges as souvenirs. Holbrook wrote that each year a guide named Johnny Govan and his wife, Bo-Ka-Dos, "tanned over a hundred deer hides for settlers and hunters, and stacked them in their cabin."[77] Some women accompanied spouses or male relatives on guiding trips and cooked for hunting or fishing parties. Mary Gheen hauled a heavy sheet-iron camp stove and cooked meals when her husband, Joe, guided sportsmen on hunting and fishing trips.[78]

But there is no indication that Ojibwe or other Native women worked as hunting or fishing guides. In her study of twentieth-century big-game hunting in British Columbia, Tina Loo suggests that few women participated in sports hunting because it was considered a masculine activity; many sportsmen considered women "disruptive" or "ridiculous" on hunting trips.[79] White men aggressively expressed their masculinity and sexuality through the conquest of game and fish.[80] Under these conditions, it seems unlikely that guiding would have been appealing to Ojibwe women.

Working for vacationers was often a family endeavor. Holbrook recalled a group of Ojibwe families "who lived in their tents, huts, and wigwams on the river bank opposite near Muskikiwiininni Lodge: The Antoine Dennis family lived in this little village, as did the Joe La Pointe family and some of the Morrisons, with a number of others whom I do not recall." In 1891, Holbrook took the hides from the deer that he had shot "to this little community where the wives of Antoine Dennis and Joe La Pointe soaked, stretched, scraped, and tanned the skins."[81] Living together provided these families with support and economic stability as well as a larger combined income. Family members also passed the guide work to younger generations since kinship structured this labor. There are several examples of guiding families. John Morrison and his sons rented out cabins for travelers near the Brule River and provided their guiding services.[82] Antoine Dennis and his son Ed Dennis both worked as guides in the area. Individuals became familiar with the tourist industry because of family associations with guiding. Families known for their work as guides developed steady relationship with vacationers who returned to the region each summer. The Holbrook family, for example, employed Antoine and Ed Dennis each year. These relationships ensured employment opportunities for Ojibwe families every year.

OJIBWE WORKERS AND TOURIST EMPLOYERS

Although many Ojibwes found work in the tourist industry, the tensions surrounding tourist and state efforts to rewild northern Wisconsin and restrict Ojibwe livelihoods permeated individual interactions between Ojibwes and tourist employers. Tourists who vacationed in this region envisioned a vacation in a wilderness, and they expected Indian employees to adhere to this vision. Tourist employers not only pressed Indians to perform work in ways that catered to these expectations, but they also disapproved of their taking other forms of labor.[83] Building and paddling birch-bark canoes, performing dances in regalia, telling stories around the campfire, making moccasins for an employer, and guiding sportsmen to fish and game using "traditional" tracking skills were all considered acceptable forms of labor, ones that enriched the tourists' sense that they were indeed vacationing among a primitive people who were close to nature. Hunting and fishing for one's own living, using modern equipment or techniques, or working in an occupation outside of tourism were not acceptable, or at least they were not recognized as valid forms of labor. In essence, employers attempted to rewild Indian employees as they attempted to restore the wilderness of the Lake Superior region.

Tourists believed that they were entitled to these experiences because they were patrons; they insisted that the wages or goods they paid Indian employees obligated them to accommodate their desires. Grant Arndt writes, for example, that white audience members who attended Ho-Chunk dances considered themselves patrons because they paid admission and were thus entitled to see a "good show."[84] Indians employees were reluctant to openly criticize the expectations of their employers because they depended on tourism for their livelihoods.[85] Tourists hired and re-hired Indian employees based on their perceived loyalty and attachment to families. Rebekah Knight Cochran, for example, emphasized the loyalty and emotional ties that she believed her Ojibwe employees felt toward her family vacationing on the Brule River.[86]

When describing the men and women who worked for them, employers often used racist and gendered language. These descriptions were most often applied to guides and domestic servants perhaps because tourists spent extended periods of time with them in their summer homes and on camping, hunting, or fishing trips.[87] Holbrook, for example, made a point of stressing that his guides and servants were Indians or had "Chippewa blood." He referred to Mary Gheen, Mary Bouskey, and other Ojibwe women he encountered as "squaws" or described them as "squaw-like." He also emphasized the masculinity of guides and their natural skillfulness in the woods, writing, for example, that Johnny Govan was regarded by sportsmen as "tough guy" and that Alex Sevalia "was a handsome, dashing, daredevil type of full-blooded Chippewa Indian."[88] He marveled at the pace with which Joe Gheen trekked through the woods, commenting, "Although I am sure that those Indians thought they were going slow enough for our unaccustomed, it was a tough job to keep up."[89] Descriptions like these naturalized Ojibwe connections to the land and defined what constituted an authentic experience in the wilderness.

Rebekah Knight Cochran also commented on the racial qualities of guides, often emphasizing their masculinity. She spent many summers during her childhood on the Brule River, and she later married Percy Cochran, the son of Judge Joseph Cochran, whose family vacationed nearby. The families employed many of the same guides. Cochran described guide Jack Condecon as "a handsome tall full-blooded Chippewa Indian, who never drank and took a dip every morning in the river."[90] She went on to write that Condecon "never worked as a guide for anyone else on the river, emphasizing his loyalty" and noted that he was "always immaculate in dress and manners"; he was "One of Nature's noblemen." She described John La Rock, in a similar manner, noting that he "was a famous and outstanding man" and that he was "Part French and Chippewa."[91] Cochran focused on Condecon and La Rock's masculinity, revealing her possible sexual attraction to the men. For Cochran, the "Indian-blood" of the guides was part of their identity and thus made them genuine and authenticated their connections to the wilderness.

In the process of laying claim to the lands they explored and built summer homes on, tourists appropriated and refashioned American Indian culture. Philip Deloria has argued that Euro-Americans utilized what they saw as "Indianness" and "played Indian" in order to redefine their own identities.[92] Tourists who visited the region were no exception. Sports hunters and sports fishermen adopted Indian culture as way of staking their claim to the north woods. For example, Holbrook described an incident when he and Ojibwe guide Joe Gheen were carrying home a deer that Holbrook had killed and ran into Christopher O'Brien. O'Brien raised an arm, bowed, and exclaimed, "Hail Joseph of the Tribe of the Chippewas and Arthur the younger of the Tribe of the Gitche Gumees. Greeting from the wigwam of the Great Spirit Winneboujou. Put aside your pack, O Arthur, son of the mighty fisherman, and kneel before me; close your eyes and receive from the hands of his humble messenger the rites of the Great Spirit Winneboujou, which will admit you to the sacred circle of those whom he chooses to be his mightiest hunters." O'Brien then marked Holbrook's forehead, cheeks, and chin with the deer's blood and assured him that he was "a trusted hunter" and that "the Great Spirit Winneboujou" would always be at his side.[93] O'Brien invented a new ritual to recognize Holbrook's accomplishments and to admit him to the club or elite group of sportsmen. Holbrook did not mention Gheen's reaction to this event, so we do not know whether he was accustomed to such displays or found them annoying or offensive.

Ojibwe employees did not always accommodate the desires of sportsmen like Holbrook but rather utilized subtle forms of resistance to disrupt the fantasies of their employers. Holbrook described an instance in which he excitedly anticipated showing guests in his fishing party how well his Ojibwe guide, Antoine Dennis, could make a fire after they had traveled through a rainstorm. He told his companions: "Too bad we had to get soaked; but this will give you fellows a chance to see some genuine woodcraft. Just you watch Antoine and see how an Indian builds a fire with drenched fire wood and drizzle like this."[94] Holbrook expected to see Dennis use a knife to scrape off the wet bark on some kindling and demonstrate what he described as "aboriginal instincts that could meet any emergency."[95] However, he was embarrassed when Dennis went to the canoe, procured a box of dry kindling, set it into the fireplace, and then sprinkled it with a generous amount of kerosene before setting in on fire. Holbrook commented, tongue in cheek, that his guests "never got over that demonstration of pure, primitive Indian woodcraft."[96]

Eliza Morrison faced similar expectations working as a cook and housekeeper for the Gray family at their summer camp by the St. Croix River at the turn of the century.[97] Morrison had become friends with Mrs. Gray, and she related many of the stories of her life to the Gray family. When Mrs. Gray learned that Morrison and her husband planned to sell their farm on Spider Lake and to take an allotment on the Bad River reservation, she asked Eliza to write down her stories for posterity. Because Morrison had accepted clothing and food from the family each winter, she felt obligated to repay them. She recorded her stories in a series of letters that she sent to Mrs. Gray.[98]

The Gray family believed that Morrison's stories would provide a lens into a way of life and culture that was becoming part of the past.[99] Instead, Morrison provided them with a narrative of her experiences as a mixed-blood Ojibwe woman who had eagerly embraced the changes of the twentieth century. She wrote about building a farm at Spider Lake and taking a train on her own to the bustling harbor town of Ashland, Wisconsin. She wrote in her first letter, "I don't know much about the Indians myself only what my mother used to tell me."[100] In another letter she paused to ask, "Is this too much nonsense?" and then continued with her story.[101] Morrison's letters suggest that the stories she had been asked to write were not an accurate portrayal of her life and that she was trying to mitigate the differences between what the Grays expected from her and what she had actually experienced.

Tensions over the kinds of labor tourists thought Ojibwes should perform and the kinds of labor they were willing to perform surfaced in more overt ways when President Calvin Coolidge visited northern Wisconsin in 1928. Coolidge's visit also precipitated debates within tribal communities about how far they were willing to go to make a living in tourist industry and to ingratiate themselves to powerful political figures. The troubles began when the Wisconsin Conservation Commission recommended Antoine Dennis, who was at this point well into his eighties, as a guide for the president. The local and national press swarmed around Dennis's cabin for a few days; but, as one newspaper reported, Dennis did not "care for the glare of publicity." When reporters approached Dennis, he told them that "he couldn't be bothered with them," and after responding to a few of their questions, he "declared he was too busy [and then]swung a sack of potatoes over his shoulder and started off."[102]

The commission appointed John La Rock as the president's guide instead. La Rock seemed to tolerate and perhaps even enjoy the attention from the press. It is likely that he saw guiding the president as a way to publicize his experience and skills in order to generate more opportunities for work. However, the press was more interested in La Rock's physical appearance and his reports on the fishing abilities of the president, or "the big chief," rather than La Rock's skills as a guide. One reporter described La Rock as a "tall solidly framed man," who was not "a great talker" but possessed "a natural dignity and reserve" that was occasionally broken by a "twinkle of his shining black eyes."[103]

Some members of local tribal communities saw Coolidge's visit to the area as an opportunity to influence or get aid from the federal government and wanted to invite him to their reservations or host events in his honor. But not everyone saw it that way. Lac Courte Oreilles elder Bill Baker recalled that the tribal council came up with the idea of giving the president a name at a tribal induction ceremony so that Coolidge would put in a "good word" for the community.[104] However, in order to give the president a name they had to seek the help of a person who had the ceremonial authority to do so. When they asked John Mink, a respected elder, for his assistance, Mink responded, "You want me to try to dream up a name for some goddamn white man? I don't care what he is president of." Because John Mink stood up to the council and told them that their request was disrespectful, Baker explained, no other community member would "dare offer their services."[105]

Similarly, Bad River tribal member Charles Armstrong used a reporter's question about whether Bad River people would use Coolidge's visit as an opportunity to criticize tourists' expectations and the assimilation initiatives of federal Indian policy. He replied sharply, "You expect us to tool ourselves in the ways of the white man, but still you want us to put on feathers and paint for things such as this," which "[is] an insult to the Indians who have attempted to become civilized." There were "plenty of bootlegger chiefs" who would be glad to adopt (that is, as an honorary member of the tribe) the president for what "they can get out of it," he continued. "Some Indian agents probably will help them, for if the agents can make it appear that the Chippewas are still savages it will show that the Indian agents are still needed and will make their jobs more secure."[106]

Armstrong also criticized Ojibwes who celebrated the president's visit. He remarked that he would advise Ojibwe bands against adopting the president but that there were "enough Chippewas willing to sacrifice their dignity for a few dollars." He explained, "I have advised my people not to go about to pageants but still some of them go. I think I can say though that the real Chippewas will not have any hand in adopting the president. We respect him as a president, but we must respect ourselves too."[107] As Armstrong indicated, not all Ojibwes shared Armstrong's views, but he made an important point about how this work reinforced conventional notions about Indians that were implicit in tourist colonialism in the north woods.

In the early twentieth century, tourist and state efforts to restore the environment focused not only on transforming the landscape but also the lives and livelihoods of people living in the region. This process centered on Ojibwe people. As Patricia Jasen has argued, Native presence was central to tourism and "the beginnings of the tourist industry coincided, not accidentally, with the process of securing control over this vast territory from its established inhabitants."[108]

Tourist fascination with Indians and their assumptions about the primitiveness of Native people and their connections to the wilderness provided Ojibwes with jobs that were not open to local whites. Ojibwes utilized work in the tourist industry for their own ends in diverse and creative ways. Tourism provided a chance for them not only to earn an income but to sustain and revitalize culture and community, to travel off-reservation, to assert their connections to their homelands, and to resist the initiatives of assimilation policy.

However, these opportunities could also turn out to be what Hal Rothman terms "devil's bargains."[109] Tourist expectations about Indians extended beyond their personal interactions with the Native peoples they watched in pageants, purchased souvenirs from, or employed in their households to influence state Indian policies. Behind the conservation goals of wealthy tourists and state officials was the desire to privatize land and control natural resources, and they saw treaty rights as undermining their power. The ideology of Indian primitiveness served as a rationale for confining Ojibwe labor to the tourist industry and criminalizing Ojibwe livelihoods that were protected by treaty rights. But Ojibwes questioned the motives behind tourist expectations and determined what work they were indeed willing to perform.

Tourism has remained one of the most important industries in northern Wisconsin and Minnesota. After World War II, with the development of the highway system and automobile travel, the area became increasingly accessible to working- and middle-class visitors after World War II. Tourism has had a mixed impact on Ojibwe communities. Although the tourist industry continues to be a critical source of income for Ojibwe people, until just recently, it exacerbated struggles over treaty rights. In particular, following the *Voigt* decision in 1983, anti–treaty rights groups, including local whites who made a living from the tourist industry and sportsmen, violently rallied against Ojibwes who exercised their rights to spearfish in northern Wisconsin; they crowded around boat landings, threw rocks and pipe bombs, rammed boats, and otherwise harassed the spearers. Like their early-twentieth-century predecessors, these groups claimed that treaty rights enabled Ojibwes to take more than their fair share of fish (despite statistics that have demonstrated otherwise). At present, many non-Indians continue to express opposition to indigenous treaty rights based on similar arguments.

Today, thousands of tourists travel to the Lake Superior region to hunt, fish, hike, camp, canoe, and kayak, and they continue to be drawn to Ojibwe culture. In contrast to the early twentieth century, though, Ojibwe communities exercise a great deal more power in their relationships with tourists. This is due to in part to the introduction of gaming following the Indian Gaming Regulatory Act in 1988. Grand Portage, Fond du Lac, Red Cliff, and Bad River and surrounding Ojibwe reservations operate casinos, as well as hotels or campgrounds where tourists stay while sightseeing in the area. Casinos have become places where Ojibwes can present their own versions of their culture and history to tourists. For example, at Red Cliff's Legendary Waters Casino, photographs document Red Cliff history related to treaty rights, as well as the prominent leader Chief Buffalo's role in defending them after Sandy Lake in the 1850s.

However, gaming is not the only reason for the changed dynamics between Ojibwes and tourists. Indeed, some gaming operations have been more successful than others. Fond du Lac reservation's proximity to Duluth makes its casino a popular destination. Grand Portage's casino thrives because the reservation is located on Highway 61, a major thoroughfare between Minnesota and Ontario. Conversely, the casinos at Red Cliff and Bad River have been less successful because of their remote locations. Another and perhaps more important reason is that Ojibwe communities have creatively engaged in tourism outside of gaming and in the process have exercised greater self-determination and sovereignty.

In the early twentieth century, conservationists and historians representing the state of Minnesota pushed for greater control over the restoration of an eighteenth-century fur post on the Grand Portage reservation and the creation of a national monument at the site. In 1958, the combination of pressure exerted by these parties and the band's economic difficulties led the band to cede the site to the federal government.[110] However, the band has worked cooperatively with the National Park Service in the management of the site. Today, the National Park Service and the Grand Portage Band jointly run the National Monument Heritage Center (built in 2007), which introduces hundreds visitors to the monument each year and features exhibits on Ojibwe and fur-trade history. This endeavor is only one example of the Grand Portage Ojibwes' historical efforts to exercise self-governance over federal programs within their reservation.[111]

Similarly, in 2012, the Red Cliff Band created the Frog Bay Tribal National Park when it purchased eighty-seven acres of Lake Superior shoreline that had been privately owned but was historically part of the reservation.[112] The band obtained a grant from the federal Coastal and Estuarine Land Conservation Program to purchase the land, which it manages in partnership with the Bayfield Regional Conservancy. As part of this partnership, the tribal government, a committee of elders, natural resource professionals, and conservancy staff oversee the management of the park, and tribal wardens and police have jurisdiction over the park. The park is open to the public.[113] Frog Bay is the first park of its kind and marks Red Cliff Ojibwes' assertion of self-determination in their efforts to protect and conserve the environment of northern Wisconsin in the interest of the entire population.

Both the Grand Portage National Monument Heritage Center and the Frog Bay Tribal National Park are inspiring examples of how Ojibwe communities have engaged in innovative relationships with the federal government and local organizations and demonstrate how tribes might implement and promote conservation projects on their own terms. Moreover, they represent a future in which Ojibwe engagement in the tourist industry creates new avenues for tribal sovereignty rather than tourist colonialism.

Conclusion

In 1934, federal representatives convened the Hayward Indian Congress near the Lac Courte Oreilles reservation in Wisconsin at the request of Commissioner of Indian Affairs John Collier. The congress was ostensibly set up as a forum for tribal representatives from Minnesota, Wisconsin, and Michigan to discuss concerns related to the provisions of the proposed Wheeler-Howard Bill, which was designed to create a solid economic foundation for American Indian communities and to support tribal self-governance, but the real purpose of the congress was to promote the legislation. One hundred and sixty-seven tribal representatives from twenty-five delegations and Indian Service agents gathered in the Hayward Indian School gymnasium to participate in the conference proceedings as 250 spectators looked on.[1]

The Ojibwe delegates from Wisconsin, including Jerome Arbuckle and Thomas St. Germaine, were among the most vocal representatives. They raised concerns about whether the legislation would protect tribal treaty rights in the face of increasing state encroachment on reservation lands. They were worried that the bill would abolish Ojibwe treaty rights, especially since the state government had recently argued before the Wisconsin Supreme Court that it should have jurisdiction over all navigable waterways, including those located within the boundaries of the reservation. If this were to come to pass, the state to could make it illegal for Ojibwes to trap, fish, and harvest resources such as wild rice on waterways on- and off-reservation. Thomas St. Germaine informed federal officials that water rights were critical to Ojibwe survival and suggested that if the federal government truly wanted to improve the welfare of Ojibwe people, it should pass a law giving the tribes exclusive jurisdiction over waterways on reservations. Jerome Arbuckle asserted, "If this bill takes away our hunting and fishing rights it takes everything away from us and will be of no benefit to us."[2] When Arbuckle asked federal officials whether Ojibwes passing over these waters with game out season would be arrested and was answered in the affirmative, he said: "I would like to know what good our treaty is then."[3] Ojibwes from other Wisconsin reservations voiced similar concerns. Their reply was that these were "deep legal waters" that did not apply to the bill and would be more appropriately settled in state and federal courts. Thus, though it had the opportunity to address them, the federal government disregarded treaty rights as important aspect of tribal welfare and economic revitalization.

What was it like for St. Germaine, Arbuckle, and other delegates to witness this chance for redress come to a rapid end? We do not know how the other delegates reacted to the meeting, but it is apparent that it haunted Jerome Arbuckle. In a discussion of the treaty rights litigation that was taking place around the same time of the meeting, Arbuckle stated: "Technical questions arose as a result of these cases, which to date have never been satisfactorily settled while publicity given to these cases in court and in the press seemed to furnish 'ads' for ever increasing white trespassers. The Indians raised their voices in complaint against these grievances, but to no avail."[4] For Ojibwes, the congress ultimately represented the federal government's refusal to address or even acknowledge that treaty rights were central to their economies and their sovereignty. Writing about the congress, Ronald Satz concluded, "The BIA's failure to address these issues had dramatic consequences for Wisconsin's Indians as is exemplified in the long struggle of the state's six Chippewa bands to practice their hunting and fishing regulations free from state regulation."[5]

Ironically, precisely during the period when federal policy was shifting toward promoting tribal self-governance and economic development, the government disregarded the extent to which Ojibwe sovereignty and their livelihoods were intertwined. Although the Indian New Deal focused on programs designed to invigorate tribal economies and to generate work, the federal representatives at the congress did not acknowledge that Ojibwes had depended on their treaty rights to exercise political and economic self-determination since the mid-nineteenth century. By brushing treaty rights aside as a strictly legal matter to be in settled the courts, they disregarded the role that treaties had played in defining Ojibwe relationships with the federal government.

In fact, the treaties played a critical role in shaping the political relations between Ojibwes and the United States, as well as the structure of the regional economy in which both Ojibwes and settlers worked. Ojibwe headmen and U.S. officials both had economic interests in mind during treaty negotiations in the mid-nineteenth century. Ojibwe leaders saw traditional livelihoods and access to their homelands as critical to their people's survival as well as to their sovereignty. They reserved the right to hunt, fish, and gather in the 1837, 1842, and 1854 treaties in an effort to guarantee both. They were well aware of the changes brought by the fur trade as well as increasing American interest in acquiring lands and resources within their territory. The treaties, then, had presented Ojibwes the opportunity to mitigate American desires for timber and mineral resources while sustaining their indigenous life ways. They granted American citizens access to timber and other resources with the understanding that they would not interfere with the seasonal round. The United States, however, utilized the treaties as way to claim title to ceded territory and to extend power over the region; the treaties became the vehicle through which the United States asserted its own settler sovereignty in the western Great Lakes. As a result, Ojibwes became an indigenous nation encompassed by the boundaries of the United States.

The nineteenth century brought some of the most dramatic changes that Ojibwes had ever experienced. The focus of the regional economy shifted from the fur trade to industrial capitalism and settlement, bringing new forms of economic production and new people to their lands. In just a few decades, towns and cities emerged along the shores of Lake Superior as businesses took advantage of the land and resources that were ceded in the treaties of 1837, 1842, and 1854. At the same time, the federal government imposed an intricate system of colonial policy designed to erode the Ojibwe way of life and to facilitate Euro-American acquisition of additional lands and resources in Ojibwe hands.

Within this context, many different forms of labor became critical to Ojibwe survival and resistance; Ojibwes transformed their traditional livelihoods to meet the demands of the market; they engaged in commerce and adopted wage labor in a manner that served their own interests. Ojibwe men took up new occupations in the lumber industry in order to alleviate the economic instability caused by the loss of land and resources and their containment on reservations. Moreover, many Ojibwes performed work that involved mobility or took advantage of modern transportation to exercise treaty rights, to sustain community, and to avoid the assimilation efforts of Indian agents. They also relied on their treaty rights to resist federal Indian policy initiatives and to make a living in the capitalist market. They transformed hunting, fishing, and gathering into commercial activities while continuing to practice the social and ceremonial traditions connected to this labor. Ojibwes constructed an identity around these mixed economic strategies and asserted a distinct connection to the places in which they worked as they undermined U.S. efforts to constrain their autonomy. Although Ojibwes worked in many of the same occupations as their settler neighbors, they attributed unique meanings to and found their own purposes for this work based on their cultural traditions and their struggles with colonialism.

In the early twentieth century, tourism grew to be the most prominent industry in the region, filling in the gaps that the lumber industry left behind. The ascendance of tourism marked a major shift in both the economy and state and federal policy. Tourism bolstered state conservation efforts and criminalized of indigenous livelihoods. But tourism also presented Ojibwes with many economic opportunities. Ojibwes made a living as guides, domestic servants, or performers or by selling handicrafts like beadwork and birch baskets or commodities like maple sugar or wild rice. At the same time, however, tourism restricted the kinds of labor that Indians could perform. Wealthy summer residents employed Indians because they saw them as primitive and exotic. They believed that the presence of Ojibwe people enhanced their experiences in the wilderness. Consequently, they restricted Indians to certain forms of labor that they deemed authentic and nonthreatening. Treaty rights stood in the way of tourists' and state governments' desire to gain access and control over the region's natural resources. Because of the political clout of wealthy tourists and monopolies in the fishing industry, Minnesota and Wisconsin fish and game laws catered to conservation interests while restricting Ojibwe livelihoods.

By the early twentieth century, the decline of several prominent industries coupled with fish and game laws made it ever more difficult for Ojibwes to make a living and compounded poverty in their communities. Times were indeed grim when Ojibwe representatives spoke at the Hayward Indian Congress, and the future likely did not look much better. Despite the federal government's attempts to alleviate American Indian poverty through relief programs that provided employment and improved the infrastructure of reservation communities, policy-makers did not acknowledge the centrality of treaty rights to Ojibwe economic survival. In the following decades, the tourist industry continued to grow. In the 1950s, almost 4 million out-of-state residents and 2 million in-state residents vacationed in Wisconsin alone. In 1960, Wisconsin issued 925,000 fishing licenses, more than twice the number issued only twenty years before.[6] Ojibwes bore the brunt of the industry as states continued to step up the enforcement of regulations targeting Indians and increasingly extended enforcement to reservations.

Still, Ojibwes continued to contest state infringement on their rights and confront the political motivations that lay behind these policies. They exercised self-determination and defined their sovereignty by hunting, fishing, and gathering in resistance to state laws. Their resistance to state laws, however, led to dire economic consequences. Ojibwes rarely received compensation or redress for their arrests or fines or equipment confiscated by state wardens. The political climate of the 1960s and the rise of the American Indian movement opened new doors for Ojibwes to assert their sovereignty. Beginning in the 1970s, Ojibwes once again fought in state and federal courts for the recognition of their treaty rights and redress for the depredations caused by state policy. They were successful because they had greater access to Judicare funds that allowed them to pursue litigation in the federal courts and because their strategies were more confrontational than those of previous generations. From the 1970s to the 1990s, treaty rights activism ushered in major shifts in state and federal policy. Ojibwes endured a long process of litigation and violent protest on the part of anti–treaty rights groups, but they persevered. In 1991, after eight years of litigation, the state of Wisconsin announced that it would no longer appeal the rulings of the *Voigt* decision of 1983, which confirmed Chippewa rights to hunt, fish, and gather in ceded territory. In 1999, in *Minnesota v. Mille Lacs*, the United States Supreme Court upheld Chippewa treaty rights in Minnesota.

Larry Nesper argues that the rearticulation of Ojibwe identity was central to the treaty rights activism in the late twentieth century and that struggles of past generations played a key role. Elders who supported younger generations of Ojibwe activists during the 1970s, 1980s, and 1990s came of age during the Indian Reorganization Act of the 1930s. Although through their "accommodation" this generation of Ojibwes gave up significant cultural traditions, Nesper writes, their actions "also permitted the continual re-definition and endurance of other aspects of Ojibwe culture, like hunting and fishing, and it has fostered a social coherence and continuity that made a cultural revival thinkable in the late 1980s."[7] Older generations of Ojibwes clearly played a critical role in shaping the articulation of self-determination and sovereignty associated with these livelihoods.

Activists in the late twentieth century were motivated by their own early experiences or the stories related to them by family members. These stories centered on labor. Ojibwes drew from a long history of harassment and resistance to explain why they continued to assert their treaty rights. Indeed "violating," or what Ojibwes call their resistance to state laws, has become an important part of Ojibwe identity; it symbolizes both their refusal to accept infringement on their rights and their survival.[8] That labor associated with treaty rights became a form of resistance under these conditions illustrates how Ojibwe livelihoods were uniquely defined by their struggles with colonialism.

Grand Portage Ojibwe Bill Myers described how state game wardens' treatment of elders in the 1950s influenced his efforts to challenge them: "When I was younger, I got arrested for exercising my treaty rights to fish. The game warden at the time was constantly badgering the old people, and he would only pick on the old-timers when they were trying to get fish. I didn't like that, so I thought I'd see if he wanted to pick on me instead of the old-timers." After consulting with his attorney so he would be prepared to go to court, Myers set nets on Vermilion Lake and was promptly arrested by the warden and his fish and nets were confiscated. Because the state did not want to go to court, the judge ordered the warden to return Myers's nets and "told not to harass the Indians at Vermilion Lake."[9]

Ojibwe Esther Nahganub recalled the injustice of state encroachment among Fond du Lac people in the early twentieth century. Nahganub's grandfather shot bears and sold the surplus meat. When on one occasion he attempted to sell the meat to a game warden, Nahganub, recalled, "The game warden immediately arrested him because he had shot something. Grandpa took the case to court and the court dismissed it, citing the 1854 treaty that you could hunt, fish, and gather in ceded territory." She suggested that many Fond du Lac residents were not aware that their treaty rights were valid: "They didn't realize that we still had these rights because the game wardens and everyone had inflicted all these rules on us." For example, the authorities told them: "'Yes you can go hunt anywhere you want but you have to eat it right there because you can't take it over a county road.'"[10]

Nahganub described a time in the 1980s when she was arrested by a Minnesota game warden for ricing. "I was arrested along with Bob Diver, for ricing by Floyd Jaros," she explained. "He wanted to cite me and Bob for the canoe being a couple of inches too wide and was a little bit too long and the knockers weren't right." The warden confiscated their rice, so they went to court. When Nahganub brought a copy of the treaty of 1854 to the court, the judge threw out the case out, but since she did not have a state license to rice within in the reservation, the rice was never returned, nor was she compensated for it. "That was another thing we were doing wrong and we were ricing at the wrong time," she commented.[11] Nahganub "There was just an endless list of what we had done wrong. But Grandpa was a treaty fighter and from the time I can remember, I always was told, 'the treaty will protect us, the treaty will protect us.' I didn't even know what the treaty was . . . through those years and that['s] why in 1988, when I heard all the stuff happening with treaty rights, I went ballistic. But he was such a staunch defender of that because he knew the time would come that they would want (because it was happening then) everything we have, except us."[12] In her own efforts to fight for treaty rights, Nahganub clearly drew inspiration from her grandfather.

Myers's and Nahganub's experiences reflected a long history of resistance that linked generations of Ojibwes. Ojibwes continue express a sense of identity and nationhood based on their historical struggles to exercise their sovereignty. The seasonal round of subsistence had always been central to Ojibwe life, encompassing an intricate matrix of ceremonial beliefs, social relations, and a sense of place. But Ojibwe livelihoods took on new forms and meaning as the United States extended power over the western Great Lakes, using resources and lands ceded in the treaties to bolster regional economic development. In treaty negotiations, Ojibwe leaders defined their relationship with the United States in economic terms as a way of provisioning for their people's survival and maintaining autonomy under U.S. jurisdiction.

Ojibwes transformed labor not just to make a living but to resist the colonial initiatives of federal Indian policy in the nineteenth and twentieth centuries. They sustained their connections to territory, cultural practices, and social relations that defined their identity through their labor. In the face of state encroachment on treaty rights, labor encompassed by the treaties only grew in importance. Hunting, fishing, and, to a lesser extent, gathering were the primary means through which Ojibwes articulated and exercised their sovereignty in defiance of state laws.

Today, treaty rights remain critical to Ojibwe economies. They continue to link the challenges they face at present to the struggles of past generations. Commenting on the importance of these rights during the economic recession in 2010, Mic Isham, the chairman of the Great Lakes Indian Fish and Wildlife Commission, referenced this history: "Our Chiefs who negotiated the treaties sure had foresight! They knew our reliance on hunting, fishing, and gathering would get us through even the toughest times. Times today are not as tough for us as they were in the late 1800s and early 1900s, but lately they have been pretty rough. Tribal revenues are down all over, and other funding sources are less readily available. Jobs for our people in cities have been lost due to massive layoffs. Our members have been coming back home to survive and rely on our old reliable ways of life. Chimiigwech to our Chiefs for thinking seven generations into the future!"[13]

By considering the relationship between Ojibwe labor and their sovereignty, we begin to understand how American Indian labor history is unique yet intertwined with American history as a result of the treaties. The cession of Ojibwe land and resources fueled industrial development and structured the labor markets in which Ojibwes and Euro-Americans worked. However, Ojibwes became part of American labor history as indigenous peoples colonized by the United States. It was through their struggles to challenge colonialism on their own economic and political terms that Ojibwes have become the resilient and vibrant people that they are today.

Treaties with the Chippewa, 1837, 1842, and 1854

The following are excerpts of the treaties of 1837, 1842, and 1854, adapted from Kappler, *Indian Affairs*, vol. 2. For ease of reading, I have adjusted the formatting as necessary and silently added and/or corrected punctuation and corrected spelling errors.

Treaty of 1837

Articles of a treaty made and concluded at St. Peters (the confluence of the St. Peters and Mississippi rivers) in the Territory of Wisconsin, between the United States of America, by their commissioner, Henry Dodge, Governor of said Territory, and the Chippewa nation of Indians, by their chiefs and headmen.

ARTICLE 1.

The said Chippewa nation cede to the United States all that tract of country included within the following boundaries:

Beginning at the junction of the Crow Wing and Mississippi rivers, between twenty and thirty miles above where the Mississippi is crossed by the forty-sixth parallel of north latitude, and running thence to the north point of Lake St. Croix, one of the sources of the St. Croix river; thence to and along the dividing ridge between the waters of Lake Superior and those of the Mississippi, to the sources of the Ocha-sua-sepe, a tributary of the Chippewa river; thence to a point on the Chippewa river, twenty miles below the outlet of Lake De Flambeau; thence to the junction of the Wisconsin and Pelican rivers; thence on an east course twenty-five miles; thence southerly, on a course parallel with that of the Wisconsin river, to the line dividing the territories of the Chippewas and Menomonees; thence to the Plover Portage; thence along the southern boundary of the Chippewa country, to the commencement of the boundary line dividing it from that of the Sioux, half a days march below the falls on the Chippewa river; thence with said boundary line to the mouth of Wah-tap river, at its junction with the Mississippi; and thence up the Mississippi to the place of beginning.

ARTICLE 2.

In consideration of the cession aforesaid, the United States agree to make to the Chippewa nation, annually, for the term of twenty years, from the date of the ratification of this treaty, the following payments.

1. Nine thousand five hundred dollars, to be paid in money.

2. Nineteen thousand dollars, to be delivered in goods.

3. Three thousand dollars for establishing three blacksmiths shops, supporting the blacksmiths, and furnishing them with iron and steel.

4. One thousand dollars for farmers, and for supplying them and the Indians, with implements of labor, with grain or seed; and whatever else may be necessary to enable them to carry on their agricultural pursuits.

5. Two thousand dollars in provisions.

6. Five hundred dollars in tobacco.

The provisions and tobacco to be delivered at the same time with the goods, and the money to be paid; which time or times, as well as the place or places where they are to be delivered, shall be fixed upon under the direction of the President of the United States. The blacksmiths shops to be placed at such points in the Chippewa country as shall be designated by the Superintendent of Indian Affairs, or under his direction.

If at the expiration of one or more years the Indians should prefer to receive goods, instead of the nine thousand dollars agreed to be paid to them in money, they shall be at liberty to do so. Or, should they conclude to appropriate a portion of that annuity to the establishment and support of a school or schools among them, this shall be granted them.

ARTICLE 3.

The sum of one hundred thousand dollars shall be paid by the United States, to the half-breeds of the Chippewa nation, under the direction of the President. It is the wish of the Indians that their two sub-agents Daniel P. Bushnell and Miles M. Vineyard, superintend the distribution of this money among their half-breed relations.

ARTICLE 4.

The sum of seventy thousand dollars shall be applied to the payment, by the United States, of certain claims against the Indians; of which amount twenty-eight thousand dollars shall, at their request, be paid to William A. Aitkin, twenty-five thousand to Lyman M. Warren, and the balance applied to the liquidation of other just demands against them—which they acknowledge to be the case with regard to that presented by Hercules L. Dousman, for the sum of five thousand dollars; and they request that it be paid.

ARTICLE 5.

The privilege of hunting, fishing, and gathering the wild rice, upon the lands, the rivers and the lakes included in the territory ceded, is guaranteed to the Indians, during the pleasure of the President of the United States.

ARTICLE 6.

This treaty shall be obligatory from and after its ratification by the President and Senate of the United States.

Done at St. Peters in the Territory of Wisconsin the twenty-ninth day of July eighteen hundred and thirty-seven.

Henry Dodge, Commissioner.

From Leech lake:
Aish-ke-bo-ge-koshe, or Flat Mouth,
R-che-o-sau-ya, or the Elder Brother.
Chiefs.
Pe-zhe-kins, the Young Buffalo,
Ma-ghe-ga-bo, or La Trappe,
O-be-gwa-dans, the Chief of the Earth,
Wa-bose, or the Rabbit,
Che-a-na-quod, or the Big Cloud.
Warriors.

From Gull lake and Swan river:
Pa-goo-na-kewe-zhig, or the Hole in
    the Day,
Songa-ko-mig, or the Strong Ground.
Chiefs.
Wa-boo-jig, or the White Fisher,
Ma-cou-da, or the Bear's Heart.
Warriors.

From St. Croix river:
Pe-zhe-ke, or the Buffalo,
Ka-be-ma-be, or the Wet Month.
Chiefs.
Pa-ga-we-we-wetung, Coming Home
    Hollowing,
Ya-banse, or the Young Buck,
Kis-ke-ta-wak, or the Cut Ear.
Warriors.

From Lac Courte Oreilles:
Pa-qua-a-mo, or the Wood Pecker.
Chief.

From Lac du Flambeau:
Pish-ka-ga-ghe, or the White Crow,
Na-wa-ge-wa, or the Knee,
O-ge-ma-ga, or the Dandy,
Pa-se-quam-jis, or the Commissioner,
Wa-be-ne-me, or the White Thunder.
Chiefs.

From La Pointe (on Lake Superior):
Pe-zhe-ke, or the Buffalo,
Ta-qua-ga-na, or Two Lodges Meeting,
Cha-che-que-o.
Chiefs.

From Mille Lacs:
Wa-shask-ko-kone, or Rats Liver,
Wen-ghe-ge-she-guk, or the First Day.
Chiefs.
Ada-we-ge-shik, or Both Ends of the
    Sky,
Ka-ka-quap, or the Sparrow.
Warriors.

From Sandy lake:
Ka-nan-da-wa-win-zo, or Le Brocheux,
We-we-shan-shis, the Bad Boy, or Big
    Mouth,
Ke-che-wa-me-te-go, or the Big
    Frenchman.
Chiefs.
Na-ta-me-ga-bo, or the Man that
    Stands First,
Sa-ga-ta-gun, or Spunk.
Warriors.

From Snake river:
Naudin, or the Wind,
Sha-go-bai, or the Little Six,
Pay-ajik, or the Lone Man,
Na-qua-na-bie, or the Feather.
Chiefs.
Ha-tau-wa,
Wa-me-te-go-zhins, or the Little
    Frenchman,
Sho-ne-a, or Silver.
Warriors.

From Fond du Lac (on Lake Superior):
Mang-go-sit, or the Loons Foot,
Shing-go-be, or the Spruce.
Chiefs.

From Red Cedar lake:
Mont-so-mo, or the Murdering Yell.
From Red lake:
Francois Goumean (a half breed).
From Leech lake:
Sha-wa-ghe-zhig, or the Sounding Sky,
Wa-zau-ko-ni-a, or Yellow Robe.
Warriors.

Signed in presence of—
Verplanck Van Antwerp, Secretary to
the Commissioner.
M. M. Vineyard, U.S. Sub-Indian
Agent.
Daniel P. Bushnell.
Law. Taliaferro, Indian Agent at St.
Peters.
Martin Scott, Captain, Fifth Regiment
Infantry.
J. Emerson, Assistant Surgeon, U.S.
Army.
H. H. Sibley.
H. L. Dousman.
S. C. Stambaugh.
E. Lockwood.
Lyman M. Warren. J.
N. Nicollet.
Harmen Van Antwerp.
Wm. H. Forbes.
Jean Baptiste Dubay, Interpreter.
Peter Quinn, Interpreter.
S. Campbell, U.S. Interpreter.
Stephen Bonga, Interpreter.
Wm. W Coriell.
(To the Indian names are subjoined a
mark and seal.)

Treaty of 1842

Articles of a treaty made and concluded at La Pointe of Lake Superior, in the Territory of Wisconsin, between Robert Stuart, commissioner on the part of the United States, and the Chippewa Indians of the Mississippi, and Lake Superior, by their chiefs and headmen.

ARTICLE 1.

The Chippewa Indians of the Mississippi and Lake Superior, cede to the United States all the country within the following boundaries; viz: beginning at the mouth of Chocolate river of Lake Superior; thence northwardly across said lake to intersect the boundary line between the United States and the Province of Canada; thence up said Lake Superior, to the mouth of the St. Louis, or Fond du Lac river (including all the islands in said lake); thence up said river to the American Fur Company's trading post, at the southwardly bend thereof, about 22 miles from its mouth; thence south to intersect the line of the treaty of 29th July 1837, with the Chippewas of the Mississippi; thence along said line to its southeastwardly extremity, near the Plover portage on the Wisconsin river; thence northeastwardly, along the boundary line, between the Chippewas and Menomonees, to its eastern termination (established by the treaty held with the Chippewas, Menomonees, and Winnebagoes, at Butte des Morts, August 11th 1827) on the Skonawby river of Green Bay; thence northwardly to the source of Chocolate river; thence down said river to its mouth, the place of beginning; it being the intention of the parties to this treaty, to include in this cession, all the Chippewa lands eastwardly of the aforesaid line running from the American Fur Company's trading post on the Fond du Lac river to the intersection of the line of the treaty made with the Chippewas of the Mississippi July 29th 1837.

ARTICLE 2.

The Indians stipulate for the right of hunting on the ceded territory, with the other usual privileges of occupancy, until required to remove by the President of the United States, and that the laws of the United States shall be continued in force, in respect to their trade and intercourse with the whites, until otherwise ordered by Congress.

ARTICLE 3.

It is agreed by the parties to this treaty, that whenever the Indians shall be required to remove from the ceded district, all the unceded lands belonging to the Indians of Fond du Lac, Sandy Lake, and Mississippi bands, shall be the common property and home of all the Indians, party to this treaty.

ARTICLE 4.

In consideration of the foregoing cession, the United States, engage to pay to the Chippewa Indians of the Mississippi, and Lake Superior, annually, for twenty-five years, twelve thousand five hundred (12,500) dollars, in specie, ten thousand five hundred (10,500) dollars in goods, two thousand (2,000) dollars in provisions and tobacco, two thousand (2,000) dollars for the support of two blacksmiths shops, (including pay of smiths and assistants, and iron steel &c.) one thousand (1,000) dollars for pay of two farmers, twelve hundred (1,200) for pay of two carpenters, and two thousand (2,000) dollars for the support of schools for the Indians party to this treaty; and further the United States engage to pay the sum of five thousand (5,000) dollars as an agricultural fund, to be expended under the direction of the Secretary of War. And also the sum of seventy-five thousand (75,000) dollars, shall be allowed for the full satisfaction of their debts within the ceded district, which shall be examined by the commissioner to this treaty, and the amount to be allowed decided upon by him, which shall appear in a schedule hereunto annexed. The United States shall pay the amount so allowed within three years.

Whereas the Indians have expressed a strong desire to have some provision made for their half-breed relatives, therefore it is agreed, that fifteen thousand (15,000) dollars shall be paid to said Indians, next year, as a present, to be disposed of, as they, together with their agent, shall determine in council.

ARTICLE 5.

Whereas the whole country between Lake Superior and the Mississippi, has always been understood as belonging in common to the Chippewas, party to this treaty; and whereas the bands bordering on Lake Superior, have not been allowed to participate in the annuity payments of the treaty made with the Chippewas of the Mississippi, at St. Peters July 29th 1837, and whereas all the unceded lands belonging to the aforesaid Indians, are hereafter to be held in common, therefore, to remove all occasion for jealousy and discontent, it is agreed that all the annuity due by the said treaty, as also the annuity due by the present treaty, shall henceforth be equally divided among the Chippewas of the Mississippi and Lake Superior, party to this treaty, so that every person shall receive an equal share.

ARTICLE 6.

The Indians residing on the Mineral district, shall be subject to removal therefrom at the pleasure of the President of the United States.

ARTICLE 7.

This treaty shall be obligatory upon the contracting parties when ratified by the President and Senate of the United States.

In testimony whereof the said Robert Stuart, commissioner, on the part of the United States, and the chiefs and headmen of the Chippewa Indians of the Mississippi and Lake Superior, have hereunto set their hands, at La Pointe of Lake Superior, Wisconsin Territory this fourth day of October in the year of our Lord one thousand eight hundred and forty-two.

Robert Stuart, Commissioner.
Jno. Hulbert, Secretary.

Crow Wing River,	*Po go ne gi shik,*	*1st chief*
Do.	*Son go com ick,*	*2d do.*
Sandy Lake,	*Ka non do ur uin zo,*	*1st do.*
Do.	*Na tum e gaw bon,*	*2d do.*
Gull Lake,	*Ua bo jig,*	*1st do.*
Do.	*Pay pe si gon de bay,*	*2d do.*
Red Cedar Lake,	*Kui ui sen shis,*	*1st do.*

Do.	*Ott taw wance,*	*2d do.*
Po ke gom maw,	*Bai ie jig,*	*1st do.*
Do.	*Show ne aw,*	*2d do.*
Wisconsin River,	*Ki uen zi,*	*1st do.*
Do.	*Wi aw bis ke kut te way,*	*2d do.*
Lac du Flambeau,	*A pish ka go gi,*	*1st do.*
Do.	*May tock cus e quay,*	*2d do.*
Do.	*She maw gon e,*	*2d do.*
Lake Bands,	*Ki ji ua be she shi,*	*1st do.*
Do.	*Ke kon o tum,*	*2d do.*
Fond du Lac,	*Shin goob,*	*1st do.*
Do.	*Na gan nab,*	*2d do.*
Do.	*Mong o zet,*	*2d do.*
La Pointe,	*Gitchi waisky,*	*1st do.*
Do.	*Mi zi,*	*2d do.*
Do.	*Ta qua gone e,*	*2d do.*
Onlonagan,	*O kon di kan,*	*1st do.*
Do.	*Kis ke taw wac,*	*2d do.*
Ance,	*Pe na shi,*	*1st do.*
Do.	*Guck we san sish,*	*2d do.*
Vieux Desert,	*Ka she osh e,*	*1st do.*
Do.	*Medge waw gwaw wot,*	*2d do.*
Mille Lacs,	*Ne qua ne be,*	*1st do.*
Do.	*Ua shash ko kum,*	*2d do.*
Do.	*No din,*	*2d do.*
St. Croix,	*Be zhi ki,*	*1st do.*
Do.	*Ka bi na be,*	*2d do.*
Do.	*Ai aw bens,*	*2d do.*
Snake River,	*Sha go bi,*	*1st do.*
Chippewa River,	*Ua be she shi,*	*1st do.*
Do.	*Que way zhan sis,*	*2d do.*
Lac Courte Oreilles,	*Ne na nang eb,*	*1st do.*
Do.	*Be bo kon uen,*	*2d do.*
Do.	*Ki uen zi.*	*2d do.*

In presence of—

Henry Blanchford, interpreter.
Samuel Ashmun, interpreter.
Justin Rice.
Charles H. Oakes.
William A. Aitkin.
William Brewster.
Charles M. Borup.
Z. Platt.
C. H. Beaulieau.
L. T. Jamison.

James P. Scott.

Cyrus Mendenhall.

L. M. Warren.

(To the Indian names are subjoined marks.)

Schedule of claims examined and allowed by Robert Stuart, commissioner, under the treaty with the Chippewa Indians of the Mississippi and Lake Superior, concluded at La Pointe, October 4th 1842, setting forth the names of claimants, and their proportion of allowance of the seventy-five thousand dollars provided in the fourth article of the aforesaid treaty, for the full satisfaction of their debts, as follows:

No. of Claim	Name of claimant.	Proportion of $75,000. set apart in 4th article of treaty.
1	Edward F. Ely	$50.80
2	Z. Platt, esq., attorney for George Berkett	484.67
3	Cleveland North Lake Co.	1,485.67
4	Abraham W. Williams	75.03
5	William Brewster	2,052.67
	This claim to be paid as follows, viz:	
	William Brewster, or order	1, 929.77
	Charles W. Borup, or order	122.90
		$2,052.67
6	George Copway	61.67
7	John Kahbege	57.55
8	Alixes Carpantier	28.58
9	John W. Bell	186.16
10	Antoine Picard	6.46
11	Michael Brisette	182.42
12	Francois Dejaddon	301.48
13	Pierre C. Duvernay	1,101.00
14	Jean Bts. Bazinet	325.46
15	John Hotley	69.00
16	Francois Charette	234.92
17	Clement H. Beaulieu, agent for the estate of Bazil Beaulieu, dec'd	596.00
18	Francois St. Jean and George Bonga	366.84
19	Louis Ladebauche	322.52
20	Peter Crebassa	499.27
21	B. T. Kavanaugh	516.82
22	Augustin Goslin	169.05
23	American Fur Company	13,365.00
	This claim to be paid as follows, viz:	
	American Fur Company	12,565.10
	Charles W. Borup	800.20
		13,365.00

24	William A. Aitken	935.67
25	James P. Scott	73.41
26	Augustin Bellanger	192.35
27	Louis Corbin	12.57
28	Alexes Corbin	596.03
29	George Johnston	35.24
30	Z. Platt, esq., attorney for Sam'l Ashman	1,771.63
31	Z. Platt, esq., attorney for Wm. Johnson	390.27
32	Z. Platt, esq., attorney for estate of Dan'l Dingley	1,991.62
33	Lyman M. Warren	1,566.65
34	Estate of Michael Cadotte, *disallowed.*	
35	Z. Platt, esq., attorney for the estate of E. Roussain	959.13
36	Joseph Dufault	144.32
37	Z. Platt, esq., attorney for Antoine Mace	170.35
38	Michael Cadotte	205.60
39	Z. Platt, esq., att'y for Francois Gauthier	167.05
40	Z. Platt, esq., att'y for Joseph Gauthier	614.30
41	Z. Platt, esq., attorney for J. B. Uolle	64.78
42	Jean Bts. Corbin	531.50
43	John Hulbert	209.18
44	Jean Bts. Couvellion	18.80
45	Nicholas Da Couteau, *withdrawn.*	
46	Pierre Cotté	732.50
47	W. H. Brockway and Henry Holt, executors to the estate of John Holliday, dec'd	3,157.10
48	John Jacob Astor	37,994.98
	This claim is to be paid as follows, viz Charles Borup	1,676.90
	Z. Platt, esq.	2,621.80
	John Jacob Astor	23,696.28
		27,994.98
49	Z. Platt. esq., attorney for Thos. Connor	1,118.60
50	Charles H. Oakes	4,309.21
51	Z. Platt., esq., attorney for Wm. Morrison	1,074.70
52	Z. Platt, esq., att'y for Isaac Butterfield	1,275.56
53	J. B. Van Rensselaer	62.00
54	William Brewster and James W. Abbot	2,067.10
	The parties to this claim request no payment be made either without their joint consent or until the decision of the case be had, in a court of justice.	
55	William Bell	17.62
		75,000.00

Robert Stuart, Commissioner.

Jno. Hulbert, Secretary.

Treaty of 1854

Articles of a treaty made and concluded at La Pointe, in the State of Wisconsin, between Henry C. Gilbert and David B. Herriman, commissioners on the part of the United States, and the Chippewa Indians of Lake Superior and the Mississippi, by their chiefs and head-men.

ARTICLE 1.

The Chippewas of Lake Superior hereby cede to the United States all the lands heretofore owned by them in common with the Chippewas of the Mississippi, lying east of the following boundary-line, to wit: Beginning at a point, where the east branch of Snake River crosses the southern boundary-line of the Chippewa country, running thence up the said branch to its source, thence nearly north, in a straight line, to the mouth of East Savannah River, thence up the St. Louis River to the mouth of East Swan River, thence up the East Swan River to its source, thence in a straight line to the most westerly bend of Vermillion River, and thence down the Vermillion River to its mouth.

The Chippewas of the Mississippi hereby assent and agree to the foregoing cession, and consent that the whole amount of the consideration money for the country ceded above, shall be paid to the Chippewas of Lake Superior, and in consideration thereof the Chippewas of Lake Superior hereby relinquish to the Chippewas of the Mississippi, all their interest in and claim to the lands heretofore owned by them in common, lying west of the above boundary-line.

ARTICLE 2.

The United States agree to set apart and withhold from sale, for the use of the Chippewas of Lake Superior, the following-described tracts of land, viz:

1st. For the L'Anse and Vieux Desert bands, all the unsold lands in the following townships in the State of Michigan: Township fifty-one north range thirty-three west; township fifty-one north range thirty-two west; the east half of township fifty north range thirty-three west; the west half of township fifty north range thirty-two west, and all of township fifty-one north range thirty-one west, lying west of Huron Bay.

2d. For the La Pointe band, and such other Indians as may see fit to settle with them, a tract of land bounded as follows: Beginning on the south shore of Lake Superior, a few miles west of Montreal River, at the mouth of a creek called by the Indians Ke-che-se-be-we-she, running thence south to a line drawn east and west through the centre of township forty-seven north, thence west to the west line of said township, thence south to the southeast corner of township forty-six north, range thirty-two west, thence west the width of two townships, thence north the width of two townships, thence west one mile, thence north to the lake shore, and thence along the lake shore, crossing Shag-waw-me-quon Point, to the place of beginning. Also two hundred acres on the northern extremity of Madeline Island, for a fishing ground.

3d. For the other Wisconsin bands, a tract of land lying about Lac du Flambeau, and another tract on Lac Courte Oreilles, each equal in extent to three townships, the boundaries of which shall be hereafter agreed upon or fixed under the direction of the President.

4th. For the Fond du Lac bands, a tract of land bounded as follows: Beginning at an island in the St. Louis River, above Knife Portage, called by the Indians Paw-paw-sco-me-me-tig, running thence west to the boundary-line heretofore described, thence north along said boundary-line to the mouth of Savannah River, thence down the St. Louis River to the place of beginning. And if said tract shall contain less than one hundred thousand acres, a strip of land shall be added on the south side thereof, large enough to equal such deficiency.

5th. For the Grand Portage band, a tract of land bounded as follows: Beginning at a rock a little east of the eastern extremity of Grand Portage Bay, running thence along the lake shore to the mouth of a small stream called by the Indians Maw-ske-gwaw-caw-maw-se-be, or Cranberry Marsh River, thence up said stream, across the point to Pigeon River, thence down Pigeon River to a point opposite the starting-point, and thence across to the place of beginning.

6th. The Ontonagon band and that subdivision of the La Pointe band of which Buffalo is chief, may each select, on or near the lake shore, four sections of land, under the direction of the President, the boundaries of which shall be defined hereafter. And being desirous to provide for some of his connections who have rendered his people important services, it is agreed that the chief Buffalo may select one section of land, at such place in the ceded territory as he may see fit, which shall be reserved for that purpose, and conveyed by the United States to such person or persons as he may direct.

7th. Each head of a family, or single person over twenty-one years of age at the present time of the mixed bloods, belonging to the Chippewas of Lake Superior, shall be entitled to eighty acres of land, to be selected by them under the direction of the President, and which shall be secured to them by patent in the usual form.

ARTICLE 3.

The United States will define the boundaries of the reserved tracts, whenever it may be necessary, by actual survey, and the President may, from time to time, at his discretion, cause the whole to be surveyed, and may assign to each head of a family or single person over twenty-one years of age, eighty acres of land for his or their separate use; and he may, at his discretion, as fast as the occupants become capable of transacting their own affairs, issue patents therefor to such occupants, with such restrictions of the power of alienation as he may see fit to impose. And he may also, at his discretion, make rules and regulations, respecting the disposition of the lands in case of the death of the head of a family, or single person occupying the same, or in case of its abandonment by them. And he may also assign other lands in exchange for mineral lands, if any such are found in the tracts herein set apart. And he may also make such changes in the boundaries of such reserved tracts or otherwise, as shall be necessary to prevent interference with any vested rights. All necessary roads, highways, and railroads, the lines of which may run through any of the reserved tracts, shall have the right of way through the same, compensation being made therefor as in other cases.

ARTICLE 4.

In consideration of and payment for the country hereby ceded, the United States agree to pay to the Chippewas of Lake Superior, annually, for the term of twenty years, the following sums, to wit: five thousand dollars in coin; eight thousand dollars in goods, household furniture and cooking utensils; three thousand dollars in agricultural implements and cattle, carpenter's and other tools and building materials, and three thousand dollars for moral and educational purposes, of which last sum, three hundred dollars per annum shall be paid to the Grand Portage band, to enable them to maintain a school at their village. The United States will also pay the further sum of ninety thousand dollars, as the chiefs in open council may direct, to enable them to meet their present just engagements. Also the further sum of six thousand dollars, in agricultural implements, household furniture, and cooking utensils, to be distributed at the next annuity payment, among the mixed bloods of said nation. The United States will also furnish two hundred guns, one hundred rifles, five hundred beaver-traps, three hundred dollars' worth of ammunition, and one thousand dollars' worth of ready-made clothing, to be distributed among the young men of the nation, at the next annuity payment.

ARTICLE 5.

The United States will also furnish a blacksmith and assistant, with the usual amount of stock, during the continuance of the annuity payments, and as much longer as the President may think proper, at each of the points herein set apart for the residence of the Indians, the same to be in lieu of all the employees to which the Chippewas of Lake Superior may be entitled under previous existing treaties.

ARTICLE 6.

The annuities of the Indians shall not be taken to pay the debts of individuals, but satisfaction for depredations committed by them shall be made by them in such manner as the President may direct.

ARTICLE 7.

No spirituous liquors shall be made, sold, or used on any of the lands herein set apart for the residence of the Indians, and the sale of the same shall be prohibited in the Territory hereby ceded, until otherwise ordered by the President.

ARTICLE 8.

It is agreed, between the Chippewas of Lake Superior and the Chippewas of the Mississippi, that the former shall be entitled to two-thirds, and the latter to one-third, of all benefits to be derived from former treaties existing prior to the year 1847.

ARTICLE 9.

The United States agree that an examination shall be made, and all sums that may be found equitably due to the Indians, for arrearages of annuity or other thing, under the provisions of former treaties, shall be paid as the chiefs may direct.

ARTICLE 10.

All missionaries, and teachers, and other persons of full age, residing in the territory hereby ceded, or upon any of the reservations hereby made by authority of law, shall be allowed to enter the land occupied by them at the minimum price whenever the surveys shall be completed to the amount of one quarter-section each.

ARTICLE 11.

All annuity payments to the Chippewas of Lake Superior, shall hereafter be made at L'Anse, La Pointe, Grand Portage, and on the St. Louis River; and the Indians shall not be required to remove from the homes hereby set apart for them. And such of them as reside in the territory hereby ceded, shall have the right to hunt and fish therein, until otherwise ordered by the President.

ARTICLE 12.

In consideration of the poverty of the Bois Forte Indians who are parties to this treaty, they having never received any annuity payments, and of the great extent of that part of the ceded country owned exclusively by them, the following additional stipulations are made for their benefit. The United States will pay the sum of ten thousand dollars, as their chiefs in open council may direct, to enable them to meet their present just engagements. Also the further sum of ten thousand dollars, in five equal annual payments, in blankets, cloth, nets, guns, ammunitions, and such other articles of necessity as they may require.

They shall have the right to select their reservation at any time hereafter, under the direction of the President; and the same may be equal in extent, in proportion to their numbers, to those allowed the other bands, and be subject to the same provisions.

They shall be allowed a blacksmith, and the usual smithshop supplies, and also two persons to instruct them in farming, whenever in the opinion of the President it shall be proper, and for such length of time as he shall direct.

It is understood that all Indians who are parties to this treaty, except the Chippewas of the Mississippi, shall hereafter be known as the Chippewas of Lake Superior. *Provided*, That the stipulation by which the Chippewas of Lake Superior relinquishing their right to land west of the boundary-line shall not apply to the Bois Forte band who are parties to this treaty.

ARTICLE 13.

This treaty shall be obligatory on the contracting parties, as soon as the same shall be ratified by the President and Senate of the United States.

In testimony whereof, the said Henry C. Gilbert, and the said David B. Herriman, commissioners as aforesaid, and the undersigned chiefs and headmen of the Chippewas of Lake Superior and the Mississippi, have hereunto set their hands and seals, at the place aforesaid, this thirtieth day of September, one thousand eight hundred and fifty-four.

Henry C. Gilbert,
David B. Herriman,
Commissioners.
Richard M. Smith, Secretary.

La Pointe Band:

Ke-che-waish-ke, or the Buffalo, 1st chief, his x mark.

Chay-che-que-oh, 2d chief, his x mark.

A-daw-we-ge-zhick, or Each Side of the Sky, 2d chief, his x mark.

O-ske-naw-way, or the Youth, 2d chief, his x mark.

Maw-caw-day-pe-nay-se, or the Black Bird, 2d chief, his x mark.

Naw-waw-naw-quot, headman, his x mark.

Ke-wain-zeence, headman, his x mark.

Waw-baw-ne-me-ke, or the White Thunder, 2d chief, his x mark.

Pay-baw-me-say, or the Soarer, 2d chief, his x mark.

Naw-waw-ge-waw-nose, or the Little Current, 2d chief, his x mark.

Maw-caw-day-waw-quot, or the Black Cloud, 2d chief, his x mark.

Me-she-naw-way, or the Disciple, 2d chief, his x mark.

Key-me-waw-naw-um, headman, his x mark.

She-gog headman, his x mark.

Ontonagon Band:

O-cun-de-cun, or the Buoy 1st chief, his x mark.

Waw-say-ge-zhick, or the Clear Sky, 2d chief, his x mark.

Keesh-ke-taw-wug, headman, his x mark.

L'Anse Band:

David King, 1st chief, his x mark.

John Southwind, headman, his x mark.

Peter Marksman, headman, his x mark.

Naw-taw-me-ge-zhick, or the First Sky, 2d chief, his x mark.

Aw-se-neece, headman, his x mark.

Vieux Desert Band:

May-dway-aw-she, 1st chief, his x mark.

Posh-quay-gin, or the Leather, 2d chief, his x mark.

Grand Portage Band:

Shaw-gaw-naw-sheence, or the Little Englishman, 1st chief, his x mark.

May-mosh-caw-wosh, headman, his x mark.

Aw-de-konse, or the Little Reindeer, 2d chief, his x mark.

Way-we-ge-wam, headman, his x mark.

Fond du Lac Band:

Shing-goope, or the Balsam, 1st chief, his x mark.

Mawn-go-sit, or the Loon's Foot, 2d chief, his x mark.

May-quaw-me-we-ge-zhick, headman, his x mark.

Keesh-kawk, headman, his x mark.

Caw-taw-waw-be-day, headman, his x mark.

O-saw-gee, headman, his x mark.

Ke-che-aw-ke-wain-ze, headman, his x mark.

Naw-gaw-nub, or the Foremost Sitter, 2d chief, his x mark.

Ain-ne-maw-sung, 2d chief, his x mark.

Naw-aw-bun-way, headman, his x mark.

Wain-ge-maw-tub, headman, his x mark.

Aw-ke-wain-zeence, headman, his x mark.

Shay-way-be-nay-se, headman, his x mark.

Paw-pe-oh, headman, his x mark.

Lac Courte Oreilles Band:

Aw-ke-wain-ze, or the Old Man, 1st chief, his x mark.

Key-no-zhance, or the Little Jack Fish, 1st chief, his x mark.

Key-che-pe-nay-se, or the Big Bird, 2d chief, his x mark.

Ke-che-waw-be-shay-she, or the Big Martin, 2d chief, his x mark.

Waw-be-shay-sheence, headman, his x mark.

Quay-quay-cub, headman, his x mark.

Shaw-waw-no-me-tay, headman, his x mark.

Nay-naw-ong-gay-be, or the Dressing Bird, 1st chief, his x mark.

O-zhaw-waw-sco-ge-zhick, or the Blue Sky, 2d chief, his x mark.

I-yaw-banse, or the Little Buck, 2d chief, his x mark.

Lac du Flambeau Band:

Aw-mo-se, or the Wasp, 1st chief, his x mark.

Ke-nish-te-no, 2d chief, his x mark.

Me-gee-see, or the Eagle, 2d chief, his x mark.

Kay-kay-co-gwaw-nay-aw-she, headman, his x mark.

O-che-chog, headman, his x mark.

Nay-she-kay-gwaw-nay-be, headman, his x mark.

O-scaw-bay-wis, or the Waiter, 1st chief, his x mark.

Que-we-zance, or the White Fish, 2d chief, his x mark.

Ne-gig, or the Otter, 2d chief, his x mark.

Nay-waw-che-ge-ghick-may-be, headman, his x mark.

Quay-quay-ke-cah, headman, his x mark.

Bois Forte Band:

Kay-baish-caw-daw-way, or Clear Round the Prairie, 1st chief, his x mark.

Way-zaw-we-ge-zhick-way-sking, headman, his x mark.

O-saw-we-pe-nay-she, headman, his x mark.

The Mississippi Bands:

Que-we-san-se, or Hole in the Day, head chief, his x mark.

Caw-nawn-daw-waw-win-zo, or the Berry Hunter, 1st chief, his x mark.

Waw-bow-jieg, or the White Fisher, 2d chief, his x mark.

Ot-taw-waw, 2d chief, his x mark.

Que-we-zhan-cis, or the Bad Boy, 2d chief, his x mark.

Bye-a-jick, or the Lone Man, 2d chief, his x mark.

I-yaw-shaw-way-ge-zhick, or the Crossing Sky, 2d chief, his x mark.

Maw-caw-day, or the Bear's Heart, 2d chief, his x mark.

Ke-way-de-no-go-nay-be, or the Northern Feather, 2d chief, his x mark.
Me-squaw-dace, headman, his x mark.
Naw-gaw-ne-gaw-bo, headman, his x mark.
Wawm-be-de-yea, headman, his x mark.
Waish-key, headman, his x mark.
Caw-way-caw-me-ge-skung, headman, his x mark.
My-yaw-ge-way-we-dunk, or the One who carries the Voice, 2d chief, his x mark.
John F. Godfroy, Interpreter.
Geo. Johnston, Interpreter.
S. A. Marvin, Interpreter.
Louis Codot, Interpreter.
Paul H. Beaulieu, Interpreter.
Henry Blatchford, Interpreter.
Peter Floy, Interpreter.

Executed in the presence of—
Henry M. Rice,
J. W. Lynde,
G. D. Williams,
B. H. Connor,
E. W. Muldough,
Richard Godfroy,
D. S. Cash,
H. H. McCullough,
E. Smith Lee,
Wm. E. Vantassel,
L. H. Wheeler.

Notes

BIAR   Records of the Bureau of Indian Affairs, Record Group 75

BR-WPA   Bad River Works Progress Administration Project

CIHPR   United States Works Progress Administration, Chippewa Indian Historical Project Records

GFCM   Game and Fish Commission of Minnesota

GLIFWC   Great Lakes Indian Fish and Wildlife Commission

JB-WPA   John Bardon Works Progress Administration Project

MGFDR   Minnesota Game and Fish Department Records

MHSA   Minnesota Historical Society Archives, St. Paul

NAGL   National Archives, Great Lakes Region, Chicago, Ill.

NAKC   National Archives, Kansas City, Mo.

NAWA   National Archives, Washington, D.C., and College Park, Md.

RKCS   Rebekah Knight Cochran Scrapbook

WCDR   Wisconsin Conservation Department Records

WHSA   Wisconsin Historical Society Archives, Madison, Wisc.

INTRODUCTION

1. For example, Public Law 280, passed on August 15, 1953, transferred federal jurisdiction over tribes to six states, including Minnesota and Wisconsin. Note that I refer to "Ojibwes" rather than "the Ojibwe" to indicate that Ojibwe society was diverse and that Ojibwe people had a variety of perspectives on and understandings of what it meant to be Ojibwe.

2. Bad River Tribal Council, "A Declaration of War," November 10, 1959, WHSA; Satz, *Chippewa Treaty Rights*, 89–90.

3. Littlefield and Knack, *Native Americans and Wage Labor*. See also Knight, *Indians at Work*.

4. O'Neill, *Working the Navajo Way*; Hosmer, *American Indians in the Marketplace*; Raibmon, *Authentic Indians*; Bauer, *We Were All Like Migrant Workers Here*. See also Hosmer and O'Neill, *Native Pathways*; Pickering, *Lakota Culture, World Economy*; and Heaton, *Shoshone-Bannocks*.

5. For an overview of this historiography, see Fink, "American Labor History."

6. Harmon, O'Neill, and Rosier, "Interwoven Economic Histories," 704.

7. Ibid.

8. Fink, "American Labor History"; Thompson, *Making of the English Working Class*. Examples of this work include Gutman, *Work, Culture, and Society*; Montgomery, *Fall*

of the House of Labor; Montgomery, *Worker's Control in America*; and Cohen, *Making a New Deal*.

9. Harmon, O'Neill, and Rosier, "Interwoven Economic Histories," 717. Seth Rockman's *Scraping By* challenges these categories (outside of American Indian labor history). Rockman utilizes the category of subsistence to examine the histories of people who worked to get by and were not represented by organized labor. He argues that in order for the Early Republic to be a prosperous place, the economy depended on the exploitation of a population of workers paid the lowest wages in society, indentured servants, and slaves. In American Indian Studies, Harmon's innovative study *Rich Indians* (2010) problematizes conventional assumptions about American Indians and wealth, and Usner's book *Indian Work* (2009) explores how the language and ideologies constructed around American Indian work have been employed to serve the colonial initiatives of Euro-Americans.

10. Useful overviews of these transitions can be found in Shifferd, "Study in Economic Change," and Danziger, *Great Lakes Indian Accommodation*.

11. I continue along the same lines as scholars of American Indian history who have focused on the ways in which American Indian communities became the modern nations and the ways in which American Indian nationhood changed over time. For example, in his book *Parading Through History*, Frederick Hoxie has shown how the Crow became a modern Indian nation in the twentieth century as a result of their participation in the American economic and political system. By engaging with new opportunities and creating new structures within their society, they protected their interests. Similarly, in his book *We Are an Indian Nation*, Jeffrey Shepherd explores how the Haulapai people constructed their nationhood in the face of U.S. colonialism. He demonstrates how this nation building was a complex process influenced by the internal dynamics of the community, as well as their resistance to external forces.

12. I see this as an emerging effort among scholars to frame Ojibwe history and identity in more fluid ways. For example, in his book *The Walleye War*, Larry Nesper demonstrates how, as a result of their struggle to exercise spearfishing and treaty rights, Lac du Flambeau Ojibwes "re-imagined" their identity. He connects this to the longer, dynamic history of Lac du Flambeau people's articulation of their distinctiveness as they interacted with external forces. In his book *An Infinity of Nations*, Michael Witgen challenges Euro-American mythologies about discovery and conquest in the Great Lakes by showing how, through their shifting political and social organization and alliances, Ojibwes and other people in the region retained their power until the mid-nineteenth century.

13. Gross, "Bimaadiziwin, or the 'Good Life,'" 16.

14. National Oceanic and Atmospheric Administration, "NowData."

15. National Oceanic and Atmospheric Administration, "About Our Great Lakes."

16. Treaty with the Chippewa, 1837. See appendix.

17. Treaty with the Chippewa, 1842. See appendix.

18. Residents of the region refer to the western shore of Lake Superior as the north shore.

19. In his book *Crimes against Nature*, Karl Jacoby demonstrates that conservation laws criminalized and colonized populations whose ways of life did not fit the aims of American conservationists.

20. There is a large body of literature that explores Ojibwe struggles to exercise treaty rights and the interpretation of treaty rights in a legal context. The works that I have found

most useful to this study include Silvern, "Nature, Territory and Identity"; Silvern, "Geography of Ojibwe Treaty Rights"; Silvern, "Negotiating Ojibwe Treaty Rights"; White, "Early Game and Fish Regulation"; Satz, *Chippewa Treaty Rights*; McClurken and Cleland, *Fish in the Lakes*; and Nesper, *Walleye War*.

21. Berger, *Village Journeys*, 51.

22. Usner, *Indian Work*, 13.

23. See also Chambers and Conway, *Sustainable Livelihoods*, and Wisner et al., *At Risk*.

24. Usner, *Indian Work*, 3.

25. Ibid., 13.

26. See also Cattelino, *High Stakes*, 15.

27. Simpson, "Paths Towards a Mohawk Nation," 116.

28. Ngai, *Impossible Subjects*; Glenn, *Unequal Freedom*; Deutsch, *No Separate Refuge*; Fink, *Maya of Morganton*. See also Jung, *Coolies and Cane*, and Meeks, *Border Citizens*.

29. Jones, *Labor of Love*; Jones, *Dispossessed*; Jones, *American Work*; Kessler-Harris, *In Pursuit of Equity*, 10. See also Roediger, *Wages of Whiteness*.

30. Wolfe, "Land, Labor, and Difference," 867, 868, 887.

31. Ibid., 868. See also Mikdashi, "What is Settler Colonialism?" Mikdashi writes about settler colonialism as an ongoing process that shapes the complex experiences that define her family's history and her Arab, Swedish, and Ojibwe background. In particular, she describes traveling to the Bad River reservation where her family holds an allotment and the sense of ambivalence and uncertainty that accompanied this visit based on her grandfather's struggles with the past and his Native American ancestry.

32. Fink, *Workers Across the Americas*, x.

33. Parnaby, "Indigenous Labor," 126.

34. Weaver, "More Light Than Heat," 237.

35. Greene, "Transnational Forces," 13; Bayly et al., "*AHR* Conversation," 1444.

36. For a useful discussion on the possibilities and pitfalls of transnational history, see Bayly et al., "*AHR* Conversation."

37. Ibid.

38. Wilkins, *American Indian Politics*, 339.

39. Ibid.

40. Kamper, *Work of Sovereignty*, 14, 18.

41. Hämäläinen's *Comanche Empire*, Miles's *House on Diamond Hill*; and Sturm's *Blood Politics* stand out as presenting strong examples of how indigenous peoples have exercised power and/or in some instances adopted practices of the American nation-state.

42. See Simpson, "Paths Towards a Mohawk Nation," 115, and Witgen, *Infinity of Nations*, 21.

43. Witgen, *Infinity of Nations*, 15, 19.

44. Ibid., 17–18.

45. Ibid., 19–20. Witgen argues that the fluidity of Ojibwe social and political organization allows them to act as a collective, transregional social formation or to mobilize power on a local level as members of clans holding jurisdiction over specific territories and resources.

46. Simpson, *Paths Towards a Mohawk Nation*, 116.

47. I use the term "expectation" based on the definition that Deloria has put forth in his book *Indians in Unexpected Places*, 14. Deloria uses the term "expectation" to

examine non-Indians' assumptions about American Indians and their existence in modern contexts.

48. Nesper, *Walleye War*, xii; Warren, *History of the Ojibway People*, 36.

49. Nesper, *Walleye War*, xii; Hickerson, *Southwestern Chippewa*, 78; Schenk, *Voice of the Crane Echoes Far*.

50. Nesper, *Walleye War*, xii; Day and Trigger, "Algonquin," 792–97; Clifton, "Potawatomi," 725–42.

51. Cleland, "Preliminary Report," 9.

52. Ibid., 19.

53. Warren, *History of the Ojibway People*, 38–39.

54. Treaty with the Chippewa, 1837. See appendix.

55. Treaty with the Chippewa, 1842. See appendix.

56. Treaty with the Chippewa, 1854. See appendix.

57. Godfrey, *Forestry History*, 10.

58. Cleland, "Preliminary Report," 85.

59. Ross, *La Pointe*, 117.

CHAPTER 1

1. Florina Denomie, "Blueberry Picking among the Chippewas," BR-WPA, CIHPR.

2. Ibid.

3. I recognize that the term "gathering" implies a passive activity that stands in contrast to the work that the harvest, processing, and preserving resources actually entailed. However, I use the term throughout the book to refer to a category of livelihood designated as rights in the treaties.

4. Verplanck Van Antwerp, "Proceedings of Council Held by Governor Henry Dodge, with the Chiefs and Principal Men, of the Chippewa Nation of Indians," quoted in Satz, *Chippewa Treaty Rights*, 19.

5. Cleland, "Preliminary Report," 39; Alfred Brunson to James Doty, January 8, 1843, with enclosure by Marten, Correspondence to the Office of Indian Affairs (Central Office) and Related Records, Letters Received, 1824–81, Microcopy 234, Roll 388: 390–407, BIAR, NAWA.

6. Ibid.

7. Meyer, "White Earth Women," 247.

8. Ibid., 248; Densmore, *Strength of the Earth*, ix, x.

9. Child, *Holding Our World Together*, 103. Brenda Child argues (referring to ricing): "Ojibwe women constructed an extraordinary legal framework and an orderly system of ecological guardianship to manage the wild rice economy." This included the supervision of specific family territories; determining the correct time to harvest wild plants, including wild rice; and determining which individuals harvested plants.

10. Vennum, *Wild Rice and the Ojibway People*, 134; Warren, *History of the Ojibway*, 186.

11. Frances Densmore listed many of these in her study of Ojibwe uses of plants. See Densmore, *How the Indians Use Wild Plants*.

12. Densmore, *Chippewa Customs*, 127.

13. Densmore, *Strength of the Earth*, 321.

14. Florina Denomie, "Picking Blueberries in Northern Michigan," BR-WPA, CIHPR.

15. Densmore, *Chippewa Customs*, 127.

16. Cleland, "Preliminary Report," 9.

17. Keller, "America's Native Sweet," 123.

18. Densmore, *Strength of the Earth*, 321.

19. Vennum, *Wild Rice and the Ojibway People*, 160.

20. Meyer, "White Earth Women," 248.

21. Roufs, "When Everybody Called Me *Gah-bay-bi-nayss*."

22. Vennum, *Wild Rice and the Ojibway People*, 188.

23. Auger and Driben, *Grand Portage Chippewa*, 58.

24. Roufs, "When Everybody Called Me *Gah-bay-bi-nayss*."

25. Benton-Banai, *Mishomis Book*, chap. 14.

26. Vennum, *Wild Rice and the Ojibway People*, 70.

27. Ibid.; Densmore, *Chippewa Customs*, 124.

28. Vennum, *Wild Rice and the Ojibway People*, 78–79.

29. These varying kinds of subsistence relate to Seth Rockman's definition of the term in his book *Scraping By*. Rockman explores the unskilled labor that essentially enabled the poorest population of Baltimore to survive. He argues that these people have been largely overlooked because they did not fit within the optimistic picture that equated labor with independence and stability in Early Republic America. Rockman's focus on labor that constituted "survival" provides the opportunity to think about how the meaning of the term "subsistence" has changed over time depending on the economic conditions and contexts in which a population is located.

30. Vennum, *Wild Rice and the Ojibway People*, 203.

31. Keller, "America's Native Sweet," 123.

32. Vennum, *Wild Rice and the Ojibway People*, 199–206.

33. Cleland, "Preliminary Report," 15.

34. Ibid.

35. Satz, *Chippewa Treaty Rights*, 80.

36. Christine Carlson, "Marceline (Couture) Champagne: Granddaughter of a Medicine Man Earned Reputation for Excellence as a Midwife in Late 1800s," *Fond du Lac Na gah chi wa nong Di bah ji mowin nan*, July 2009, 12.

37. Ibid., 13.

38. Shifferd, "Study in Economic Change," 33.

39. Vennum, *Wild Rice and the Ojibway People*, 211, 213.

40. Ibid., 228–50.

41. Ibid., 250.

42. Keller, "America's Native Sweet," 120.

43. Ibid., 127; Pinchot, *Breaking New Ground*, 411–12.

44. Cullon, "Landscapes of Labor and Leisure," 22.

45. Parker, "Bayfield in Rythme."

46. Shifferd, "Study in Economic Change," 33; *Bayfield Press*, September 16, 1871.

47. Shifferd, "Study in Economic Change," 33; *North Wisconsin News*, July 13, 1883.

48. Shifferd, "Study in Economic Change," 33; *North Wisconsin News*, August 3, 1883.

49. Shifferd, "Study in Economic Change," 33; *North Wisconsin News*, September 21, 1883.

50. Annual Report of the Commissioner of Indian Affairs, 1873, 163, BIAR, NAWA.

51. Ibid., 1875, 371.

52. Reports of Inspection of the Field Jurisdictions of the Office of Indian Affairs, September 26, 1883, Records of the Office of Indian Affairs, BIAR, NAWA.

53. Annual Report of the Commissioner of Indian Affairs, 1876, 150, BIAR, NAWA.

54. J. A. Stack to M. A. Leahy, November 4, 1889, Letters Received from the Fond du Lac Reservation, General Records of the La Pointe Agency, BIAR, NAGL.

55. Ibid.

56. John Anamosing to W. A. Mercer, July 20, 1894, Letters Received from the Fond du Lac Reservation, General Records of the La Pointe Agency, BIAR, NAGL.

57. Annual Report of the Commissioner of Indian Affairs, 1878, 147, BIAR, NAWA.

58. Ibid., 1889, 304.

59. Roufs, "When Everybody Called Me *Gah-bay-bi-nayss*."

60. Jerome Arbuckle, "Qui-Ka-Ba-No-Kwe, 'Dawn Woman,'" BR-WPA, CIHPR.

61. John Condecon, "Life History of John Condecon," BR-WPA, CIHPR.

62. Kegg and Nichols, *Portage Lake*, 46.

63. Some gathering activities like wild rice harvesting were targeted by state officials, as Esther Nahganub's story demonstrates in the conclusion of this book. I found no evidence of Ojibwe being targeted by state wardens for harvesting berries.

64. Florina Denomie, "Blueberry Picking among the Chippewas," BR-WPA, CIHPR.

65. Godfrey, *Forestry History*, 59.

66. Ibid., 62.

67. Duchesne and Wetzel, "Effect of Fire Intensity," 195–200.

68. Marie Livingston, "Blueberrying Forty-Five Years Ago—Strange but True," BR-WPA, CIHPR.

69. Ibid.

70. Florina Denomie, "Picking Blueberries in Northern Michigan," BR-WPA, CIHPR.

71. Gough, *Farming the Cutover*, 2–3.

72. Ibid., 3.

73. Danbom, *Resisted Revolution*, vii.

74. Ibid., 23–24.

75. Knight, *Tales of Bayfield Pioneers*, 48–55, 58–67.

76. Ibid., 64.

77. Ibid.

78. Feldman, "View from Sand Island," 20.

79. Information provided to author by Bob Nelson, Bayfield Heritage Association, July 8, 2010.

80. Godfrey, *Forestry History*, 107.

81. Ibid.

82. Annual Report of the Commissioner of Indian Affairs, 1905, 376, BIAR, NAWA.

83. Ibid., 375.

84. Ibid.

85. "Narrative and Statistical Report for the Red Cliff Reservation," 1915, File: Annual Reports of Red Cliff and Bad River, 1911–21, Records of the Great Lakes Consolidated Indian Agency, BIAR, NAGL.

86. "Annual Statistical and Narrative Report for the Red Cliff Agency," 1922, File: Reports of 1922–26, Annual Reports of Red Cliff and Bad River, 1911–26, Records of the Great Lakes Consolidated Agency and Bad River Agency, BIAR, NAGL. Unfortunately, I have not been able to find additional information on the Bayfield Fruit Association.

87. Ibid., 1926.

88. Foulk et al., "Commercial Blueberry Production in Minnesota and Wisconsin."

89. Vennum, *Wild Rice and the Ojibwe People*, 215–17.

90. James Scott, "Early Settlement of the Bad River Indian Reservation," BR-WPA, CIHPR.

91. Child, *Holding Our World Together*, 97–120.

92. Simonsen, *Making Home Work*, 4. For a more extensive discussion of how this focus on domesticity impacted women's roles in Ojibwe society, see also Kugel, "Leadership Within the Women's Community."

93. Caroline Parker, "History of John Bear, Noted Lacrosse Player," BR-WPA, CIHPR.

94. Roufs, "When Everybody Called Me *Gah-bay-bi-nayss*."

95. Gough, *Farming the Cutover*, 179–80.

96. Ibid., 218–19.

97. Knight, *Tales of Bayfield Pioneers*, 64.

98. "Mino Bi Ma De Se Win Farm," Red Cliff Community Health website, http://www.red-cliff-health.com/americorps-vista.shtml (February 6, 2013).

99. Godfrey, *Forestry History*, 158.

100. Vennum, *Wild Rice and the Ojibway People*, 228.

101. Child, *Holding Our World Together*, 112–15.

102. Asbury, McKinsey, and Mani, "Economic Survey," MHSA.

103. Florina Denomie, "Blueberry Picking among the Chippewas," BR-WPA, CIHPR.

104. Ibid.

105. Ibid.

106. "Chippewa and Winnebago Tribes to Meet as Friends for First Time at Odanah Friday," *Ashland Daily Press*, August 10, 1933.

107. Auger and Driben, *Grand Portage Chippewa*, 107.

108. Peacock, *Forever Story*, 63.

109. Ibid., 65.

CHAPTER 2

1. Norrgard, *Waasa Inabidaa*.

2. For an extensive discussion of the ways in which Euro-Americans employed their beliefs about the savagery of Indian hunting practices in order to justify confiscating Indian lands and resources, see Usner, *Indian Work*, 18–41.

3. Meyer, "White Earth Women," 247; Buffalohead, "Farmers, Warriors, and Traders," 31.

4. Meyer, "White Earth Women," 248.

5. Ray, *Indians in the Fur Trade*.

6. White, "Skilled Game of Exchange," 231.

7. Ray, *Canadian Fur Trade*, 3–29, 113–38. Ray discusses the kinds of animals trapped and furs sold in particular regions of Canada and along the U.S. border. He also discusses the international marketing of furs.

8. Ibid.

9. Some fur trade enterprises like the Hudson Bay Company managed to survive by diversifying their economic activities, selling other products in addition to furs. (The Hudson Bay Company is now the name of a department store chain in Canada.)

10. White, "Early Game and Fish Regulation," 31.

11. Farrow, "Extinction and Market Forces." Farrow discusses how railroad economic policy and development affected buffalo and passenger pigeons, for example.

12. Bardon, "Odd Characters of Old Superior," JB-WPA, vol. 1, p. 47, CIHPR.

13. Bardon, "Wau-Beh-Meh-Shay-Way," JB-WPA, vol. 2, p. 72, CIHPR.

14. Annual Report of the Commissioner of Indian Affairs, 1874, 188, BIAR, NAWA.

15. Ibid., 1881, 472.

16. Ibid., 1890, 237.

17. See Shifferd, "Study in Economic Change," 16–41, for more information about how diversifying economic activities enabled Ojibwes to survive during the latter half of the nineteenth century.

18. Annual Report of the Commissioner of Indian Affairs, 1875, BIAR, NAWA.

19. Ibid., 1878, 147.

20. Lancaster, *John Beargrease*, 27–28.

21. Ibid., 23.

22. Ibid., 34.

23. Raff, *Pioneers in the Wilderness*, 298.

24. Raff acknowledges that "the legends about the invincibility of John Beargrease are probably rooted in the service he gave the North Shore in the second half of the 1890's" and that mail carriers "were nearly invulnerable to criticism whatever their personal peculiarities or shortcomings, for their service had such great importance for everyone who depended on them for the only contact possible with the outside world" (ibid., 300). See also the *Herald*, November 30, 1895; and Dwan, "Growth of the Postal System on the North Shore," 9, MHSA.

25. John Beargrease Marathon website.

26. Auger and Driben, *Grand Portage Chippewa*, 82.

27. Peacock, *Forever Story*, 224.

28. Bob Wilson, "First Kill," BR-WPA, CIHPR.

29. Ibid.

30. Florina Denomie, "An Indian Huntress," BR-WPA, CIHPR.

31. White, "Early Game and Fish Regulation," viii.

32. Ibid., 6.

33. Samuel F. Fullerton, GFCM, Fifth Annual Report, 1896, 503, MHSA. The Minnesota Game and Fish Commission was established in 1874.

34. Cullon, "Landscapes of Labor and Leisure," 12.

35. Ibid.; Loo, "Of Moose and Men," 298.

36. Cullon, "Landscapes of Labor and Leisure," 12; Loo, "Of Moose and Men," 300.

37. Jacoby, *Crimes against Nature*, 2.

38. In his invaluable book *Hunting and Fishing in the New South*, Scott Giltner explores the importance of hunting in African American communities in the South and the ways in which white southerners restricted this labor, which they saw as a threat to the South's labor system and racial hierarchy.

39. White, "Early Game and Fish Regulation," 6.

40. Ibid.; Tober, *Who Owns the Wildlife?*, 53, 125–26, 208–9.

41. White, "Early Game and Fish Regulation," 6.

42. GFCM, Report of the Board of the Game and Fish Commissioners of Minnesota, 1906, 5, MHS SH11. M63 A314, MHSA.

43. GFCM, Report of the Board of the Game and Fish Commissioners of Minnesota, 1895, 4, MHS SH11.M63 A312, MHSA.

44. Ibid., 1890, 22, MHS SH11.M63 A3, MHSA.

45. White, "Early Game and Fish Regulation," 28–29; GFCM, Report of the Board of the Game and Fish Commissioners of Minnesota, 1892, 967, MHS SH11.M63 A3, MHSA.

46. GFCM, Report of the Board of the Game and Fish Commissioners of Minnesota, 1892, 967, MHS SH11.M63 A3, MHSA.

47. Wisconsin Historical Society, "Killing of Chief Joe White (Gishkitawag), 1894"; Child, *Holding Our World Together*, 84. See also Redix, "Murder of Joe White."

48. Nesper, *Walleye War*, 53.

49. Peacock, *Forever Story*, 224.

50. Ibid.

51. White, "Early Game and Fish Regulation," 46; *Minneapolis Journal*, April 8, 1897. White explains that Beaulieu was probably referring to the 1842 and 1854 treaties.

52. Ibid., 47.

53. U.S. Supreme Court, *Ward v. Racehorse*, U.S. 504 (1896), no. 841.

54. White, "Early Game and Fish Regulation," 49, 50.

55. Ibid., 54–58. White also discusses these cases in his report as examples of state encroachment on off-reservation treaty rights.

56. Ibid., 53.

57. Ibid., 53–54; *Selkirk v. Stephens*, 72 Minn. Rep. 335, 1898.

58. White, "Early Game and Fish Regulation," 54–57; *Minnesota v. Al Cooney*, 77 Minn. Rep. 518, October 30, 1899.

59. White, "Early Game and Fish Regulation," 55; *Minnesota v. Al Cooney*, 77 Minn. Rep. 518, October 30, 1899.

60. White, "Early Game and Fish Regulation," 56. It is unclear what happened to the case after the Supreme Court ruling.

61. Section 6 of U.S. Congress, Dawes Act.

62. White, "Early Game and Fish Regulation," 95; H. H. Kattman to H. A. Rider, January 15, 1913, GFCM, MHS 103.H.11.1B, MHSA.

63. White, "Early Game and Fish Regulation," 96; Executive agent C. W. Cross to H. H. Kattman enclosed with Kattman to Rider, January 17, 1913, GFCM, MHS 103.H.11.1B, MHSA.

64. White, "Early Game and Fish Regulation," 168; Carlos Avery to Thomas Savoy, December 2, 1920, MGFDR, MHS 103.F.8.12F, MHSA.

65. White, "Early Game and Fish Regulation," 170; George Cross to Carlos Avery, January 3, 1921, MGFDR, MHS 103.F.8.6 F, MHSA.

66. White, "Early Game and Fish Regulation," 170.

67. James Sharlow to Col. L. B. Nagler, April 30, 1928, copied in James Sharlow to William A. Mauthe, November 30, 1928, WHS, Subject Files, 1917–67, Series 271, WHSA.

68. Ibid., August 13, 1928.

69. State Conservation Commission to James Sharlow, August 15, 1928, WCDR, Subject Files, 1917–67, Series 271, WHSA.

70. GFCM, Report of the Board of the Game and Fish Commissioners of Minnesota, 1909, 4, MHS SH11. M63 A315, MHSA; White, "Early Game and Fish Regulation," 82.

71. GFCM, Report of the Board of the Game and Fish Commissioners of Minnesota, 1916, 20, MHS SH11. M63 A316, MHSA; White, "Early Game and Fish Regulation," 31.

72. Weygant, *John (Jack) Linklater*, 13–14.

73. *State of Wisconsin v. Frank Decoteau Johnson*, no. 212 Wis. 301.

74. U.S. Congress, Major Crimes Act, 1885. The Major Crimes Act reflected federal erosion of tribal sovereignty. It removed the power of tribes to try and to punish individuals for committing certain crimes committed in their territory and established the federal government's jurisdiction over seven major crimes, including murder, manslaughter, rape, assault with the intent to commit murder, arson, burglary, and larceny.

75. *State of Wisconsin v. Frank Decoteau Johnson*, Brief of Defendant by Amicus Curiae—Thomas L. St. Germaine, January Term, 1933, State no. 5.

76. *State of Wisconsin v. John LaBarge*, no. 234 Wis. 449.

77. *State of Wisconsin v. John LaBarge*, Brief of Defendant by Counsel Thomas L. St. Germaine, 1939; *United States v. Winans*, 198 U.S. 371, 49 L. ed. 1089.

78. Daniel Morrison, "Hunting Deer on the Bad River Reservation," BR-WPA, CIHPR. Though the word "privilege" may not have been the most accurate characterization of treaty rights, Morrison stressed their validity.

79. Jerome Arbuckle, "Trapping," BR-WPA, CIHPR.

80. Jerome Arbuckle, "Duck Hunting on the Bad River Reservation," BR-WPA, CIHPR.

CHAPTER 3

1. Auger and Driben, *Grand Portage Chippewa*, 16.

2. Ibid.

3. See appendix.

4. Cleland, "Inland Shore Fishery," 765.

5. Ibid., 766.

6. Ibid., 767.

7. Densmore, *Chippewa Customs*, 124–25.

8. Morrisseau, *Legends of My People*, 33–38.

9. Kohl, *Kitchi-Gami*, 325.

10. Florina Denomie, "Fishermen's Wind Indicator," BR-WPA, CIHPR. Denomie noted that many Euro-American fishers also adopted this practice.

11. Quinlan, "Taking Care of Name' (Lake Sturgeon)."

12. Nute, "American Fur Company's Fishing Enterprises," 486–87; Ramsey Crooks to George Wildes and Company, London, December 9, 1835, Letterbook 2:224–26, American Fur Company Papers, New York Historical Society.

13. Nute, "American Fur Company's Fishing Enterprises," 487; Ramsey Crooks to George Wildes and Company, London, December 9, 1835, Letterbook 2:224–26, American Fur Company Papers, New York Historical Society.

14. Nute, "American Fur Company's Fishing Enterprises," 485. The company sought and exported white fish.

15. Ibid., 489–91; Ramsey Crooks to George Wildes and Company, London, December 9, 1835, Letterbook 2:224–26, American Fur Company Papers, New York Historical Society.

16. Nute, "American Fur Company's Fishing Enterprises," 489; "Register of Persons in the Employ of the American Fur Company's Northern Outfit Lapointe 10 October 1838," Miscellaneous Papers of the American Fur Company, New York Historical Society.

17. "G Francheres Journal of his voyage in the 'Brewster' with Mr. Scott to Grand Portage, Ile Royal & the Ance August 1839," Gabriel Franchere Papers, MHSA. See also Nute, "American Fur Company Enterprises," 491, and Bardon, "Captain E. C. Smith," JB-WPA, vol. 1, pp. 89–90, CIHPR.

18. Nute, "American Fur Company Enterprises," 498–99.

19. Ibid., 495–99.

20. Ibid., 498–99.

21. Satz, *Chippewa Treaty Rights*, 29–30; Lucius Lyon to Commissioner of Indian Affairs T. Hartley Crawford, December 16, 1839, in *Territorial Papers*, 28:91–98.

22. Nute, "American Fur Company's Fishing Enterprises," 501.

23. Ibid., 483.

24. Bogue, *Fishing the Great Lakes*, 31.

25. Ibid., 44.

26. Feldman, "Rewilding the Islands," 167; Goode, *Fisheries and Fishery Industries*, 45, 49.

27. John Condecon "Life History of John Condecon," BR-WPA, CIHPR.

28. Ibid. It is not clear what kinds of boxes that Condecon family used or how they boxed fish.

29. Feldman, *Storied Wilderness*, 63–64.

30. Feldman, "Rewilding the Islands," 161.

31. Ibid., 163.

32. Feldman, *Storied Wilderness*, 65; Feldman, "Rewilding the Islands," 167.

33. Annual Report of the Commissioner of Indian Affairs, 1875, 372, BIAR, NAWA.

34. Reports of Inspection of the Office of Indian Affairs, 1896, n.p, BIAR, NAWA.

35. Ibid., 331.

36. Annual Report to the Commissioner of Indian Affairs, Consolidated Chippewa Agency, Cass Lake, Minn., 1925, BIAR, NAWA.

37. Superintendent M. D. Archiquette, Grand Portage, to Commissioner of Indian Affairs, Washington, D.C., March 2, 1916, BIAR, NAWA.

38. Ibid., March 16, 1918.

39. Johnston, *Crazy Dave*, 183.

40. Ibid., 184.

41. Bogue, *Fishing the Great Lakes*, 47.

42. Ibid., 45.

43. Doherty, *Disputed Waters*, 28–30; Dominion Fishery Commission on the Fisheries of the Province of Ontario, "Report," in *Sessional Papers of the Parliament of Canada*, vol. 26, 1893, no. 10C, pt. 2, "Evidence," p. 116, https://archive.org/details/sessional1010ds-1893cana (accessed November 17, 2013); T. H. Elliot to the Deputy Minister of Marine and

Fisheries, July 4, 1898, File 140, pt. 1, frames 57–58, reel 2734, Records of the Department of Marine and Fisheries, Record Group 23, National Archives of Canada, Ottawa.

44. Doherty, *Disputed Waters*, 53.

45. Ibid., 90.

46. Feldman, *Storied Wilderness*, 86–87.

47. Feldman, "Rewilding the Islands," 208.

48. Ibid., 208, 155.

49. Chapple, "'Herring Boom' at Bayfield," 32.

50. "Annual Statistical and Narrative Report for the Red Cliff agency," 1922, File: Reports of 1922–26, Annual Reports of Red Cliff and Bad River, 1911–26, Records of the Great Lakes Consolidated and Bad River Agency, BIAR, NAGL.

51. Feldman, "Rewilding the Islands," 186; Scott and Reitz, *Wisconsin Warden*.

52. Bogue, *Fishing the Great Lakes*, 57.

53. Boxberger, *To Fish in Common*, 183.

54. Bogue, *Fishing the Great Lakes*, 72–73.

55. Ibid., 65.

56. Ibid., 64; M. B. Johnson, Agent for the A. Booth Packing Company, interview with Richard Rathbone, Bayfield, Wisconsin, 10 July 1894; Joseph La Belle interview with Richard Rathbone, Bayfield, Wisconsin, 10 July 1894, 3, Lake Superior Interviews and Field Notes, Notes and Files of the Joint Commission Relative to the Preservation of the Fisheries of in Waters Contiguous to Canada and the United States, Records of the U.S. Fish and Wildlife Service, Record Group 22, NAWA.

57. Bogue, *Fishing the Great Lakes*, 64; M. B. Johnson, Agent for the A. Booth Packing Company, interview with Richard Rathbone, Bayfield, Wisconsin, 10 July 1894; Joseph La Belle interview with Richard Rathbone, Bayfield, Wisconsin, 10 July 1894, 3, Lake Superior Interviews and Field Notes, Notes and Files of the Joint Commission Relative to the Preservation of the Fisheries of in Waters Contiguous to Canada and the United States Records of the U.S. Fish and Wildlife Service, Record Group 22, NAWA.

58. Feldman, *Storied Wilderness*, 80; Feldman, "Rewilding the Islands," 190; *Bayfield County Press*, October 20, 1983.

59. Bogue, *Fishing the Great Lakes*, 70–71. According to Bogue, the statements made by the Booth Company's representatives revealed "not only the firm's ideas, but the typical commercial fisher's view of how state and national government could help by subsidized restocking and how state regulation could help by establishing rules that hampered the operations of competitors."

60. Feldman, *Storied Wilderness*, 80; Feldman, "Rewilding the Islands," 191.

61. Reports of Inspection of the Field Jurisdictions of the Office of Indian Affairs, 1896, Records of the Office of Indian Affairs, BIAR, NAWA; Feldman, *Storied Wilderness*, 82.

62. Reports of Inspection of the Field Jurisdictions of the Office of Indian Affairs, Records of the Office of Indian Affairs, 1896, BIAR, NAWA.

63. Feldman, "Rewilding the Islands," 192.

64. Ibid., 193.

65. Feldman, *Storied Wilderness*, 81; Feldman, "Rewilding the Islands," 194; D. M. Browning, Commissioner, to Lieut. W. A. Mercer, June 25, 1894, Wisconsin Department of Justice, Closed Case Files, Series 644, Box 2, Folder 5 (36), WHSA.

66. Feldman, *Storied Wilderness*, 81; Feldman, "Rewilding the Islands," 194; W. A. Mercer to H. E. Briggs, June 6, 1896, Wisconsin Department of Justice, Closed Case Files, Series 644, Box 2, Folder 5 (36), WHSA.

67. Feldman, *Storied Wilderness*, 82; Feldman, "Rewilding the Islands," 194–95; W. H. Mylrea to G. H. McCloud, June 26, 1896, Wisconsin Department of Justice, Closed Case Files, Series 644, Box 2, Folder 5 (36), WHSA.

68. Feldman, *Storied Wilderness*, 82; Feldman, "Rewilding the Islands," 193–94; W. A. Mercer to H. E. Briggs, June 6, 1896, and D. M. Browning, Commissioner, to Lieut. W. A. Mercer, June 25, 1894, Wisconsin Department of Justice, Closed Case Files, Series 644, Box 2, Folder 5 (36), WHSA.

69. Feldman, *Storied Wilderness*, 82; Feldman, "Rewilding the Islands," 193–94; W. A. Mercer to H. E. Briggs, June 6, 1896, Wisconsin Department of Justice, Closed Case Files, Series 644, Box 2, Folder 5 (36), WHSA.

70. Feldman, *Storied Wilderness*, 82; Feldman, "Rewilding the Islands," 193–94; Attorney General to G. H. McCloud, Esq., June 26, 1896, Wisconsin Department of Justice, Closed Case Files, Series 644, Box 2, Folder 5 (36), WHSA.

71. Feldman, *Storied Wilderness*, 82; Attorney General to G. H. McCloud, Esq., June 26, 1896, Wisconsin Department of Justice, Closed Case Files, Series 644, Box 2, Folder 5 (36), WHSA.

72. *Ashland Daily Press*, April 23, 1901.

73. *Re Blackbird*, No. 602 District Court, W.D. Wisconsin 109 F. 139, 1901; Satz, *Chippewa Treaty Rights*, 83; Feldman, *Storied Wilderness*, 82–83.

74. *Re Blackbird*, No. 602 District Court, W.D. Wisconsin 109 F. 139, 1901; Satz, *Chippewa Treaty Rights*, 83; Feldman, *Storied Wilderness*, 82–83.

75. *Re Blackbird*, No. 602 District Court, W.D. Wisconsin 109 F. 139, 1901; Satz, *Chippewa Treaty Rights*, 83.

76. *Re Blackbird*, No. 602 District Court, W.D. Wisconsin 109 F. 139, 1901; Satz, *Chippewa Treaty Rights*, 83.

77. *State v. Morrin*, No. 136 Wisconsin Supreme Court, *Wisconsin Reports*, 552–57, 1908; Satz, *Chippewa Treaty Rights*, 85; Feldman, *Storied Wilderness*, 83.

78. See Section 6 of U.S. Congress, Dawes Act; Satz, *Chippewa Treaty Rights*, 85; Feldman, *Storied Wilderness*, 83. According to Sec. 6, every member of the bands or tribes taking a land allotment was subject to laws of the state or territory in which they lived. Any Indian who took a land allotment and "adopted the habits of civilized life" became a U.S. citizen. However, the act was not supposed to impair or otherwise affect "the right of any such Indian to tribal or other property."

79. State Supreme Court of Wisconsin, "State v. Morrin"; Satz, *Chippewa Treaty Rights*, 85.

80. Wilkins, *American Indian Politics*, 96.

81. U.S. District Court, Western District, Wisconsin, "Re Blackbird"; Satz, *Chippewa Treaty Rights*, 83.

82. See Harmon, *Rich Indians*. Harmon explores American society's uncertainty about Indian identity and wealth. She notes that wealthy Indians have been viewed as less authentic than Indians living in poverty based on conventional assumptions about Native people.

83. Cleland, "Preliminary Report," 106.

84. Ibid.

85. Ibid.; *Kennedy v. Becker; Ward v. Racehorse*. In *Kennedy v. Becker* the court ruled that the Seneca were subject to the fish and game laws of the state of New York. In *Ward v. Racehorse*, the court found that Bannock treaty rights did not enable Bannock people to exercise these rights within the boundaries of the state of Wyoming in violation of its laws.

86. Cleland, "Preliminary Report," 106.

87. Ibid.; E. Meritt to P. Everest, December 10, 1925, *State of Minnesota, Mille Lacs v. Minnesota*, 004394.

88. Cleland, "Preliminary Report," 106; Chiefs to C. Burke, December 16, 1925, *State of Minnesota, Mille Lacs v. Minnesota*, MN004187; J. Hammitt to Commissioner of Indian Affairs, December 21, 1925, *State of Minnesota, Mille Lacs v. Minnesota*, 008194.

89. Memorandum from H. W. Mackenzie to Paul Kelleter, April 28, 1932, WCDR, Subject Files, 1917–67, Box 419, Series 271, WHSA.

90. Today, a number of independent Ojibwe commercial fishers are selling fish caught on Lake Superior. They are promoting their catch through funding from the Administration for Native Americans, and they also work in collaboration with the Great Lakes Indian Fish and Wildlife Commission. They operate a website about their enterprise. See Lake Superior White Fish Fishermen, "Lake Superior White Fish." See also Charlie Otto Rasmussen, "Ice Opens Up Apostle Islands Fishery, Red Cliff Brothers, Sons Continue Legacy," *GLIFWC Mazina'igan*, Spring 2008, 5.

91. Bogue, *Fishing the Great Lakes*, 327–30.

92. Ibid., 330.

93. Joe Stoddard to Jerome Arbuckle, "Fishing Then and Now," BR-WPA, CIHPR.

94. Ibid.

95. Ibid.

96. Jerome Arbuckle, "Qui-Ka-Ba-No-Kwe 'Dawn Woman,'" BR-WPA, CIHPR.

97. Jerome Arbuckle, "Hunting and Fishing on the Bad River Reservation Today," BR-WPA, CIHPR.

98. Satz, *Chippewa Treaty Rights*, 93; *State v. Gurnoe et al.* and *State v. Connors et al.* 53 *Wisconsin Reports*, 2d, 390–492.

99. Satz, *Chippewa Treaty Rights*, 94.

100. *Lac Courte Oreilles v. State of Wisconsin*, 700 F.2d 341 (7th Cir., 1983), cert. denied 464 U.S. 805, 105 S.Ct. 53, 78 L.Ed.2d 72 (1983)

101. Satz, *Chippewa Treaty Rights*, 94–100; *Lac Courte Oreilles Band of Lake Superior Chippewa Indians et al. v. State of Wisconsin et al.*, 1991.

102. For further explanation of the use of this term, see Nesper, *Walleye War*, 99–100, and Whaley, *Walleye Warriors*.

CHAPTER 4

1. Deloria, *Indians in Unexpected Places*, 3–6. William Cadreau pursued a short-lived career in baseball, pitching in his last game for the Chicago White Sox in 1910 at the age of twenty-two. See "Baseball Almanac." Cadreau's death certificate from 1946 simply listed

his occupation as a "laborer," suggesting that after playing baseball, he returned to Clo-quet to find work.

2. Deloria, *Indians in Unexpected Places*, 3–6.

3. Ibid.

4. Satz, *Chippewa Treaty Rights*, 13; Henry Dodge to Commissioner of Indian Affairs Carey Allen Harris, August 7, 1837, Documents Relating to the Negotiations of Ratified and Unratified Treaties with Various Indian Tribes, 1801–69, Microcopy T494, Roll 3, BIAR, NAWA.

5. *United States v. Cook*, 86 U.S. 19 Wall 591 (1873).

6. See Hosmer, *American Indians in the Marketplace*. See also Beck, *Struggle for Self-Determination*. Hosmer has explored how the neighboring Menominee tribe in Wisconsin established successful lumber operations on their reservation during the same period. He demonstrates that through this work Menominees created a self-sufficient community and retained many of their traditional social structures. See p. 3. I see Ojibwe strategies as being similar, but the success of reservation timber operations in Ojibwe communities was rapidly undermined by the dispossession of their timber within a matter of decades.

7. Hosmer, *American Indians in the Marketplace*, 56.

8. Ibid., 58.

9. Treaty with the Chippewa, 1854. See appendix. Castle McLaughlin has described a similar process that accompanied cattle ranching on the Fort Berthold reservation during the same period. Ranching became an important way to make a living on the reservation, but, combined with allotment and, later, New Deal Indian policies, it exacerbated class divisions within the community as well as the economic difficulties of many tribal members. See McLaughlin, "Nation, Tribe, and Class."

10. Kurt Peters describes comparative strategies among the Laguna Pueblo people who took on wage labor with the Santa Fe Railroad. They engaged in this work based on an agreement in which they permitted the railroad to use lands within their territory in exchange for work on the railroads. Peters writes about how they reproduced indigenous practices and community within the context of railroad work and off-reservation mobility. He also describes the sense of pride that many Pueblo people expressed in this work. See Peters, "Watering the Flower."

11. White, *Organic Machine*, 4.

12. Godfrey, *Forestry History*, 27.

13. Annual Report of the Commissioner of Indian Affairs, 1871, 601, BIAR, NAWA.

14. Godfrey, *Forestry History*, 27.

15. *Bayfield Press*, July 22, 1871; Feldman, "Rewilding the Islands," 96.

16. Annual Report of the Commissioner of Indian Affairs, 1871, 601, BIAR, NAWA.

17. Godfrey, *Forestry History*, 26.

18. W. P. Bigboy, "Recollections of Joseph Bell, Member of Lost Tribe," BR-WPA. The Indian agent to which Bell referred was most likely Selden Clark. It is unclear why Bell's female relatives could not support themselves or what their contributions were to the household.

19. Ibid.

20. Treaty of 1854.

21. Annual Report of the Commissioner of Indian Affairs, 1882, 174, BIAR, NAWA; Godfrey, *Forestry History*, 29.

22. Annual Report of the Commissioner of Indian Affairs 1882, 174, BIAR, NAWA.

23. Annual Report of the Commissioner of Indian Affairs, 1884, lv, BIAR, NAWA; Godfrey, *Forestry History*, 29.

24. Annual Report of the Commissioner of Indian Affairs, 1884, liii, BIAR, NAWA; Godfrey, *Forestry History*, 31.

25. Feldman, *Storied Wilderness*, 49.

26. BIA, Annual Report of the Commissioner of Indian Affairs, 1886, 256, BIAR, NAWA; Godfrey, *Forestry History*, 32.

27. Annual Report of the Commissioner of Indian Affairs, 1888, lv, BIAR, NAWA; Godfrey, *Forestry History*, 33.

28. Godfrey, *Forestry History*, 34; Newell, Clow, and Ellis, *Forest in Trust*, sec. 1, pp. 21–22; Annual Report of the Commissioner of Indian Affairs, 1888, lv, BIAR, NAWA.

29. Annual Report of the Commissioner of Indian Affairs, 1884, lv, BIAR, NAWA; Godfrey, *Forestry History*, 34.

30. Godfrey, *Forestry History*, 34.

31. Ibid., 60; Kinney, *Indian Forest and Range*, 33, 75.

32. Godfrey, *Forestry History*, 113. The extent to which the non-Indian population grew on the reservation as a result of logging operations is unclear, but when the lumber mill closed in 1922, most of the non-Indians left the reservation. At that time, they numbered about 1,000 people.

33. "J. S. Stearns Lumber Co. Letterhead," 1905, Letterhead Collection 1850s–1975, Image ID: 88849, WHSA.

34. Godfrey, *Forestry History*, 68. See also Steen-Adams, Langston, and Mladenhoff, "Logging the Great Lakes Indian Reservations," 53. Steen-Adams, Langston, and Mladenhoff explain that lack of tribal autonomy and the management of the Indian Agency led to the loss of revenue for Bad River Band members. Indian Agent S. W. Campbell (who was appointed in 1898) gained control over $2 million in tribal accounts and blocked tribal members access to them. He swindled approximately $33,328 from the Bad River people.

35. Meyer, *White Earth Tragedy*, 137.

36. Peacock, *Forever Story*, 51.

37. Meyer, *White Earth Tragedy*, 142–43.

38. Ibid., 137–72.

39. Indian Land Tenure Foundation, "Allotment Information for Midwest BIA Region."

40. Annual Report of the Commissioner of Indian Affairs, 1882, 174, BIAR, NAWA.

41. Knight, *Tales of Bayfield Pioneers*, 260.

42. *Bayfield Press*, November 1906, quoted in ibid. Knight did not cite the specific article in which she found this quotation.

43. Sister M. Macaria Murphy, "Life History of John Condecon," BR-WPA, CIHPR.

44. RKCS, WHSA.

45. "Chance to Guide President Came Too Late for Old Antoine Dennis," Associated Press, date unspecified, summer 1928, RKCS, WHSA.

46. Daniel Morrison, "Recollection of Early Days, Told by George Starr Age 96 to Daniel Morrison," BR-WPA, CIHPR.

47. Ibid.

48. Roufs, "When Everybody Called Me *Gah-bay-bi-nayss*."

49. For more information on the structures of surveillance in place on reservations, see Biolsi, "Birth of the Reservation," and Hoxie, "From Prison to Homeland."

50. Annual Report of the Commissioner of Indian Affairs, 1875, 371, BIAR, NAWA.

51. Reports of the Inspection of the Field Jurisdictions of the Office of Indian Affairs, 1881, Records of the Office of Indian Affairs, BIAR, NAWA.

52. Rosholt, *Wisconsin Logging Book*, 82. For photographs documenting this, see Wisconsin Historical Society Online Image Collections, http://wisconsinhistory.org/whi/advancedsearch.asp (accessed July 30, 2012), and Minnesota Historical Society Visual Resource Database, http://www.collections.mnhs.org/visualresources/search.cfm?bhcp=1 (accessed July 30, 2012).

53. Rosholt, *Wisconsin Logging Book*, 82; Larson, *History of the White Pine Industry*, 194.

54. Roufs, "When Everybody Called Me *Gah-bay-bi-nayss*."

55. Agnes Larson describes examples of this violence, including fights between lumberjacks, and a cook who had scars around his throat "left by those who sought his destruction" (Larson, *History of the White Pine Industry*, 200–201).

56. Vennum, *Just Too Much of an Indian*, 88.

57. Rosholt, *Wisconsin Logging Book*, 101.

58. Ibid., 104–5.

59. Ibid., 105.

60. Ibid., 112.

61. Ibid., 166, 167.

62. The development of a distinct sense of Ojibwe identity surrounding work in the lumber industry parallels similar developments among indigenous workers on the Northwest coast in the early twentieth century. Andrew Parnaby has written about Aboriginal men who specialized in lumber work on the Vancouver waterfront. He has demonstrated how their place in the labor market was attached to their identity as Aboriginal workers and how race became a vehicle through which they defended their position as skilled workers. These workers also organized under the Industrial Workers of the World (IWW) and asserted their identity and autonomy through union organizing. See Parnaby, *Citizen Docker*, 75–99. I have found little information on Ojibwe involvement in unions or distinct Ojibwe-organized unions. This may have been because Ojibwe lumber workers did not necessarily occupy a particular niche in the industry.

63. Knight, *Tales of Bayfield Pioneers*, 260.

64. Roufs, "When Everybody Called Me *Gah-bay-bi-nayss*."

65. Lankton, *Cradle to Grave*, 212.

66. Duluth Public Library, "Duluth's Early Days."

67. See Zarnowsky, "Working at Play."

68. Christine Carlson, "1900s Fast Foot Work: FDL Men Employed by the Logging Industry Became Champion Log Rollers," *Fond du Lac Na gah chi wa nong Di bah ji mowin nan*, May 2009, 9.

69. Ibid.; *Cloquet Pine Knot*, August 12, 1905.

70. Christine Carlson, "1900s Fast Foot Work: FDL Men Employed by the Logging Industry Became Champion Log Rollers," *Fond du Lac Na gah chi wa nong Di bah ji mowin nan*, May 2009, 9; *Duluth News Tribune*, August 18, 1906.

71. Christine Carlson, "1900s Fast Foot Work: FDL Men Employed by the Logging Industry Became Champion Log Rollers," *Fond du Lac Na gah chi wa nong Di bah ji mowin nan*, May 2009, 9; *Duluth News Tribune*, August 19, 1906.

72. Bardon, "Henry La Prairie, Log Burler," JB-WPA, vol. 1, p. 186, CIHPR.

73. Annual Report of the Commissioner of Indian Affairs, 1878, 145, BIAR, NAWA.

74. Knight, *Tales of Bayfield Pioneers*, 29.

75. Annual Report of the Commissioner of Indian Affairs, 1896, 320, BIAR, NAWA.

76. Godfrey, *Forestry History*, 113.

77. Jerome Arbuckle, "The Bad River Reservation," BR-WPA, CIHPR.

78. Ibid., 97.

79. Gilman, *Grand Portage Story*, 118.

80. Godfrey, *Forestry History*, 107.

81. U.S. Congress, Senate Subcommittee on Indian Affairs, *Survey on the Conditions of the Indians of the United States: Hearing on Senate Resolution 79*, pt. 5, 71st Cong., 1st sess., July 10, 1929; Godfrey, *Forestry History*, 107.

82. Godfrey, *Forestry History*, 149.

83. U.S. Congress, Indian Reorganization Act. In his article "Sustained Yield Forest Management," Stephen L. McDonald defines sustained yield forestry as "the systematic limitation of periodic drain on timber to an amount equivalent to periodic growth of timber on a given managerial unit of forest land" (389).

84. Florina Denomie, "The Chippewa Indian Was Always Self-Supporting," BR-WPA, CIHPR.

85. La Fernier, quoted in ibid.

86. Roufs, "When Everybody Called Me *Gah-bay-bi-nayss*." In the late nineteenth and early twentieth centuries, Finnish immigrants were the target of prejudice in northern Minnesota and Michigan. Many of them intermarried or became friends with Ojibwes, perhaps due to the prejudice that both groups faced. Indeed there are still tribal members who call themselves "Finndians," claiming both Finnish and Ojibwe heritage.

87. Morrison, *Little History of My Forest Life*, 36.

88. Daniel Morrison, "The Indian as a Skilled Laborer," BR-WPA, CIHPR.

CHAPTER 5

1. Feldman, *Storied Wilderness*, 9.

2. Ibid., 11.

3. Yoshihara, "Political Economy of Tourist Colonialism in Hawai'i." See also Butler and Hinch, *Tourism and Indigenous Peoples*.

4. Feldman, *Storied Wilderness*, 10.

5. Shapiro, "Up North on Vacation," 3; Cullon "Landscapes of Labor and Leisure," 75; Ross, *La Pointe*, 159.

6. Feldman, *Storied Wilderness*, 10.

7. Shapiro, "Up North on Vacation," 3; Jakle, *Tourist*, 84–100.

8. Shapiro, "Up North on Vacation," 3; Jakle, *Tourist*, 146–70.

9. Feldman, *Storied Wilderness*, 7.

10. Ibid., 7.

11. Bogue, *Fishing the Great Lakes*, 124.

12. Feldman, *Storied Wilderness*, 7; Harlan P. Kelsey, "Report on the Apostle Island National Park Project," January 20, 1931, Record Group 79, Box 634, National Park Service, General Classified Files, 1907–32, Proposed National Parks, 0–32, NAWA.

13. Feldman, *Storied Wilderness*, 10.

14. Cullon, "Landscapes of Labor and Leisure," 75–76.

15. Shapiro, "Up North on Vacation," 3–7; Ross, *La Pointe*, 137.

16. Feldman, *Storied Wilderness*, 10; Cullon, "Landscapes of Labor and Leisure,"3.

17. Ibid.; Lock, "A Summer Place," 33.

18. Cullon, "Landscapes of Labor and Leisure," 83–86.

19. Ross, *La Pointe*, 159.

20. Cullon, "Landscapes of Labor and Leisure,"78.

21. See O'Brien, *There Were Four of Us*.

22. Knight, *Tales of Bayfield Pioneers*, 55; Godfrey, *Forestry History*, app. 1.

23. Wisconsin State Historical Society, "Dictionary of Wisconsin History."

24. "Brule Country Rich in Political Lore As Well As in Quiet Beauty, Says Pioneer Wisconsin Editor," *Wisconsin State Journal*, 1928. The discussion in this article was triggered by President Calvin Coolidge's visit to the region.

25. GFCM, Report of the Game and Fish Commission of Minnesota 1895, 7, MHS SH11. M63, MHSA.

26. Patricia C. Albers, "From Legend to Land to Labor: Changing Perspectives on Native American Work," in Littlefield and Knack, *Native Americans and Wage Labor*, 249.

27. Feldman, *Storied Wilderness*, 61; Cullon "Landscapes of Labor and Leisure," 127–36.

28. White, "Early Game and Fish Regulation," 14–15; Satz, *Chippewa Treaty Rights*, 83–90; Silvern, "Negotiating Ojibwe Treaty Rights," 161.

29. Nesper, "Simulating Culture"; Arndt, "Ho-Chunk 'Indian Powwows' "; Ellis, "Five Dollars a Week," 184–208; Troutman, *Indian Blues*.

30. Raibmon, *Authentic Indians*.

31. Cattelino, "Casino Roots."

32. Loo, "Of Moose and Men."

33. Rohde, "Living and Working in Enchanted Lands."

34. Jasen, *Wild Things*, 80–81.

35. Rohde, "Living and Working in Enchanted Lands," 60; *My Rambles in the Enchanted Summer Land of the Great Northwest during the Tourist Season of 1881* (Chicago: Rand McNally, 1882).

36. Holbrook, *From the Log of a Trout Fisherman*, 94.

37. RKCS, 1, WHSA.

38. Ellis, "Five Dollars a Week," 184–208.

39. Nesper, "Simulating Culture."

40. Sister M. Macaria Murphy, "Chief Anakwadoons' Peace Pipe," BR-WPA, CIHPR.

41. Olmanson, *Future City on the Inland Sea*, 170–71; Roy L. Martin, *History of the Wisconsin Central*, Bulletin no. 54 (Boston: Railroad and Locomotive Historical Society, 1941),

25; *Ashland Daily Press*, September 11, 1896; *Ashland News*, September 11, 1896; *Ashland Daily Press*, September 11, 1896; *Ashland Daily Press*, September 12, 1896.

42. Kenneth M. Ellis, "Ke-wa-de-no-kwa: First Apostle Island Indian Pageant," 1924, Pamphlet Collection, WHSA; *Bayfield County Press*, July 20, 1923; Olmanson, "Romantics, Scientists, Boosters," 340–53; Feldman, "Rewilding the Islands," 250–52, 257.

43. Kenneth M. Ellis, "Ke-wa-de-no-kwa: First Apostle Island Indian Pageant," 1924, Pamphlet Collection, WHSA.

44. Rohde, "Living and Working in Enchanted Lands," 94.

45. Diane Bear told these stories at a storytelling event on March 21, 2012, at Northland College in Ashland, Wisconsin, as part of "Native American Awareness Days."

46. See Arndt, "Ho-Chunk 'Indian Powwows' "; Rohde, "Living and Working in Enchanted Lands."

47. Arndt, "Ho-Chunk 'Indian Powwows,' " 51–52.

48. Daniel Morrison, "Fiftieth Anniversary of the Signing of the Treaty of 1854," BR-WPA, CIHPR.

49. Albers and James, "Images and Reality"; Albers and James, "Wisconsin Indians on the Picture Postcard"; Albers and James, "Tourism and the Changing Image of the Great Lakes Indian."

50. Albers and James, "Images and Reality," 232.

51. White, *We Are at Home*, 10.

52. Roufs, "When Everybody Called Me *Gah-bay-bi-nayss*." A turn table is a tool used to turn locomotives around for return trips. They consisted of a circular, rotating base on which there was a track. The track could be rotated in order to turn the locomotive.

53. White, *We Are at Home*, 162.

54. Ibid.

55. Roufs, "When Everybody Called Me *Gah-bay-bi-nayss*"; White, *We Are at Home*, 162.

56. Albers and James, "Images and Reality," 231; White, *We Are at Home*, 162–64.

57. Roufs, "When Everybody Called Me *Gah-bay-bi-nayss*."

58. For a full discussion of non-Indian ideas about "authenticity" as they related to Indigenous peoples, see Raibmon, *Authentic Indians*, 1–14.

59. Newspaper unspecified, RKCS, WHSA.

60. Holbrook, *From the Log of a Trout Fisherman*," 45–46.

61. Annual Report of the Commissioner of Indian Affairs, 1895, 320, BIAR, NAWA.

62. Lyford, *Ojibwa Crafts*, 30. There is no evidence to suggest that these activities were associated with the Indian Arts and Crafts Board, though Ojibwe produced art for tribally owned cooperatives or for New Deal programs like the WPA at Grand Portage. The term "traders" most likely refers to entrepreneurs who would buy items from individuals and resell them (at a higher price) in local stores or arrange to sell an individual's items in a store and collect a portion of the profit.

63. Simonsen, *Making Home Work*, 103–9.

64. Ibid., 103.

65. Annual Report of the Commissioner of Indian Affairs, 1905, 376, BIAR, NAWA.

66. Lac du Flambeau Indian Agency, Lac du Flambeau, Wisconsin, "Surveys of Indian Industry, 1920–1922," BIAR, NAGL. See also Rohde, "Living and Working in Enchanted Lands," 84.

67. See, for example, Lyford, *Ojibwa Crafts*, and Densmore, *Chippewa Customs*.

68. Lyford, *Ojibwa Crafts*, 30.

69. Holbrook, *From the Log of a Trout Fisherman*, 83.

70. Ibid., 49–54; RKCS, WHSA; Loo, "Of Moose and Men," 298, 311, 314.

71. Cullon, "Landscapes of Labor and Leisure," 53.

72. Holbrook, *From the Log of a Trout Fisherman*, 93.

73. Ibid., 53.

74. Ibid., 200–201.

75. Ibid., 202.

76. Morrison, *Little History of My Forest Life*, x–45. Eliza Morrison later moved to the Bad River reservation. Mary Bouskey was an Ojibwe woman from northern Wisconsin, but it is unclear where she lived when she was not working for the Grays and Purcells.

77. Holbrook, *From the Log of a Trout Fisherman*, 89.

78. Ibid., 43.

79. Loo, "Of Moose and Men," 301.

80. Holbrook, *From the Log of a Trout Fisherman*, 44–45.

81. Ibid.

82. Cullon, "Landscapes of Labor and Leisure," 73.

83. Patricia C. Albers, "From Legend to Land to Labor: Changing Perspectives on Native American Work," in Littlefield and Knack, *Native Americans and Wage Labor*, 248–49.

84. Arndt, "Ho-Chunk 'Indian Powwows,'" 52.

85. Loo, "Of Moose and Men," 298.

86. RKCS, 2, 3, WHSA.

87. Writing about tourism among Ojibwes in Ontario, Patricia Jasen observes, "In no aspect of Ontario tourism did ideas about civilization and the primitive come under more sustained scrutiny than in the relations between white tourists and Native guides" (Jasen, *Wild Things*, 133). The same can be said for relations between tourists and Ojibwe guides on the other side of the border.

88. Holbrook, *From the Log of a Trout Fisherman*, 89.

89. Ibid., 50.

90. RKCS, 2, WHSA.

91. Ibid., 3–4.

92. Deloria, *Playing Indian*, 94, 127.

93. Holbrook, *From the Log of a Trout Fisherman*, 60.

94. Ibid., 154.

95. Ibid., 154–55.

96. Ibid., 155.

97. Morrison, *Little History of My Forest Life*, 17, 21.

98. Ibid., 17.

99. Ibid.

100. Ibid., 49.

101. Ibid., 42.

102. Unidentified newspaper clipping, RKCS, WHSA.

103. Ibid.

104. Vennum, *Just Too Much of An Indian*, 321.

105. Ibid., 322.

106. "Battle of the Brule was Fought Near Cedar Island Retreat," unidentified newspaper clipping, n.d., RKCS, WHSA. In 1909, Charles Armstrong was the chairman of a committee appointed to press the federal government to address conflicts between the Bad River Band and the J. S. Stearns Lumber Company.

107. Ibid.

108. Jasen, *Wild Things*, 80.

109. Rothman, *Devil's Bargains*, 11, 13.

110. Cockrell, *Grand Portage National Monument*, 35.

111. "Grand Portage National Monument Heritage Center."

112. The term "Tribal National" was the band's own designation to suggest that it is run by the tribe but open to the public. It is not part of the National Park System. George Wright Society, "Red Cliff Tribe in Wisconsin Creates Frog Bay Tribal National Park."

113. "A New Shoreline Tribal Park," *Lake Superior Magazine*, January 16, 2012.

CONCLUSION

1. Satz, " 'Tell Those Gray Haired Men What They Should Know,' " 196.

2. U.S. Interior Department, "Testimony Taken at Hayward," in Wheeler-Howard Bill, Congress (Hayward, Wisc.), Conference Proceedings, April 23–24, 1934, 38 MHS P1580, MHSA.

3. Ibid., 39.

4. Jerome Arbuckle, "Hunting and Fishing on the Bad River Reservation Today," BR-WPA, CIHPR.

5. Satz, " 'Tell Those Gray Haired Men What They Should Know,' " 201.

6. Satz, *Chippewa Treaty Rights*, 89.

7. Nesper, *Walleye War*, 203.

8. Ibid., 53–54.

9. Auger and Driben., *Grand Portage Chippewa*, 53.

10. Peacock, *Forever Story*, 177.

11. Ibid., 177–78.

12. Ibid., 178.

13. Mic Isham, "Treaty Harvests Really Count in Tough Economic Times: A Commentary by Chairman Mic Isham, GLIFWC Board of Commissioners," *GLIFWC Mazina'igan*, Spring/Summer 2010, 2.

Bibliography

PRIMARY SOURCES

Archival Collections

Minnesota Historical Society Archives, St. Paul, Minnesota
    F. A. Asbury, S. N. McKinsey, and D. D. Mani, "Economic Survey of the Consolidated
        Chippewa Jurisdiction of Minnesota," 1938
    Dennis Dwan, "Growth of the Postal System on the North Shore," Address delivered
        at the North Shore Historical Assembly, Listen, Minn., August 21, 1933,
        Manuscript Notebooks
    Gabriel Franchere Papers, 1835-39
    Game and Fish Commission of Minnesota, Board of the Game and Fish
        Commissioners of Minnesota Reports, 1891-1915
    Minnesota Conservation Department Records, 1931-42
    Minnesota Game and Fish Department Records, 1915-23
    Minnesota Historical Society, "Visual Resource Database," http://www.collections.
        mnhs.org/visualresources/search.cfm?bhcp=1
    Olga Soderberg, "Grand Portage the Great Carrying Place," Pageant script for the
        Minnesota Territorial Centennial Celebration, 1949
    Wheeler-Howard Bill, Congress (Hayward, Wisc.), Conference Proceedings, April
        23-24, 1934
National Archives, Great Lakes Region, Chicago, Illinois
    Records of the Bureau of Indian Affairs, Record Group 75
        Records of the Bad River Agency, Wisconsin, 1887-1958
        Records of the Great Lakes Consolidated Agency, 1887-1963
        Records of the La Pointe Agency, Minnesota and Wisconsin, 1869-1931
        Records of the Red Cliff School and Agency, Wisconsin, 1878-1955
National Archives, Kansas City, Missouri
    Records of the Bureau of Indian Affairs, Record Group 75
        Records of the Consolidated Chippewa Agency, Minnesota, 1881-1969
National Archives, Washington, D.C., and College Park, Maryland
    Records of the Bureau of Indian Affairs, Record Group 75
        Annual Reports of the Commissioner of Indian Affairs, 1839-1943
        Documents Relating to the Negotiations of Ratified and Unratified Treaties with
            Various Indian Tribes, 1801-69
        Records of the Office of Indian Affairs
            Correspondence of the Office of Indian Affairs (Central Office) and Related
                Records, Letters Received, 1836-48

Reports of Inspection of the Field Jurisdictions of the Office of Indian Affairs,
1873–1900
Records of the U.S. Fish and Wildlife Service, Record Group 22
Notes and Files of the Joint Commission Relative to the Preservation of the
Fisheries in Waters Contiguous to Canada and the United States
New York Historical Society, New York
American Fur Company Papers
Wisconsin Historical Society Archives, Madison, Wisconsin
Bad River Tribal Council, "A Declaration of War," November 10, 1959, Record Series
27, Box 419, Folder 4
John A. Bardon Papers, 1921–37
Kenneth M. Ellis, "Ke-wa-da-no-kwa: First Annual Apostle Islands Indian Pageant,"
1924, Pamphlet Collection
"J. S. Stearns Lumber Co. Letterhead," 1905, Letterhead Collection 1850s–1975, Image
ID: 88849
Rebekah Knight-Cochran, President Coolidge Brule River Scrapbook, 1928 and 1978
Vincent Roy, Miscellany, 1861–62, 1892, 1921
"Statement of Treaties Between the Chippewas and the United States from 1825 to
1864, from the Chippewa Standpoint, as Presented to the Commissioner of
Indian Affairs," Small Collections–Oversize, File 40
United States Works Progress Administration, Chippewa Indian Historical Project
Records, 1936–42
Wisconsin Conservation Department Records
Commission Secretary's Correspondence, 1927–31
Subject Files, 1917–67
Wisconsin Department of Justice, Division of Legal Services, Closed Case Files,
1885–1976
Wisconsin Governor, Reports, 1848–1926
Wisconsin Historical Society online image collections, http://wisconsinhistory.org/
whi/advancedsearch.asp

Published Primary Sources

Auger, Donald J., and Paul Driben, eds. *Grand Portage Chippewa: Stories and
Experiences of Grand Portage Band Members.* Grand Portage, Minn.: Grand Portage
Tribal Council and Sugarloaf Interpretive Center Association, 2000.
Baraga, Frederick. *Frederic Baraga's Short History of the North American Indians.*
Translated by Graham MacDonald. 1837. Calgary: University of Calgary Press,
2004.
Copway, George. *Life, Letters, and Speeches: George Copway (Kahgegagabowh).* Edited
by A. LaVonne Brown Ruoff and Donald B. Smith. Lincoln: University of Nebraska
Press, 1997.
Holbrook, Arthur Tenney. *From the Log of a Trout Fisherman.* Norwood, Mass.:
Plimpton Press, 1949.
Johnston, Basil. *Crazy Dave.* St. Paul: Minnesota Historical Society Press, 2002.

Kappler, Charles, comp. and ed. *Indian Affairs: Laws and Treaties*. 5 vols. Washington, D.C.: Government Printing Office, 1904–41.

Kegg, Maude, and John D. Nichols. *Portage Lake: Memories of an Ojibwe Childhood*. Minneapolis, Minn.: University of Minnesota Press, 1993.

Knight, Eleanor. *Tales of Bayfield Pioneers: A History of Bayfield*. Bayfield, Wisc.: Beedlow Media, 2008.

Kohl, Johann Georg. *Kitchi-Gami: Life among Lake Superior Ojibway*. London: Chapman and Hall, 1860. Reprinted with an introduction by Robert E. Bieder. St. Paul: Minnesota Historical Society Press, 1985.

Lewis, Herbert S., and Gordon L. McLester, eds. *Oneida Lives: Long-Lost Voices of the Wisconsin Oneida*. Lincoln: University of Nebraska Press, 2005.

Lyford, Carrie L. *Ojibwa Crafts*. Washington, D.C.: Branch of Education, Bureau of Indian Affairs, 1943.

Lyon, Lucius. Lucius Lyon to Commissioner of Indian Affairs T. Hartley Crawford, December 16, 1839. *Territorial Papers* 28:91–98.

Morrison, Eliza. *A Little History of My Forest Life*. Edited by Victoria Brehm. Tustin, Mich.: Ladyslipper Press, 2002.

Morrisseau, Norval. *Legends of My People, The Great Ojibway*. Toronto: Ryerson Press, 1965.

Nichols, John D., ed. *"Statements Made by the Indians": A Bilingual Petition of the Chippewas of Lake Superior*. 1864. London, Ontario: Centre for Research and Teaching of Canadian Native Languages, 1988.

O'Brien, Thomas D. *There Were Four of Us, or Was it Five*. St. Paul, Minn.: T. D. O'Brien, 1936.

Peacock, Thomas D., ed. *A Forever Story: The People and Community of Fond du Lac Reservation*. Cloquet, Minn.: Fond du Lac Band of Lake Superior Chippewa, 1998.

Purcell, William Gray. *St. Croix Country: Recollections of Wisconsin*. Minneapolis: University of Minnesota Press, 1967.

Schoolcraft, Henry Rowe. *The American Indians: Their History, Conditions, and Prospects*. Buffalo, N.Y.: George H. Derby, 1851.

Schoolcraft, Jane Johnston. *The Sound the Stars Make Rushing Through the Sky: The Writings of Jane Johnston Schoolcraft*. Edited by Robert Dale Parker. Philadelphia: University of Pennsylvania Press, 2007.

Van Antwerp, Verplanck. "Negotiations for the Chippewa Treaty of July 29, 1837." In Satz, *Chippewa Treaty Rights*, app. 1.

Warren, William W. *History of the Ojibway People*. 1885. Reprinted with an introduction by W. Roger Buffalohead. St. Paul: Minnesota Historical Society Press, 1984.

Newspapers and Popular Periodicals

Ashland (Wisconsin) Daily Press
Ashland (Wisconsin) News
Bayfield (Wisconsin) Press
Bayfield County (Wisconsin) Press
Duluth (Minnesota) News Tribune

Fond du Lac Na gah chi wa nong Di bah ji mowin nan
GLIFWC Mazina'igan
The (Grand Marais, Minn.) Herald
Lake Superior Magazine
Milwaukee (Wisconsin) Journal
Minneapolis (Minnesota) Journal
North Wisconsin News
Cloquet (Minnesota) Pine Knot
St. Paul (Minnesota) Pioneer Press
Wisconsin State Journal

Federal Reports, Legislation, and Litigation

Brookings Institution. Institute for Government Research. *The Problem of Indian Administration. Report of a Survey Made at the Request of Honorable Hubert Work, Secretary of the Interior and Submitted to Him February 21, 1928.* Baltimore, Md.: Johns Hopkins University Press, 1928.

Cockrell, Ron. *The Grand Portage National Monument: An Administrative History.* Omaha, Neb.: National Park Service Midwest Regional Office, Office of Planning and Resource Preservation, 1983.

Godfrey, Anthony. *A Forestry History of Ten Wisconsin Indian Reservations under the Great Lakes Agency.* Salt Lake City: U.S. West Research, for BIA Branch of Forestry, 1996.

Goode, George Brown. *The Fisheries and Fishery Industries of the United States.* Washington, D.C.: Government Printing Office, 1884–87.

United States Commissioner of Indian Affairs. *Annual Reports of the Commissioner of Indian Affairs, 1850–1905.* Washington, D.C.: Government Printing Office.

United States Commission of Fish and Fisheries. *Annual Reports,* 1872–1905. U.S. Senate and House Docs.

United States Congress. Dawes Act, February 8, 1887. *U.S. Statutes at Large* 24 (1887): 388–91.

———. Indian Citizenship Act (Snyder Act), June 2, 1924. *U.S. Statutes at Large* 43 (1924): 253.

———. Indian Reorganization Act, June 18, 1934, *U.S. Statutes at Large* 48 (1934): 984–88.

———. Major Crimes Act, March 3, 1885. *U.S. Statutes at Large* 23 (1885): 385.

———. Nelson Act, January 14, 1889. *U.S. Statutes at Large* 25 (1889): 642.

———. Public Law 83-280, August 15, 1953. *U.S. Statutes at Large* 67 (1953): 588–90.

———. Treaty of La Pointe. October 4, 1842. *U.S. Statutes at Large* 7 (1842): 591.

———. Treaty of La Pointe. September 30, 1854. *U.S. Statutes at Large* 10 (1854): 1109.

———. Treaty of St. Peters. July 29, 1837. *U.S. Statutes at Large* 7 (1837): 536.

United States Supreme Court. *Kennedy v. Becker,* 241 U.S. 556 (1916).

———. *Minnesota v. Mille Lacs Band of Chippewa Indians,* 526 U.S. 172 (1999).

———. *Ward v. Racehorse,* 163 U.S. 504 (1896).

Minnesota Litigation

Minnesota Supreme Court. "Minnesota v. Al Cooney." *Minnesota Reports* 518 (1899): 77.

———. "Selkirk v. Stephens." *Minnesota Reports* 335 (1898): 72.

Wisconsin Litigation

Supreme Court of Wisconsin. "State v. Morrin." *Wisconsin Reports* 136 (1908): 552–57.

United States District Court, Western District, Wisconsin. "Re Blackbird." *Federal Reporter* 109 (1901): 139–45.

———. "Lac Courte Oreilles Band of Lake Superior Chippewa Indians et al. v. Voigt et al." reported sub. nom. "U.S. v. Ben Ruby." 464 F. Supp. 1316–376 (1978).

SECONDARY SOURCES

Books

Allison, Charlene J., Sue-Ellen Jacobs, and Mary A. Porter. *Winds of Change: Women in Northwest Commercial Fishing*. Seattle: University of Washington Press, 1989.

Anthes, Bill. *Native Moderns: American Indian Painting, 1940–1960*. Durham, N.C.: Duke University Press, 2006.

Armour, Robert E. *Superior, Wisconsin, 1857–1885*. Superior, Wisc.: Robert E. Armour, 1994.

Aubut, Sheldon T., and Maryanne C. Norton. *Duluth, Minnesota*. Mount Pleasant, S.C.: Arcadia Publishing, 2002.

Bal, Mieke, Jonathan Crewe, and Leo Spitzer, eds. *Acts of Memory: Cultural Recall in the Present*. Hanover, N.H.: University Press of New England, 1999.

Barnouw, Victor. *Acculturation and Personality among the Wisconsin Chippewa*. Memoirs of the American Anthropological Association 52, no. 4, pt. 2, memoir 72, 1950.

Bauer, William J., Jr. *We Were All Like Migrant Workers Here: Work, Community, and Memory in California's Round Valley Reservation, 1850–1941*. Chapel Hill: University of North Carolina Press, 2009.

Beck, David R. M. *The Struggle for Self-Determination: History of the Menominee Indians since 1854*. Lincoln: University of Nebraska Press, 2005.

Bederman, Gale. *Manliness and Civilization: A Cultural History of Gender and Race in the United States, 1880–1917*. Chicago: University of Chicago Press, 1995.

Benton-Banai, Edward. *The Mishomis Book: The Voice of the Ojibway*. St. Paul, Minn.: Little Red School House, 1988.

Berger, Thomas R. *Village Journeys: The Report of the Alaska Native Review Commission*. New York: Hill and Wang, 1985.

Brehm, Victoria. *A Fully Accredited Ocean: Essays on the Great Lakes*. Ann Arbor: University of Michigan Press, 1998.

Bruyneel, Kevin. *The Third Space of Sovereignty: The Postcolonial Politics of U.S.-Indigenous Relations*. Minneapolis: University of Minnesota Press, 2007.

Bogue, Margaret Beattie. *Fishing the Great Lakes: An Environmental History, 1783–1933*. Madison: University of Wisconsin Press, 2000.

Boxberger, Daniel. *To Fish in Common: The Ethnohistory of Lummi Indian Salmon Fishing*. Lincoln: University of Nebraska Press, 1989.

Butler, Richard, and Tom Hinch. *Tourism and Indigenous Peoples*. Boston: International Thomson Business Press, 1996.

Cattelino, Jessica. *High Stakes: Florida Seminole Gaming and Sovereignty*. Durham, N.C.: Duke University Press, 2008.

Chambers, Robert, and Gordon R. Conway. *Sustainable Livelihoods: Practical Concepts for the 21st Century*. Brighton, UK: Institute of Development Studies, 1992.

Child, Brenda J. *Boarding School Seasons*. Lincoln: University of Nebraska Press, 2000.

———. *Holding Our World Together: Ojibwe Women and the Survival of Community*. New York: Viking Press, 2012.

Cohen, Lizabeth. *Making a New Deal: Industrial Workers in Chicago, 1919–1939*. New York: Cambridge University Press, 1991.

Coleman, Sister Bernard. *Where the Water Stops: Fond du Lac Reservation*. Duluth, Minn.: College of St. Scholastica, 1967.

Cooper, Frederick, Allen F. Isaacman, Florencia E. Mallon, William C. Roseberry, and Steve J. Stern. *Confronting Historical Paradigms: Peasants, Labor, and the Capitalist World System in Africa and Latin America*. Madison: University of Wisconsin Press, 1993.

Cruikshank, Julie. *Life Lived Like a Story: Life Stories of Three Yukon Native Elders*. Lincoln: University of Nebraska Press, 1990.

———. *The Social Life of Stories: Narrative and Knowledge in Yukon Territory*. Lincoln: University of Nebraska Press, 1998.

Danbom, David. *The Resisted Revolution: Urban America and the Industrialization of Agriculture*. Ames: Iowa State University Press, 1979.

Danziger, Edmund J., Jr. *The Chippewas of Lake Superior*. Norman: University of Oklahoma Press, 1978.

———. *Great Lakes Indians Accommodation and Resistance during the Early Reservation Years*. Ann Arbor: University of Michigan Press, 2009.

Denetdale, Jennifer Nez. *Reclaiming Dine History: Legacies of Navajo Chief Manuelito and Juanita*. Tucson: University of Arizona Press, 2007.

Deloria, Philip J. *Playing Indian*. New Haven: Yale University Press, 1998.

———. *Indians in Unexpected Places*. Lawrence: University Press of Kansas, 2004.

Densmore, Frances. *How the Indians Use Wild Plants for Food, Medicine, and Crafts*. Washington, D.C.: Smithsonian Institute Bureau of American Ethnology, 1928. Reprint, New York: Dover Publications, 1974.

———. *Chippewa Customs*. Washington, D.C.: Smithsonian Institution Bureau of American Ethnology, bulletin 86, 1929. Reprint, St. Paul: Minnesota Historical Society Press, 1979.

———. *Strength of the Earth: a Classic Guide to Ojibwe Uses of Native Plants*. 1928. Reprinted with an introduction by Brenda Child. St. Paul: Minnesota Historical Society Press, 2006.

Deutsch, Sarah. *No Separate Refuge: Culture, Class, and Gender on the Anglo-Hispanic Frontier in the American Southwest*. New York: Oxford University Press, 1989.

Doherty, Robert. *Disputed Waters: Native Americans and the Great Lakes Fishery*. Lexington: University of Kentucky Press, 1990.

Feldman, James W. *A Storied Wilderness: Rewilding the Apostle Islands*. Seattle: University of Washington Press, 2011.

Fink, Leon. *The Maya of Morganton: Work and Community in the Nuevo New South.* Chapel Hill: University of North Carolina Press, 2003.

———, ed. *Workers Across the Americas: The Transnational Turn in Labor History.* New York: Oxford University Press, 2011.

Fiske, Jo-Anne, Susan Sleeper-Smith, and William Wicken, eds. *New Faces of the Fur Trade: Selected Papers of the North American Fur Trade Conference, Halifax, Nova Scotia, 1995.* East Lansing: Michigan State University Press, 1998.

Foner, Eric, ed. *The New American History.* Philadelphia: Temple University Press, 1997.

Gilman, Carolyn. *The Grand Portage Story.* St. Paul: Minnesota Historical Society Press, 1992.

Giltner, Scott. *Hunting and Fishing in the New South: Black Labor and White Leisure After the Civil War.* Baltimore, Md.: Johns Hopkins University Press, 2008.

Glenn, Evelyn Nakano. *Issei, Nisei War Bride: Three Generations of Japanese American Women in Domestic Service.* Philadelphia: Temple University Press, 1986.

———. *Unequal Freedom: How Race and Gender Shaped American Citizenship and Labor.* Cambridge: Harvard University Press, 2002.

Gough, Robert. *Farming the Cutover: A Social History of Northern Wisconsin, 1900–1940.* Lawrence: University Press of Kansas, 1997.

Gutman, Herbert G. *Work, Culture, and Society in Industrializing America.* New York: Vintage, 1977.

Hämäläinen, Pekka. *Comanche Empire.* New Haven, Conn.: Yale University Press, 2008.

Harmon, Alexandra. *Indians in the Making: Ethnic Relations and Indian Identities Around Puget Sound.* Berkeley: University of California Press, 1999.

———. *Rich Indians: Native People and the Problem of Wealth in American History.* Chapel Hill: University of North Carolina Press, 2010.

Heaton, John W. *The Shoshone-Bannocks: Culture and Commerce at Fort Hall, 1870–1940.* Lawrence: University Press of Kansas, 2005.

Hickerson, Harold. *The Chippewa and Their Neighbors: A Study in Ethnohistory.* New York: Holt, Rinehart, and Winston, 1970.

———. *The Southwestern Chippewas: An Ethnohistorical Study.* Memoirs of the American Anthropological Association. 64, no. 3, pt. 2, memoir 92, 1962.

Hickerson, Harold, and Helen Knuth. *Ethnohistory of the Chippewas of Lake Superior.* New York: Garland Publishers, 1974.

Higbie, Frank Tobias. *Indispensible Outcasts: Hobo Workers and Community in the American Midwest, 1880–1930.* Champaign: University of Illinois Press, 2003.

Hilger, Sister M. Inez. *Chippewa Child Life and Its Historical Background.* Washington, D.C.: Smithsonian Institution Bureau of American Ethnology, 1951. Reprinted with an introduction by Jean M. O'Brien. St. Paul: Minnesota Historical Society Press, 1992.

———. *Chippewa Families: A Social Study of the White Earth Reservation, 1938.* Washington, D.C.: Catholic University Press of America, 1939. Reprinted with an introduction by Brenda J. Child and Kimberly M. Blaeser. St. Paul: Minnesota Historical Society Press, 1998.

Hosmer, Brian. *American Indians in the Marketplace: Persistence and Innovation among the Menominees and Metlakatlans, 1870–1920.* Lawrence: University Press of Kansas, 1999.

Hosmer, Brian, and Colleen O'Neill, eds. *Native Pathways: American Indian Culture and Economic Development in the Twentieth Century*. Boulder: University Press of Colorado, 2004.

Hoxie, Frederick E. *A Final Promise: The Campaign to Assimilate the Indians, 1880–1920*. Cambridge: Cambridge University Press, 1984.

———. *Parading Through History: The Making of the Crow Nation in America, 1805–1935*. Cambridge: Cambridge University Press, 1995.

Jacoby, Karl. *Crimes against Nature: Squatters, Poachers, Thieves, and the Hidden History of American Conservation*. Berkeley: University of California Press, 2001.

Jakle, John A. *The Tourist: Travel in Twentieth-Century North America*. Lincoln: University of Nebraska Press, 1985.

Jasen, Patricia Jane. *Wild Things: Nature, Culture, and Tourism in Ontario, 1790–1914*. Toronto: University of Toronto Press, 1995.

Jones, Jacqueline. *American Work: Four Centuries of Black and White Labor*. New York: W. W. Norton, 1998.

———. *The Dispossessed: America's Underclass from Civil War to the Present*. New York: Basic Books, 1992.

———. *A Labor of Love, A Labor of Sorrow: Black Women, Work, and the Family from Slavery to the Present*. New York: Basic Books, 1985.

Jung, Moon-Ho. *Coolies and Cane: Race, Labor, and Sugar in the Age of Emancipation*. Baltimore, Md.: Johns Hopkins University Press, 2006.

Kamper, David. *The Work of Sovereignty: Tribal Labor Relations and Self-Determination at the Navajo Nation*. Santa Fe, N.M.: School for Advanced Research Press, 2010.

Knight, Rolf. *Indians at Work: An Informal History of Native American Labor in British Columbia, 1858–1930*. Vancouver: New Star Books, 1996.

Keller, Robert H., and Michael F. Turek. *American Indians and National Parks*. Tucson: University of Arizona Press, 1998.

Kessler-Harris, Alice. *Gendering Labor History*. Urbana: University of Illinois Press, 2007.

———. *In Pursuit of Equity: Women, Men, and the Quest for Economic Citizenship in 20th-Century America*. New York: Oxford University Press, 2001.

———. *Out of Work: A History of Wage Earning Women in the U.S.* 1982. Reprint, New York: Oxford University Press, 2003.

Kinney, J. P. *Indian Forest and Range: A History of the Administration and Conservation of Redman's Heritage*. Washington, D.C.: Forestry Enterprises, 1950.

Konkle, Maureen. *Writing Indian Nations: Native Intellectuals and the Politics of Historiography, 1827–1863*. Chapel Hill: University of North Carolina Press, 2004.

Kugel, Rebecca. *To Be the Main Leaders of Our People: A History of Minnesota Ojibwe Politics, 1825–1898*. East Lansing: Michigan State University Press, 1998.

LaGrand, James B. *Indian Metropolis: Native Americans in Chicago, 1945–1975*. Urbana: University of Illinois Press, 2002.

Lancaster, Daniel. *John Beargrease: Legend of Minnesota's North Shore*. Duluth, Minn.: Holy Cow! Press, 2008.

Lankton, Larry. *Cradle to the Grave: Life, Work, and Death at the Lake Superior Copper Mines*. New York: Oxford University Press, 1991.

Larson, Agnes M. *History of the White Pine Industry in Minnesota*. Minneapolis: University of Minnesota Press, 1949.

Littlefield, Alice, and Martha C. Knack, eds. *Native Americans and Wage Labor: Ethnohistorical Perspectives*. Norman: University of Oklahoma Press, 1996.

McClurken, James M., and Charles E. Cleland, eds. *Fish in the Lakes, Wild Rice, and Game in Abundance: Testimony on Behalf of Mille Lacs Ojibwe Hunting and Fishing Rights*. East Lansing: Michigan State University Press, 2000.

McNally, Michael. *Ojibwe Singers: Hymns, Grief, and a Native Culture in Motion*. New York: Oxford University Press, 2000.

Meeks, Eric V. *Border Citizens: The Making of Indians, Mexicans, and Anglos in Arizona*. Austin: University of Texas Press, 2007.

Meyer, Melissa L. *White Earth Tragedy: Ethnicity and Dispossession at a Minnesota Anishinaabe Reservation*. Lincoln: University of Nebraska Press, 1999.

Miles, Tia. *The House on Diamond Hill: A Cherokee Plantation Story*. Chapel Hill: University of North Carolina Press, 2010.

Montgomery, David. *The Fall of the House of Labor: The Workplace, the State, and American Labor Activism, 1865–1925*. New York: Cambridge University Press, 1987.

———. *Worker's Control in America: Studies in the History of Work, Technology, and Labor Struggles*. New York: Cambridge University Press, 1980.

Nabokov, Peter. *A Forest of Time: American Indian Ways of History*. New York: Cambridge University Press, 2002.

Nesper, Larry. *The Walleye War: The Struggle for Ojibwe Spearfishing and Treaty Rights*. Lincoln: University of Nebraska Press, 2002.

Newell, Alan S., Richmond L. Clow, and Richard N. Ellis. *A Forest in Trust: Three Quarters of a Century of Indian Forestry, 1910–1986*. Washington, D.C.: U.S. Department of the Interior, Bureau of Indian Affairs Division of Forestry, 1986.

Ngai, Mai. *Impossible Subjects: Illegal Aliens and the Making of Modern America*. Princeton, N.J.: Princeton University Press, 2005.

Nora, Pierre, and Lawrence D. Kritzman, eds. ,*Realms of Memory: Rethinking the French Past*. 4 vols. New York: Columbia University Press, 1998.

Nute, Grace Lee. *Lake Superior*. New York: Bobbs-Merrill, 1944.

Olmanson, Eric D. *The Future City on the Inland Sea: A History of Imaginative Geographies of Lake Superior*. Athens: Ohio University Press, 2007.

O'Neill, Colleen. *Working the Navajo Way: Labor and Culture in the Twentieth Century*. Lawrence: University Press of Kansas, 2005.

Ostergren, Robert C., and Thomas R. Vale, eds. *Wisconsin Land and Life*. Madison: University of Wisconsin Press, 1997.

Parnaby, Andrew. *Citizen Docker: Making a New Deal on the Vancouver Waterfront, 1919–1939*. Toronto: University of Toronto Press, 2008.

Peterson, Jacqueline, and Jennifer S. H. Brown. *The New Peoples: Being and Becoming Métis in North America*. Winnipeg: University of Manitoba Press, 1985.

Pickering, Kathleen Ann. *Lakota Culture, World Economy*. Lincoln: University of Nebraska Press, 2004.

Pinchot, Gifford. *Breaking New Ground*. New York: Harcourt, Brace, 1947.

Portelli, Alessandro. *The Death of Luigi Trastulli and Other Stories*. Albany: SUNY Press, 1991.

Raff, Willis H. *Pioneers in the Wilderness*. Grand Marais, Minn.: Cook County Historical Society, 1981.

Raibmon, Paige. *Authentic Indians: Episodes of Encounter from the Late Nineteenth Century Northwest Coast*. Durham, N.C.: Duke University Press, 1985.

Rauzi, Kelli Emmerling. *Fearless John: The Story of John Beargrease*. Ely, Minn.: Singing River Publications, 2006.

Ray, Arthur J. *The Canadian Fur Trade in the Industrial Age*. Toronto: University of Toronto Press, 1990.

———. *Indians in the Fur Trade: Their Roles as Hunters, Trappers, and Middlemen in the Lands Southwest of Hudson Bay, 1660–1870*. Toronto: University of Toronto Press, 1998.

Reinfeld, Fred. *Pony Express*. Lincoln: University of Nebraska Press, 1973.

Ritzenthaler, Robert. *The Woodland Indians of the Western Great Lakes*. Garden City, N.Y.: Natural History Press, 1970.

Rockman, Seth. *Scraping By: Wage Labor, Slavery, and Survival in Early Baltimore*. Baltimore, Md.: Johns Hopkins University Press, 2008.

Roediger, David. *Wages of Whiteness: Race and the Making of the American Working Class*. New York: Verso, 1999.

Rosenzweig, Roy, and David Thelen. *The Presence of the Past: Popular Uses of History in American Life*. New York: Columbia University Press, 1998.

Rosholt, Malcolm. *The Wisconsin Logging Book, 1839–1939*. Rosholt, Wisc.: Rosholt House, 1980.

Ross, Hamilton Nelson. *La Pointe: Village Outpost on Madeline Island*. Madison: Wisconsin Historical Society, 2000.

Rothman, Hal. *Devil's Bargains: Tourism in the Twentieth-Century American West*. Lawrence: University Press of Kansas, 1998.

Satz, Ronald N. *Chippewa Treaty Rights: The Reserved Rights of Wisconsin's Chippewa Indians in Historical Perspective*. Madison: University of Wisconsin Press, 1997.

Schenk, Theresa. *The Voice of the Crane Echoes Far: The Sociopolitical Organization of Lake Superior Ojibwa, 1640–1855*. New York: Garland Publishing, 1997.

Scott, Walter E., and Thomas Reitz. *The Wisconsin Warden: Wisconsin Conservation Law Enforcement, A Centennial Chronology, 1879–1979*. Vol. 1. Madison: Wisconsin Department of Natural Resources, 1979.

Shepherd, Jeffrey P. *We Are an Indian Nation: A History of the Haulapai People*. Tucson: University of Arizona Press, 2010.

Shoemaker, Nancy, ed. *Clearing a Path: Theorizing the Past in Native American Studies*. New York: Routledge, 2001.

Simonsen, Jane E. *Making Home Work: Domesticity and Native American Assimilation in the American West, 1860–1919*. Chapel Hill: University of North Carolina Press, 2006.

Sleeper Smith, Susan. *Indian Women and French Men: Rethinking Cultural Encounter in the Great Lakes*. Amherst: University of Massachusetts Press, 2001.

Smith, Donald B. *Sacred Feathers: The Reverend Peter Jones (Kahkewahquonaby) and the Mississauga Indians*. Toronto: University of Toronto Press, 1988.

Stromquist, Shelton. *A Generation of Boomers: The Pattern of Railroad Labor Conflict in Nineteenth-Century America*. Champaign: University of Illinois Press, 1993.

Sturm, Circe. *Blood Politics: Race, Culture, and Identity in the Cherokee Nation of Oklahoma*. Berkeley: University of California Press, 2002.

Teaford, Jon C. *Cities of the Heartland: The Rise and Fall of the Industrial Midwest*. Bloomington: Indiana University Press, 1994.

Thompson, E. P. *The Making of the English Working Class*. New York: Vintage, 1966.

Thrush, Coll. *Native Seattle: Histories from the Crossing Over Place*. Seattle: University of Washington Press, 2007.

Tober, James A. *Who Owns the Wildlife?: The Political Economy of Conservation in Nineteenth-Century America*. Westport, Conn.: Greenwood Press, 1981.

Treuer, Anton. *The Assassination of Hole in the Day*. St. Paul, Minn.: Borealis Books, 2011.

Trouillot, Michele. *Silencing the Past: Power and the Production of History*. Boston: Beacon Press, 1995.

Troutman, John. *Indian Blues: American Indians and the Politics of Music, 1879–1934*. Norman: University of Oklahoma Press, 2009.

Usner, Daniel. *Indian Work: Language and Livelihood in Native American History*. Cambridge: Harvard University Press, 2009.

Vennum, Thomas, Jr. *Just Too Much of an Indian: Bill Baker, Stalwart in a Fading Culture*. La Pointe, Wisc.: Thomas Vennum Jr., 2008.

———. *Wild Rice and the Ojibway People*. St. Paul: Minnesota Historical Society Press, 1988.

Whaley, Rick, with Walter Bresette. *Walleye Warriors: An Effective Alliance against Racism and for the Earth*. Philadelphia: New Society Publishers, 1994.

Weygant, Sister Noemi. *John (Jack) Linklater: Legendary Indian Game Warden*. Duluth, Minn.: Priory Books, 1987.

White, Bruce. *We Are at Home: Pictures of the Ojibwe People*. With a foreword by Gerald Vizenor. St. Paul: Minnesota Historical Society Press, 2007.

White, Richard. *The Middle Ground: Indians, Empires, and Republics in the Great Lakes Region, 1650–1815*. New York: Cambridge University Press, 1991.

———. *The Organic Machine: The Remaking of the Columbia River*. New York: Hill and Wang, 1995.

Wilkins, David E. *American Indian Sovereignty and the U.S. Supreme Court: The Masking of Justice*. Austin: University of Texas Press, 1997.

———. *American Indian Politics and the American Political System*. New York: Rowman & Littlefield, 2002.

Wisner, Ben, Piers Blaikie, Terry Cannon, and Ian Davis. *At Risk: Natural Hazards, People's Vulnerability, and Disasters*. 2d. ed. New York: Routledge, 2004.

Witgen, Michael. *An Infinity of Nations: How the Native New World Shaped Early North America*. Philadelphia: University of Pennsylvania Press, 2011.

Wolf, Eric R. *Envisioning Power: Ideologies of Dominance and Crisis*. Berkeley: University of California Press, 1999.

Articles, Essays in Edited Volumes, and Pamphlets

Albers, Patricia C., and William R. James. "Images and Reality: Postcards of Minnesota's Ojibway People, 1900–1980." *Minnesota History* 49 (Summer 1985): 229–40.

————. "Tourism and the Changing Image of the Great Lakes Indian." *Annals of Tourism Research* 10 (1983): 128–48.

————. "Wisconsin Indians on the Picture Postcard: A History of Photographic Stereotyping." *Lore* 37 (1987): 3–19.

Arndt, Grant. "Ho-Chunk 'Indian Powwows' of the Early Twentieth Century." In *Powwow*. edited by Clyde Ellis, Luke Eric Lassiter, and Gary H. Dunham, 46–67. Lincoln: University of Nebraska Press, 2005.

Bayly, C. A., Sven Beckert, Matthew Connelly, Isabel Hofmeyr, Wendy Kozol, and Patricia Sneed. "AHR Conversation: On Transnational History." *American Historical Review* 111, no. 5 (December 2006): 1441–64.

Biolsi, Thomas. "The Birth of the Reservation: Making the Modern Individual among the Lakota." *American Anthropologist* 22, no. 1 (February 1995): 28–53.

Buffalohead, Priscilla K. "Farmers, Warriors, and Traders: A Fresh Look at Ojibway Women." *Minnesota History* 48, no. 6 (Summer 1983): 236–44.

Cattelino, Jessica. "Casino Roots: The Cultural Production of Twentieth-Century Seminole Economic Development." In *Native Pathways: American Indian Culture and Economic Development in the Twentieth Century*, edited by Brian Hosmer and Colleen O'Neill, 66–90. Boulder: University Press of Colorado, 2004.

Chapple, John C. "'Herring Boom' at Bayfield on Lake Superior." *Wisconsin Magazine of History* 30, no. 1 (September 1946): 31–38.

Cleland, Charles E. "The Inland Shore Fishery of the Great Lakes: Its Development and Importance in Prehistory." *American Antiquity* 47 (October 1982): 762–63.

————. "Preliminary Report of the Ethnohistorical Basis of the Hunting, Fishing, and Gathering Rights of the Mille Lacs Chippewa." In *Fish in the Lakes, Wild Rice, and Game in Abundance: Testimony on Behalf of Mille Lacs Ojibwe Hunting and Fishing Rights*, compiled by James M. McClurken, 3–140. East Lansing: Michigan State University Press, 2000.

Clifton, James. "Potawatomi." In *Handbook of North American Indians*. Edited by William Sturtevant. Vol. 15, *The Northeast*, edited by Bruce Trigger, 725–42. Washington D.C.: Smithsonian Institution Press, 1978.

Cruikshank, Julie. "Images of Society in Klondike Gold Rush Narratives: Skokum Jim and the Discovery of Gold." *Ethnohistory* 39 (Winter 1992): 20–41.

Day, Gordon M., and Bruce Trigger. "Algonquin." In *Handbook of North American Indians*. Edited by William Sturtevant. Vol. 15, *The Northeast*, edited by Bruce Trigger, 792–97. Washington D.C.: Smithsonian Institution Press, 1978.

Deloria, Vine Jr. "Indian Law and the Reach of History." *Journal of Contemporary Law* 4, no. 1 (Winter 1977): 1–13.

Duchesne, Luc C., and Suzanne Wetzel. "Effect of Fire Intensity and Depth of Burn on Lowbush Blueberry, *Vaccinium angustifolium*, and Velvet Leaf Blueberry, *Vaccinium myrtilloides*, Production in Eastern Ontario." *Canadian Field-Naturalist* 118, no. 2 (April-June 2004): 195–200.

Ellis, Clyde. "Five Dollars a Week to Be 'Regular Indians': Shows, Exhibitions, and the Economics of Indian Dancing, 1880–1930." In *Native Pathways: American Indian Culture and Economic Development in the Twentieth Century*, edited by Brian Hosmer and Colleen O'Neill, 184–208. Boulder: University Press of Colorado, 2004.

Farrow, Scott. "Extinction and Market Forces: Two Case Studies." *Ecological Economics* 13, no. 2 (May 1995): 115–23.

Feldman, James W. "The View from Sand Island: Reconsidering the Peripheral Economy, 1880-1940." *Western Historical Quarterly* 35, no. 3 (Autumn, 2004): 285–307.

Fink, Leon. "American Labor History." In *The New American Labor History*, edited by Eric Foner, 333–52. Philadelphia: Temple University Press, 1997.

Goodier, John L. "Fishermen and Their Trade in Canadian Lake Superior: One Hundred Years." *Inland Seas* 45 (Fall 1989): 32–48.

Greene, Julie. "Transnational Forces, Nation-States, and the Practice of U.S. History." In *Workers Across the Americas: The Transnational Turn in American Labor History*. Edited by Leon Fink. New York: Oxford University Press, 2011.

Gross, Lawrence W. "Bimaadiziwin, or the 'Good Life,' as a Unifying Concept of Anishinaabe Religion." *American Indian Culture and Research Journal* 26, no. 1 (2002): 15–32.

Hall, Thomas, D. "Patterns of Native American Incorporation into State Societies." In *Public Policy Impacts on American Indian Economic Development*, edited by C. Matthew Smith, 23–38. Albuquerque: Institute for Native American Development, University of New Mexico, 1988.

Harmon, Alexandra, Colleen O'Neill, and Paul C. Rosier. "Interwoven Economic Histories: American Indians in Capitalist America." *Journal of American History* 98, no. 3 (2011): 698–722.

Hoxie, Frederick. "From Prison to Homeland: The Cheyenne River Indian Reservation Before WWI." *South Dakota History* 10, no. 1 (Winter 1979): 1–24.

Keller, Robert H. "America's Native Sweet: Chippewa Treaties and the Right to Harvest Maple Sugar." *American Indian Quarterly* 13, no. 2 (Spring 1989): 117–35.

Klein, Kerwin Lee. "On the Emergence of Memory in Historical Discourse." *Representations* 69 (Winter 2000): 127–50.

Kugel, Rebecca. "Leadership Within the Women's Community: Susie Bonga Wright of the Leech Lake Ojibwe." In *Native Women's History in Eastern North America Before 1900: A Guide to Research and Writing*, edited by Rebecca Kugel and Lucy Eldersveld Murphy, 166–200. Lincoln: University of Nebraska Press, 2007.

Lock, Vickie. "A Summer Place: Elizabeth Hull's Madeline Island Photo Album." *Wisconsin Magazine of History*. 85, no. 2 (Summer 2000): 32–39.

Loo, Tina. "Of Moose and Men: Hunting for Masculinities in British Columbia, 1880–1939." *Western Historical Quarterly* 32, no. 3 (Autumn 2001): 296–319.

McDonald, Stephen L. "Sustained Yield Forest Management: Some Observations on its Economic Significance and Implications for Resource Policy." *American Journal of Economics and Sociology* 13, no. 4 (July 1954): 389–99.

McLaughlin, Castle. "Nation, Tribe, and Class: The Dynamics of Agrarian Transformation on the Fort Berthold Reservation." *American Indian Culture and Research Journal* 22, no. 3 (1998): 101–38.

Meyer, Melissa. "White Earth Women and Social Welfare." In *Enduring Nations: Native Americans in the Midwest*, edited by David Edmunds, 244–72. Chicago: University of Illinois Press, 2008.

Mikdashi, Maya. "What Is Settler Colonialism?" *American Indian Culture and Research Journal* 37, no. 2 (2013): 23–34.

Morgan, Mindy J. "Constructions and Contestations of the Authoritative Voice: Native American Communities and the Federal Writers' Project, 1935–41." *American Indian Quarterly* 29, nos. 1 and 2 (Winter/Spring 2005): 56–83.

Nesper, Larry. "Simulating Culture: Being Indian for Tourists in Lac du Flambeau's Indian Bowl." *Ethnohistory* 50, no. 3 (Summer 2003): 447–72.

Nora, Pierre. "Between History and Memory: Les Lieux de Memoire." *Representations* 26 (Spring 1989): 7–24.

Nute, Grace Lee. "The American Fur Company's Fishing Enterprises on Lake Superior." *Mississippi Valley Historical Review* 12, no. 4 (March 1926): 483–503.

Otis, Laurie. "Four Generations of Hausers Grow Apples at Superior View Farm." *Farm Preservation Program Newsletter* (Winter 2001).

Parnaby, Andrew. "Indigenous Labor in Mid-Nineteenth Century British North America: The Mi'KMaq of Cape Breton and the Squamish of British Columbia in Comparative Perspective." In *Workers Across the Americas*, edited by Leon Fink, 109–35. New York: Oxford University Press, 2011.

Peters, Kurt M. "Watering the Flower: Laguna Pueblo and the Santa Fe Railroad, 1880–1943." In *Native Americans and Wage Labor: Ethnohistorical Perspectives*, edited by Alice Littlefield and Martha C. Knack, 177–97. Norman: University of Oklahoma Press, 1996.

Satz, Ronald N. " 'Tell Those Gray Haired Men What They Should Know': The Hayward Indian Congress of 1934." *Wisconsin Magazine of History* 77, no. 3 (1994): 196–224.

Shapiro, Aaron. "Up North on Vacation: Tourism and Resorts in Wisconsin's North Woods, 1900–1945." *Wisconsin Magazine of History* 89, no. 4 (Summer 2006): 2–13.

Shifferd, Patricia. "A Study in Economic Change: The Chippewa of Northern Wisconsin, 1854–1900." *Western Canadian Journal of Anthropology* 6, no. 4 (1976): 16–38.

Shoemaker, Nancy. "Urban Indians and Ethnic Choices: American Indian Organizations in Minneapolis." *Western Historical Quarterly* 19, no. 4 (November 1988): 431–47.

Silvern, Steven E. "The Geography of Ojibwe Treaty Rights in Northern Wisconsin." In *Wisconsin Land and Life*, edited by Robert Ostergen and Thomas Vale, 489–504. Madison: University of Wisconsin Press, 1997.

———. "Nature, Territory, and Identity in the Wisconsin Treaty Rights Controversy." *Ecumene* 2 (1995): 267–92.

———. "Negotiating Ojibwe Treaty Rights: Towards a Critical Geopolitics of State-Tribal Relations." *American Indian Culture and Research Journal* 32, no. 3 (October 2008): 153–76.

Simpson, Audra. "Paths Towards a Mohawk Nation: Narratives of Nationhood and Citizenship in Kahnawake." In *Political Theory and the Rights of Indigenous Peoples*, edited by Duncan Ivison, Paul Patton, and Will Sanders, 113–36. New York: Cambridge University Press, 2000.

Steen-Adams, Michelle M., Nancy Langston, and David J. Mladenhoff. "Logging the Great Lakes Indian Reservations: The Case of the Bad River Band of Ojibwe." *American Indian Culture and Research Journal* 34, no. 1 (2010): 41–66.

Weaver, Jace. "More Light Than Heat: The Current State of Native American Studies." *American Indian Quarterly* 31, no. 2 (Spring 2007): 233–55.

White, Bruce M. "A Skilled Game of Exchange: Ojibway Fur Trade Protocol." *Minnesota History* 50, no. 6 (1987): 229–40.

———. "Stereotyping Minnesota's Native People." *Minnesota History* 53 (Fall 1992): 99–110.

Wilkins, David E. "Modernization, Colonialism, Dependency: How Appropriate Are These Models for Providing an Explanation of North American Indian Underdevelopment?" *Ethnic and Racial Studies* 16 (July 1993): 390–419.

Wolfe, Patrick. "Land, Labor, and Difference: Elementary Structures of Race." *American Historical Review* 106, no. 3 (June 2001): 866–905.

Zarnowsky, C. Frank. "Working at Play: The Phenomenon of 19th Century Worker-Competition." *Journal of Leisure Research* 36, no. 2 (2004): 257–81.

Theses and Dissertations

Cullon, Joseph. "Landscapes of Labor and Leisure: Common Rights, Private Property, and Class Relations Along the Boise Brule River, 1870–1940." M.A. thesis, University of Wisconsin, Madison, 1992.

Feldman, James W. "Rewilding the Islands: Nature, History, and Wilderness at Apostle Islands National Lakeshore." Ph.D. diss., University of Wisconsin, Madison, 2004.

Martin, Jay C. "Sailing the Freshwater Seas: A Social History of Life Aboard Commercial Sailing Vessels of the United States and Canada on the Great Lakes, 1815–1930." Ph.D. diss., Bowling Green State University, 1995.

Olmanson, Eric D. "Romantics, Scientists, Boosters, and the Making of the Chequamegon Bay Region on the South Shore of Lake Superior." Ph.D. diss., University of Wisconsin, Madison, 2000.

Parman, Donald L. "The Indian Civilian Conservation Corps." Ph.D. diss., University of Oklahoma, 1967.

Peters, Kurt Michael. "Watering the Flower: The Laguna Pueblo and the Atchison, Topeka, Santa Fe Railroad, 1880–1980." Ph.D. diss., University of California, Berkeley, 1994.

Redix, Erik M. "The Murder of Joe White: Ojibwe Leadership and Colonialism in Wisconsin." Ph.D. diss., University of Minnesota, 2012.

Rohde, Melissa. "Living and Working in Enchanted Lands: American Indian Tourism, Labor, Development, and Activism, 1900–1970." Ph.D. diss., University of Illinois at Urbana-Champaign, 2010.

Ronnander, Chad Delano. "Many Paths to the Pine: Mdewakanton Dakotas, Fur Traders, Ojibwes, and the United States in Wisconsin's Chippewa Valley, 1815–1837." Ph.D. diss., University of Minnesota, 2003.

Stromquist, Shelton H. "A Generation of Boomers: Work, Community Structure, and the Pattern of Industrial Conflict on Late Nineteenth-Century American Railroads." Ph.D. diss., University of Pittsburgh, 1981.

"Baseball Almanac," http://www.baseballalmanac.com/players/player. php?p=chouncho1. July 30, 2012.

Duluth Public Library. "Duluth's Early Days," http://www.duluth.lib.mn.us/History/ CorianPanels.html. June 21, 2012.

Foulk, Doug, Emily Hoover, Jim Luby, Teryl Rober, Carl Rosen, Ward Stienstra, David Wildung, and Jerry Wright. "Commercial Blueberry Production in Minnesota and Wisconsin." University of Minnesota Extension website, http://www.extension.umn. edu/distribution/horticulture/DG2241.html. July 29, 2011.

George Wright Society. "Red Cliff Tribe in Wisconsin Creates Frog Bay Tribal National Park," http://www.georgewright.org/node/7278. April 1, 2013.

"Grand Portage National Monument Heritage Center." National Park Service website, http://www.nps.gov/grpo/planyourvisit/grand-portage-national-monument-heritage-center.htm. April 1, 2013.

Indian Land Tenure Foundation. "Indian Land Tenure Curriculum, 6–8 Curriculum, Standard 3, Lesson 2," http://www.indianlandtenure.org/curriculum/6–8/ Standard3/lesson2.htm.

———. "Allotment Information for Midwest BIA Region," http://www.indianlandtenure. org/ILTFallotment/specinfo/si%20Midwest.pdf. March 15, 2007.

———. "Mino Bi Ma De Se Win Farm." Red Cliff Community Health website, http://www. red-cliff-health.com/americorps-vista.shtml.

John Beargrease Marathon website, http://www.beargrease.com. October 13, 2006.

Lake Superior Fish: Make the Purchase, Preserve the Heritage, http://www. lakesuperiorwhitefish.com/default.html. March 5, 2012.

National Oceanic and Atmospheric Administration. "About Our Great Lakes: Introduction," http://www.glerl.noaa.gov/pr/ourlakes/intro.html. April 8, 2013.

———. "NowData—NOAA Online Weather Data," http://www.nws.noaa.gov/climate/ index.php?wfo=dlh. March 29, 2012.

Quinlan, Henry. UFWS Ashland Fish and Wildlife Conservation Office. "Taking Care of Name' (Lake Sturgeon): Interagency Effort Aims to Enhance this Old Giant's Numbers." Great Lakes Indian Fish and Wildlife Commission website, http://www. glifwc.org/Accordian_Stories/Takingcareofname.html. February 13, 2012.

Roufs, Timothy G. "When Everybody Called Me *Gah-bay-bi-nayss*, 'Forever–Flying Bird': An Ethnographic Biography of Peter Paul Buffalo," http://www.d.umn.edu/cla/ faculty/troufs/Buffalo/PB14.html.

Wisconsin Historical Society. "The Killing of Chief Joe White (Gishkitawag), 1894," http://www.wisconsinhistory.org/turningpoints/search.asp?id=1626. July 1, 2012.

Wisconsin State Historical Society. "Dictionary of Wisconsin History," http://www. wisconsinhistory.org/dictionary/index.asp?action=view&term_id=2636&term_type_ id=1&term_type_text=people&letter=k. June 10, 2012.

Yoshihara, Mari. "Political Economy of Tourist Colonialism in Hawai'i: A Reading of Ikezawa Natsuki's *Hawai'I Kiko*," 19th International Congress of Historical Sciences,

Oslo, Norway, August 2000, http://www.oslo2000.uio.no/program/papers/s16/s16–yoshihara.pdf. March 28, 2013.

ADDITIONAL SOURCES

Norrgard, Lorraine, producer. *Waasa Inabidaa: We Look in All Directions.* 6 hrs. WDSE-TV, 2002. Videocassette.

Parker, Robert E., Sr. "Bayfield in Rhythm." Copy provided to the author by Bob Nelson, Bayfield Heritage Association, Bayfield, Wisconsin, July 2010.

White, Bruce. "Early Game and Fish Regulation and Enforcement in Minnesota, 1858–1920." A Report Prepared for the Mille Lacs Band of Ojibwe, December 1995. Copy courtesy of Bruce White.

Index

Cutover movement, 33, 103, 108, 109. *See also* Agriculture; Allotment

Dakota Indians, 58, 114
Davies, Cush, 111
Day, Antoine, 91
Deer, 5, 26, 45, 53, 56, 59, 60, 61, 119, 120, 122
Democratic State Central Committee, 111
Dennis, Antoine, 96, 120, 123, 124
Dennis, Ed, 119, 120
Denomie, Florina, 20, 32, 33, 39–40, 50, 66
Densmore, Frances, 24
DePerry, Michael, 75
Diver, Bob, 133,
Diver, John, 31, 50
Dodge, Henry, 87
Domesticity, 8, 36, 118, 159 (n. 92). *See also* Household economy; Material culture, Ojibwe; Women, Ojibwe
Domestic servants, 8, 113, 119, 121, 131
Duluth, Minnesota, 16, 49, 117, 127; and commercial fishing industry, 69, 73; and lumber industry, 90, 100, 101, 102; as market for Ojibwe commodities, 39, 46

Economic citizenship, 3, 10, 11, 14, 94

Fishing, 30, 31, 33, 34, 47, 48, 58, 67, 68, 96, 97, 108, 121; ceremonial beliefs about, 65, 66; commercialization of, 63, 64; contracts, 66–67, 69; court cases involving, 76–78, 81–82; environmental impacts of, 51, 53, 61, 80–81, 109; firms, 64, 65, 69, 70, 73–74, 79–80, 131; and fur trade, 26, 66–67; Indian agent attitudes toward, 64, 69–70, 76; markets for, 66, 69; and net-size regulation, 75; and Ojibwe self-determination, 27, 55, 59, 64, 65, 70, 80–82, 126, 129, 132, 133–34; for sport, 51, 52, 96, 110, 119, 120, 121, 122, 123, 124, 131; state restriction of, 27, 32, 50, 51, 52, 53, 56, 57, 65, 72–79, 108, 111–12, 131; state seasons for, 74; for subsistence, 65; technologies and methods

of, 65, 68, 71, 102; in treaties, 17, 21, 55, 64, 81–82, 130, 134; for wages, 66–67, 69, 71; violence and, 126. *See also* Herring; Lake Superior; Lake trout; Netting; Spearfishing; Sturgeon; Whitefish
Flat Mouth, 20–21
Fond du Lac reservation, 16, 19, 27, 31, 48; allotment of, 17, 19, 91, 94; berrying and, 29, 30, 41, 42; farming of, 41–42; fires on, 32; fishing and, 66, 69; gaming and, 126–27; hunting and trapping and, 49, 54, 55, 57; and lumber industry, 86–87, 92, 94, 101; physical description of, 17; production on, 29; and railroad, 30; and resistance to state jurisdiction, 133; work relief on, 104
Forest fires, 32–33, 103, 104, 109
Forestry, 104
Frog Bay Tribal National Park, 127
Fur trade, 5–6, 14, 26, 28, 45–46, 64, 127, 130. *See also* American Fur Company

Gaming, 115, 126–27
Gathering, 10, 22–24, 156 (n. 3); ceremonial beliefs about, 25, 42; fruit farming and, 33–38; and fur trade, 26; gender roles and, 22–23, 36; for medicinal purposes, 23, 27, 47; as resistance to government policies, 37; for subsistence, 22–24; and sale of wild produce, 27–29; for seasonal income, 39–42; social dynamics of, 24–25, 29–31, 37, 40–42; transformation of, 14, 20, 22, 25–26, 35–37, 42; in treaties, 6, 14, 20, 21. *See also* Agriculture; Berries; Birch bark; Maple sugar; Wild rice; Women, Ojibwe
Gervais, Frank, 59
Gheen, Joe, 119, 120, 122–23
Gheen, Mary, 120, 121
Gifts, significance of, 5–6, 45
Gitche Gumee Club, 110, 122
Govan, Johnny, 120, 121
Grand Marais, 16, 57
Grand Portage reservation, 16, 19, 49, 57; allotment of, 17, 19, 57, 91, 94, 103;

Wisconsin Conservation Commission, 57, 79, 124
Wisconsin Federal District Court, 77, 78
Wisconsin Fish Commission, 74
Wisconsin Supreme Court, 59, 77–78, 111, 128
Women, Ojibwe: conduct surrounding menstruation, 25; and fishing, 63, 72; and gardening, 27; and gathering, 22–24, 26, 29, 156 (n. 9); and hunting and trapping, 45, 48, 50, 54, 55; and material culture, 50, 117, 118; midwives, 27; racial prejudice toward, 53, 115–16, 121; resistance to state laws, 55–56, 62; self-sufficiency of, 30; shifts in roles of, 36; and tourist industry, 115–16, 117, 118–19, 120. *See also* Domesticity; Domestic servants
Woods, Frederick M., 110
Work. *See* Labor
Works Progress Administration (WPA), 16, 104
World War I, 27, 109
World War II, 21, 42, 70, 108, 126

24784612R00114

Made in the USA
Lexington, KY
31 July 2013